More than a movie : ethics in entertainment

More Than a Movie

This book emerged out of Mediascope, a nonprofit, nonpartisan media research organization based in Studio City, California, working to promote informed debate about social issues in the media.

Website: www.mediascope.org

More Than a Movie

Ethics in Entertainment

by

F. Miguel Valenti

Foreword by
Peter Bogdanovich

Edited by
Les Brown and Laurie Trotta

Westview Press
A Member of the Perseus Books Group

To Laurie, without whom this book could not have been written, and without whom, it would not have been worth writing.

Published in 2000 in the United States of America by Westview Press, 5500 Central Avenue, Boulder, Colorado 80301, and in the United Kingdom by Westview Press, 12 Hid's Copse Road, Cumnor Hill, Oxford OX2 9JJ

Find us on the World Wide Web at www.westviewpress.com

A CIP catalog record for this book is available from the Library of Congress
ISBN 0-8133-9075-3

The paper used in this publication meets the requirements of the American National Standard for Permanence of Paper for Printed Library Materials Z39.48-1984.

10 9 8 7 6 5 4 3 2

Contents

Foreword

Peter Bogdanovich

In sophisticated circles today, the mere mention of "ethics in filmmaking" is bound to get a cynical laugh, one that says there aren't any; indeed, that the very subject itself is as archaic as the old Hollywood Production Code,[1] which supposedly kept filmmakers in line throughout the 1930s, 1940s, and 1950s; a laugh that says this truly is the era of "anything goes"; specifically, anything that makes as much money as possible. An "ethic," after all (according to the *Concise Oxford English Dictionary*[2]), is "a set of moral principles," and "moral" is defined (by the same source) as "concerned with goodness or badness of human character or behavior, or with the distinction between right and wrong." Religious teachings are often thought to supply these principles, and although the word "religion" is of "doubtful" etymology, Robert Graves has traced it rather convincingly (in *The White Goddess*) to a Latin word that means "to choose, or pick, the right thing."[3]

Few people would disagree that unfortunately we are living in a largely unethical, often amoral, generally irreligious time, and so one could argue that the movies are only an accurate reflection of our fractured and confused society. Does this hypothesis, however, excuse filmmakers from any moral responsibility in their professional work? Quite apparently, many seem to think it does. I don't.

Historically, from the start of exhibited moving pictures in 1895, until around 1933, each picture maker or studio was responsible for its own work based on its own set of values. By the early 1930s, many people judged that things had gotten out of hand—there had been some nudity in the late silent films and the early talkies, as well as some sexual candor and a good deal of violence (all of it pretty tame by contemporary standards). And so, to preclude any government censorship, the U.S. studios created the so-called Hollywood Production Code as a kind of self-policing agreement.

This had quite a number of exceedingly silly restrictions and in a great many instances certainly hampered free expression. Director George Cukor once pointed out to me that the code had finally come into being not because of sexual or violent material, but rather because of simple bad taste; a film called *Convention City,*[4] he said, was "so vulgar that it brought censorship as such." The code was in force throughout the next three decades—in other words, through much of what we now look back on as the Golden Age of talking pictures (1929–1962). That's because the truly creative filmmakers seemed to have no trouble overcoming its limitations, even turning them to their advantage. It's quite clear, though obliquely stated, for example, that Humphrey Bogart and Lauren Bacall are talking of going to bed together in both Howard Hawks' *To Have and Have Not*[5] and his *The Big Sleep*[6] without having to shove their tongues down each other's throats or strip, and that Betty Hutton had been impregnated by a phony one-night stand in Preston Sturges's *The Miracle of Morgan's Creek.*[7]

With the fall of the studio system in the early 1960s, the rise of the independents, and the much-touted sexual revolution of the 1950s and 1960s, the code had been pretty thoroughly erased by the start of the 1970s, and such matters again became the concern of each individual producer, writer, or director. The irony, of course, is that the complete freedom of the screen in the last three decades has not translated into a greater degree of maturity or artistry, but rather the opposite.

The transition came not only as the studios' total authority evaporated, but also, significantly, as the first couple of generations of picture makers retired or died and their positions were eventually taken by those born shortly before or just after World War II. The earliest filmmakers generally had a substantial life experience often quite separate from show business, while the newest ones had aspired to step into the shoes of the pioneers and perhaps felt that, apart from emulating their elders, they would best be served by taking movies in directions that had previously been forbidden. In some instances, this was salutary; in most, strangely, it was not. Ethical or moral responsibility was never an issue that anyone discussed, only freedom, only lack of censorship; never if what was being made was right or wrong; or what we might be doing to the public. Already, by the mid-1970s, Orson Welles was saying to me that we were in danger of brutalizing our audiences. He used to point out that by the end of the Roman Empire, the only entertainments that could satisfy the public at the Roman Circus were real copulation and real killing.

My own personal experiences with this complicated, thorny issue might be illuminating in certain ambiguous ways. The first script I ever worked on that was actually shot was Roger Corman's popular motorcycle melodrama, *The Wild Angels.*[8] The trouble with portraying any way of life on the screen is that there cannot fail to be an inherent glorification of it, no matter how seamy: the actors' charisma or charm alone contributes here and becomes inseparable from the characters. The Hells' Angels motorcyclists we portrayed—like the outlaw cowboys of old—lived lives neither Corman nor I could really endorse, and yet they were the heroes (albeit antiheroes) of our story. The picture ended with the funeral of an Angel who had been shot by the police, and its final moments had Peter Fonda (our motorcycle club's leader) choosing not to run away as the police approached. This was the ending I wrote: His girlfriend (played by Nancy Sinatra) calls out to him, "Come on, let's go!" He is wanted by the police, but replies, "There's no place to go," and as the police sirens grow louder and louder, he stands by his friend's grave. But why didn't he leave? In life, I have to think he would have. We chose to have him give up almost as a way of renouncing his lifestyle, as a way of signaling the audience that choosing Fonda's path was ultimately a dead end, and that he had realized it.

The picture's success, however, only created more interest in outlaw motorcycle clubs, enlisted more members, spawned numerous imitations, Fonda and Dennis Hopper in *Easy Rider*[9] being only the most famous and probably the most thoughtful. It became a kind of counterculture anti-Hollywood milestone, its message being that these maverick antiheroes were preferable to redneck Middle America, and had every right to their supposedly poetic odysseys. But were most outlaw motorcyclists truly as sophisticated idealists as Fonda, Hopper, or their buddy in the film played by Jack Nicholson (in the role that made him a star)? Was their movie martyrdom—they all get killed by hypocritically violent NRA types—true to life? At best, questionable.

I remember my mother coming back from seeing Nicholas Ray's *Rebel Without a Cause*[10] and remarking that it was a dangerous, unbalanced, and potentially very harmful work. Being a pretty callow teenager at the time, not unlike the three main kids in the movie, I laughed, feeling she was overreacting, but my mother was extremely firm in her opinion, and my father agreed. She said that because there was not even one intelligent and responsible adult in the entire film, it presented an unfairly slanted view of youngsters and of life in general: the kids were completely right, the parents and other authority figures were completely wrong. I argued that maybe in these cases—the film was based on some actual instances—that's the way the grownups were. She said this wasn't relevant; the film was supposed to be a work of art, and art required a balanced representation in which the right way was dramatized at least on some level. The dissolution of the family unit in America from the mid-1950s to our current crisis certainly proves that her point was well taken. Jimmy Dean's real death[11] only increased the martyred aspect of the characters in the film, helping, with *Rebel's* countless imitators, to build an atmosphere in which the natural generation gap is exacerbated to such a degree that a schism now exists in which even the theoretical notion that maturity and age bring wisdom is totally disrespected and it is increasingly difficult after a certain age for parents to guide their children.

The first movie I directed and cowrote was a thriller released in 1968 called *Targets*.[12] In the movie, a young Vietnam veteran who collected guns goes berserk and kills first his mother and his wife and then goes on a rampage and randomly shoots a considerable number of strangers on a freeway and at a drive-in movie. His story was based on the actual Charles Whitman case in Austin, Texas, which is similar. Crosscut with this is the tale of an aging horror-film star (played by Boris Karloff in what turned out to be essentially his final role), who decides to quit the business because his Victorian kind of horror has been outdated by the modern horror of random violence in suburban settings. The two stories converge at the conclusion and, because it is a movie, Karloff actually plays a part in stopping the killer and helping to have him arrested. We considered a number of other endings, including having the murderer shot to death by patrons at the drive-in or by the police. In real life, Whitman committed suicide before the authorities could get to him. I felt that any sort of death for the killer carried an inherent glorification, and that only by his being taken off in handcuffs, subdued through his running out of weapons and ammunition, and confronted with Karloff's moral authority, could any responsible finish be created, one that perhaps wouldn't encourage an imitation of his terrible acts.

Of course, glorification of gangsters and outlaws is virtually a Hollywood tradition, from James Cagney as *The Public Enemy*[13] or Edward G. Robinson as *Little Caesar*[14] to Humphrey Bogart in *High Sierra*[15] to Warren Beatty and Faye Dunaway as *Bonnie & Clyde*.[16] Indeed, the brutal slow-motion massacre of Bonnie and Clyde was the ultimate (and much-imitated) antiauthoritarian deification. This was compounded by Sam Peckinpah's brutally revisionist outlaw western, *The Wild Bunch*,[17] which took the slow-motion pornography of violence to new heights. In each case, the inherent star personality and charisma of the actors imbues their characters with likable qualities that the actual people or characters as written may very well not have possessed, the casting alone becoming a huge factor in how these personages are perceived. Recently, this was notable in the case of two such amiable actors as Woody Harrelson and Juliette Lewis in *Natural Born Killers*,[18] tending to throw off the supposed inherent meaning of the film—a satirical look at the media's creation of celebrity—by making the characters too attractive and, therefore, causing some real incidents in which perpetrators of crimes cited the film as an inspiration.

Sometimes the construction of a movie alone can cause a different result from one the makers may have intended. In *The Accused*,[19] a gang rape sequence that is the catalyst and focus of the entire story is not actually shown until the end of the movie. Perhaps the commercial reasoning was that to put the rape where it belonged, at the beginning, would have created an anticlimactic movie, all the "action" happening at the start, leaving the work without an "exciting" enough conclusion. However, this decision completely throws the picture off balance, weakening the audience's empathy for the leading character, throwing into question throughout the film all her accusations against the perpetrators. The worst result this had, however, was to make the rape itself the object of unconscious and unwanted prurient interests on the viewers' part. As it turned out, the picture—although Jodie Foster's performance received the Academy Award for Best Actress—did not do well at the box office,[20] probably because of the innately unpleasant feeling it engendered in audiences who were placed in the position of having to be curious to see a sequence that had to be, by its very nature, highly repellent.

On my own second film, *The Last Picture Show*,[21] I was encouraged, even pressured, by the producers to make use of the new freedom of the screen by featuring nudity in a number of scenes that could certainly have been done without it. Although the exposures totaled only seven seconds (all in movement) of a two-hour film, they added to the sensational aspect of the work and probably helped at the box office. I was extremely uncomfortable with these moments while making the movie, especially after the leading lady, Cybill Shepherd, and I fell in love. The set was closed during these sequences and no one was allowed to be there except the camera operator and me, all in an attempt to make the actors more comfortable with the situation. Cybill was extremely hesitant about doing these few seconds and only agreed because of her belief in the script and in me. There were, of course, to be no still photographs taken of these scenes and because this was nearly a decade before the advent of the videocassette era, none of us imagined any possible way these few seconds could be seen except on the screen.

The film's enormous critical and popular success—it was nominated for eight Oscars including Best Picture, and won two of the acting awards—led to a greater acceptance of screen nudity, and unfortunately, assisted in opening the door to increasingly less tasteful exploitation. A year or so after the movie's release, Cybill and I were shocked to find a couple of frames from these delicate moments reproduced in *Playboy* magazine. They had been spliced—without permission from the studio or the actor or producers—from a 35mm print and blown up for use in the publication. Cybill sued and eventually won, the best result being that the Screen Actors Guild added a clause to its standard contract that no such use could be made in the future without the signed authorization of the specific player. Naturally the videocassette, the laser disk, and the Internet have made this kind of business virtually unstoppable, and therefore should give even more pause to those wanting to film such scenes.

Social acceptance of nudity in films, on cable TV, and in commercials has risen as part of the general relaxation of taboos and the proliferation of pornography, but it has done nothing to help the status of women in pictures, nor has it improved roles for women, which now are at an all-time low; nor has it decreased rape, which is at an all-time high.[22] I can't help but connect this to the patterns that began in the mid-1950s and became increasingly worse as the decades passed. Marilyn Monroe and Audrey Hepburn were the last female movie stars, except for Barbra Streisand, who began, like Frank Sinatra, as a singer, keeping her popularity on records while her screen career fluctuated. Because the mystery of women is connected in some way to nakedness, certainly the virtual obligatory nature now of nude scenes in films has deprived women of one of their inherent powers. Could such legendary goddesses of the screen like Greta Garbo or Marlene Dietrich have maintained their hold on the collective imagination if they had been forced to bare all?

That I contributed to this situation by my work in a quality picture does not make me anything but unhappy and regretful. Since *Picture Show*, I have carefully avoided such scenes, except in a release we made in Singapore, *Saint Jack*,[23] in which I shot an actual Asian transvestite prostitute and her transsexual partner performing a kind of dance routine they were in the habit of doing for customers. I shot this scene only because there was no other way to dramatize its essentially unerotic sadness than by showing the whole thing as the two were used to doing it. But this was a long way from exploiting young models or fledgling actresses who have to go on in their careers. In 1990, I did another cut of *Picture Show*, adding seven minutes and snipping out a couple of the nude moments. I'm afraid I actually hurt one scene by doing this, but feel that ethically I made the right decision, although it is a Pyrrhic victory because the real damage had been done long ago.

The financial ethics of the movies, on the other hand, seem to have been out of whack almost from the beginning. Once it became clear that in moving pictures even more than in the theater, the players were the main attraction, studios tried to keep stars in their place. The Biograph Company wouldn't give "The Biograph Girl" any other name until the public essentially demanded to know who she was; another studio lured her away by revealing the young woman's name to be Florence Lawrence, who thus became the first movie star. This was at a time when women were not yet allowed to vote. Talk about ethics! Within a decade the movies had helped to alter that immoral situation and women won the right to vote. How could they not, with women like Lillian Gish, Gloria Swanson, and Mary Pickford as leading representatives of their sex, known the world over.

Virtually the same thing that happened, in the same year, to Florence Lawrence, happened to Mary Pickford, who soon became known as "America's (and 'The World's') Sweetheart"; within a decade she co-owned a studio. Universal's early westerns hero Harry Carey (who made John Ford a director) didn't find out he was a star until he went on vacation to New York and got mobbed on the streets by fanatic screen fans, a coinage of that moment in history. Carey went right up to Universal Studios' East Coast office and demanded a raise. This was symptomatic of the studio's deep reluctance to pay the actors what they were worth, or to give them any profit participation at all. I remember Gene Kelly in the last decades of his life bemoaning the fact that he received exactly zero for home video or TV sales for all his invaluable contributions to numerous classic screen musicals in the late 1940s and 1950s. Sadly, Gene said, "None of us did. We were all just salaried employees."

From the beginning, actors were under exclusive contract to both major and minor studios and had to have permission to be loaned out for work at other places; often the loaning company took a great deal more than the salary they continued to pay the artist. Success at the box office eventually meant raises, of course, but most contracts were seven-year deals. When, in the late teens, mega-star performers Charles Chaplin, Douglas Fairbanks, and Mary Pickford and the founder of narrative film, D.W. Griffith, formed United Artists, it was a way of taking complete control of their own careers and was a unique exception to the Hollywood rule, until things began to change in the late 1940s and early 1950s.

Another singular example: After a lackluster seven-year contract with Paramount, Cary Grant, from 1936 on, never again made a long-term deal with anyone. Grant owned a hefty piece of his pictures as early as *Penny Serenade*.[24] By the last year of the 1940s, Humphrey Bogart had his own production company, and in 1950, James Stewart made the first percentage deal—for Anthony Mann's western, *Winchester 73*[25]—where Stewart took a piece of the gross in lieu of salary. This was a Lew Wassermann-negotiated deal, often credited with being the second fatal blow to the studio system; the first being the studios' forced disposition of their film theaters; the third, television.

By the start of the 1960s, however, stars were not only getting percentages, they were getting huge salaries too, and Elizabeth Taylor's overtime rate on *Cleopatra*[26] just about sunk the 20th Century Fox Company that made it. This was the beginning of the movie stars' revenge, and who better to start it than a former child contract player, as Liz Taylor was at MGM. The degree of rancor, resentment, and rage that must go with the kind of enforced servitude the actors underwent would have to be very high. And it is something passed down from one actors' generation to another, to the current situation, which has turned quite grotesquely obscene. But one of the other reasons actors began demanding such high wages is because, on percentage deals, it was known that there was often "creative accounting" on returns, so that high-grossing films barely could give off a tiny profit participation. Again, the punishment has been high in the demands players now make "up front": there's huge money in the bank long before anyone else's—and no matter what the box-office gross, the money is nonrefundable—although if the gross is big enough, they'll get even more. The ethics throughout have been so off balance that it seems difficult to envision any way to a more decent solution. And the same thing has happened with budgets and costs of marketing: everything is out of control.

The skillful craftsman side of America's directors has precipitously declined over the last three decades to a current all-time low. Among the many directors I spoke with over the years, and among all of the 18 directors I interviewed for publication—from John Ford and Alfred Hitchcock to Howard

Hawks and Orson Welles—there was a pride in achieving the illusion of expense, the illusion of an explosion, for example, rather than real expense or a real explosion. It was virtually a part of the essential discipline of the job to think of ways to economically convey something or to give an impression of something rather than simply paying the full cost of photographing reality.

Recently, the producer and director of a hot action crime picture were on TV bragging about how many real cars and real buildings they had blown up. For decades, it was the exact opposite upon which the good filmmakers prided themselves. Of course, to photograph with a dozen cameras a building being blown up is certainly considerably easier than giving the impression of blowing up a building. The first requires only money, the second only talent. To have all the money in the world at your disposal on a given project certainly makes it easier, but it doesn't guarantee quality; most often limitations on gifted artists have produced amazingly inventive results. On his Shakespeare film, *The Tragedy of Othello: The Moor of Venice*,[27] Orson Welles was stuck when costumes didn't arrive for a murder scene, so he switched locations to a Turkish bath where only towels would be required, and created one of his most memorable sequences.

The current average Hollywood production, which costs $30 to $50 million to produce[28] and another $20 to $30 million to market[29] is, by any standards, way out of the realm of ethical expense. Of course the average picture of this price is often a bomb. The success-failure ratio at studios leans heavily toward flops. The cost of actors; the cost of shooting so much footage over so many days because of the director's lack of vision or experience; his need to shoot far more material than would be necessary if he had precut the picture, either on paper or in his head (which most of the best directors did, from Griffith to Ford to Welles); all these make it so.

But with the era of MTV-video-collage kind of direction, there is no consistent point of view or style to most of the work: It's become a kind of cut-cut-cut-staccato hodgepodge that passes for hip, flashy filmmaking but gives no sense of verisimilitude or true human behavior, only a fast-paced series of manipulated, calculated (or accidental) moments trying desperately to add up to one concept, most often glued together by the ever-present musical score blatantly directing your interest and emotions in a way the images do not. Most big movies now look alike because they are all made the same way—not in the studio or on location, but in the cutting room, taking away most possibilities of players' sustained behavior working on subconscious awareness levels far more profound than the synthetic two-thrills-a-second sort of editing for its own sake now popular. Self-conscious decadence is what it suggests.

Finally, what has happened to the movies is not unique to the movies, and yet, as we noted at the outset, to say that most films' lack of ethics reflect their society's lack of ethics is not an excuse, but it is most certainly true. The only hope is quality education in the history of the world, from the true beginnings of civilization around 11,000 B.C.[30] through to the present; and then the history of the movies, from A.D. 1895 when the first exhibited film was shown in Paris by the Lumiere brothers.[31] The work, which I've seen, was a single 50-second shot of Lumiere factory workers exiting the gates at the end of a day's labors. There was something poignantly innocent about this simple beginning to a medium that would strongly influence perceptions around the globe, thus dramatically changing the world.

If we care about the world and care about the movies, it is incumbent upon us to try to improve the situation of both. Good films have that power, but so do bad ones. Hitler, don't forget, was only the first political figure created through manipulated cinematic images.

To try to improve both our current history and our current film history through education, we must make a start along some front. This is absolutely vital. The following work represents an important first step; a way to begin the exploration of the means by which we might help reverse certain of the negative trends that have seized our society. If we stop to examine the ethical implications of what we do as creators and as citizens, as advocated in these pages, and factor this circumspection into the creations we put out into the world, the start will have been made.

Notes

1 Hollywood Production Code, 1934–1966.
2 Pearsall, Judy, Ed. *Concise Oxford English Dictionary*, (Oxford: Oxford University Press, 1999).
3 Graves, Robert. *The White Goddess: A Historical Grammar of Poetic Myth*, (New York: Noonday Press, 1997).
4 1933 D: Archie Mayo, Warner Bros.
5 1944 D: Howard Hawks, Warner Bros.
6 1946 D: Howard Hawks, Warner Bros.
7 1944 D: Preston Sturges, Paramount Pictures.
8 1966 D: Roger Corman, American International Pictures.
9 1969 D: Dennis Hopper, Columbia Pictures.
10 1955 D: Nicholas Ray, Warner Bros.
11 Dean died on September 30, 1955, when his Porsche Spyder collided with another car just east of Paso Robles, California.
12 1968 D: Peter Bogdanovich, Paramount Pictures.
13 1931 D: William Wellman, Warner Bros.
14 1931 D: Mervyn LeRoy, Warner Bros.
15 1941 D: Raoul Walsh, Warner Bros.
16 1967 D: Arthur Penn, Warner Bros.
17 1969 D: Sam Peckinpah, Warner Bros.

18 1994 D: Oliver Stone, Warner Bros.
19 1988 D: Jonathan Kaplan, Paramount Pictures.
20 Box office gross was $32.069 million.
21 1971 D: Peter Bogdanovich, Columbia Pictures.
22 "Sexual assault continues to represent the most rapidly growing violent crime in America." Dupre, A.R., Hampton, H.L., Morrison, H., and Meeks, G.R. "Sexual Assault," *Obstetrical and Gynecological Survey* 48 (1993): 640–648.
23 1979 D: Peter Bogdanovich, New World Pictures.
24 1941 D: George Stevens, Columbia Pictures.
25 1950 D: Anthony Mann, Universal International Pictures.
26 1961 D: Joseph L. Mankiewicz, 20th Century Fox.
27 1952 D: Orson Wells (uncredited), United Artists.
28 Berton, Lee and Harris, Roy. "Reel-World Accounting," *CFO: The Magazine for Senior Financial Executives*, Volume 13, Number 3, March 1999, pp. 34–46.
29 Berton and Harris, 1999.
30 "11,000 B.C. This data corresponds approximately to the beginnings of village life in a few parts of the world, the first undisputed peopling of the Americas, the end of the Pleistocene Era and the last Ice Age, and the start of what geologists term the Recent Era." Diamond, Jared. *Guns, Germs, and Steel: The Fates of Human Societies* (New York: W.W. Norton & Company Inc., 1997).
31 Auguste Lumiere (B: October 19, 1862, D: April 10, 1954) and Louis Lumiere (B: October 5, 1864, D: June 6, 1948) were French inventors and pioneers of photographic equipment, who devised an early motion picture camera and projector called the cinematographic (from which "cinema" is derived). Their film *La Sortie des Ouvriers de L'usine Lumiere* (1895; *Workers Leaving the Lumiere Factory*) was shown in Paris and is considered the first motion picture. *Encyclopedia Britannica Online*: www.eb.com.

Acknowledgments

I would like to thank the following people and organizations, without whose support, hard work, and enthusiasm this book would never have been brought to fruition:

Les Brown, for everything;

Marcy Kelly, founder of Mediascope, who provided the original inspiration for this book;

David Giannovario, tireless research assistant, whose fascination with footnotes is matched only by his passion as Skeptic;

Stephanie Carbone, for graciously sharing her research and insights on various media issues;

The implacable Ivy Stone at the Fifi Oscard Agency, who believed in the book's integrity and saw it through until the end;

Westview editor Sarah Warner, for picking this book out of the pile;

Jane Olivier, for keeping it all running smoothly;

Elizabeth Monk Daly, Doe Mayer, and Carol Hodge of the University of Southern California School of Cinema-Television, for their early support and contributions;

Irina Posner of the Center for Communications;

Steven Rohde, Esq.;

Laura Blum for her vast Rolodex and interviewing talents;

Carnegie Corporation of New York and The California Wellness Foundation for supporting the Mediascope-based research and services for this project; and,

To the students I taught in my various film seminars at Yale University, for helping to articulate certain of the central theses of this book through your resolutely ceaseless questioning of everything. You know who you are.

Also, thanks to: Jon Andrews, Laurence Bortner, Alcudio Cruz, William C. Devins, Timothy Dupay, John Hart, Tom Klassen, Avi Levy, Gary Maynard of the State University of Connecticut, Professor Eugene Provenzo of the University of Miami, Mark Alan Schwartz, Linn and Barbara Stanton and … everyone else who has lent support to this project since its inception.

Interviews by Laura Blum

Interviewees and Selected Credits:

Joe Berlinger, director, *Blair Witch Two*

David Brown, producer, *Jaws, Angela's Ashes*

Charles Burnett, independent filmmaker, *To Sleep With Anger* (writer, director)

Carter Burwell, film composer, *Fargo, The General's Daughter*

Mark Gill, president, Miramax Films/L.A.

Pat Golden, casting director, *New Jack City*

Paul Hapenny, writer, *Vig*

Rob Legato, special effects director, *Titanic*

Bridget Potter, television executive, *OZ*

Bruce Sinofsky, documentary filmmaker, *Brother's Keeper*

Christine Vachon, independent producer, *I Shot Andy Warhol, Boys Don't Cry*

Gordon Willis, cinematographer, *The Godfather*

Stu Zakim, National Publicity, Universal Studios

Introduction: The Mission

"Why Are We Here?"

"Let's recap, shall we ... I ate two slices of bad pizza, went to bed and grew a conscience!" So says Tom Cruise's title character in *Jerry Maguire,*[1] explaining his "mission statement" advocating a more reasoned, ethical approach to the business of being a sports agent. Several scenes later, he loses his job for honestly expressing his opinion—an opinion shared but not spoken by his colleagues. As Maguire learns, the personal discovery of ethics and ethical choice can be jarring. So, should we play it safe and just ignore such things?

"Professions" such as law, medicine, and accounting, and "occupations" such as journalism, real estate, and business each have formal codes of ethics to be followed by those who elect to pursue these careers. Despite their tremendous combined worldwide influence, there is no such code for film and television. Why not? Should there be such a code? Is there a case to be made for self-regulation? Or, in the alternative, should all regulation be resisted?

This book, written by a filmmaker, with contributions from notable film and television professionals, as well as critics and journalists, attempts to explore and suggest answers to some of these questions.

Now, a few preliminary notes. What this book is *not*, for example.

First, this book is *not* concerned primarily with the *business* ethics of the entertainment industry or the way in which the business of producing content is conducted—production, distribution, and marketing of motion pictures and television. You will see some references to the business side of the industry, but this is an extremely broad topic, to be dealt with in a companion volume in my effort to keep this book from being 2,000 pages long!

What we are primarily interested in examining here is what I would call the ethics of *content*. At the risk of beginning this book by being overly simplistic, the two distinct worlds of ethics, those of content and those of how content comes to be realized, can and should be dealt with separately. Although they intersect at many points, there are distinct ethical issues unique to each.

The interesting thing about America is that everyone has the right to say just about anything. That's lovely. But movies are mass commercial speech. We have the ability to think about what's appropriate and what's not—which is not really to do with whether you're allowed to say it, but rather whether it's always the right thing to say.
—Mark Gill

Also, in any meaningful examination of the overall topic of ethics in entertainment, it is important to begin at the beginning. Movies and television programs begin with ideas and the artistic expression of those who create them. Although it is naive to believe that these ideas are created in a vacuum—they are most definitely influenced by the realities of the business environment in which they are nurtured—the ideas themselves are still the place where we need to begin this journey, as *they* are where production begins.

Second, this book is *not* academic in nature, per se. Although a certain amount of research is presented and discussed to illustrate the basic issues at hand, this is not in any way an attempt to put social scientists out of business. It is, rather, an attempt to extrapolate from their data and conclusions in order to provide a useful baseline for our exploration of ethical considerations.

Third, this book is also *not* designed to be a formal classroom curriculum (although it will hopefully be a tool for use in production, writing, and directing classes as a companion to more technical books on creating entertainment). Although there are ethical exercises included in many chapters, there is no formal workbook, lesson plan, or teacher's guide.

This book *is* a reader on the subject of ethical decisions faced by those who make their living creating entertainment. It is designed to stimulate thought, not to dictate it. The choice was not to attempt the *last* word in the ethics of content, but merely to start the discussion. I discovered, by teaching various film seminars at Yale University, that often just starting the discussion is enough. Others will follow to continue it, one hopes.

This book is definitely *not* intended as an academic analysis of the complex world of higher ethical principles. No "final words" will be attempted in the "absolute good" versus "situational ethics" debate—leaving aside the question as to whether, outside of religion, "absolute" ethics exist at all.

Even a cursory look at the history of the entertainment industries, along with an analysis of current trends, shows that virtually every choice is based upon situational ethics (such as "what sells," "what works," "what fits the story" and so on). Therefore, we will not delve into considerations of the nature of absolute good or other topics too broad for analysis here. We will focus instead upon what has come to be the ethical system of the entertainment industry—applied situational ethics—as our starting point.

Fourth, we are *not* attempting to dictate any sort of "morality" here. This is most definitely *not* a rule book of any kind. I would not live by that, let alone write it! In fact, we are not discussing morality (good and evil, right and wrong) at all, per se. We are trying to help develop an ethical reflex as a tool for use in the recognition and analysis of the ethical issues one faces every day in the entertainment industry.

It is open to debate whether "morality" can even be taught in a classroom or from a nonreligious text, and I want to make it clear that *this is not* the attempt here. We will not attempt to provide a blueprint containing a morally acceptable (to whom?) reasoning process that, if the formula is followed, will always lead to the correct ethical choice. This is not a "how-to" manual. In fact, you may come away scratching your head even more than when you picked up the book. Sorry, but I hope so.

The book is laid out in six sections, with roughly the first half examining arguments for considering ethics onscreen, and the latter chapters exploring specific issues involved in creating content—for example, depicting violence, sex, and stereotypes—and creating different product for different audiences, such as children and teens or documentaries.

The "Ethical Gymnastics" sections that follow most chapters are designed to provoke discussion in class or thought in the mind of the general reader. These questions provide opportunities to flex the "ethical choice reflex" we are attempting to develop.

The reputation of the motion picture industry is more than a bit tattered today. That came home to me whenever I mentioned this book project to others. Almost invariably the subject of ethics in filmmaking struck people as an oxymoron, often producing a wry chuckle or a swift remark like, "I get it—a book of empty pages," although in a serious vein, everyone, without exception, found the enterprise laudable and necessary. From all the excesses of violence and sex over the years, and the pernicious racial and gender stereotyping, many people are understandably convinced that motion pictures are being made without conscience. I think it more likely that movies are made in the misguided belief that they are just fanciful entertainment products and that no one, not even children, will mistake them for real life.

—Les Brown

> *What I would hope is that people who are going to be working in television over the next generation would be thoughtful, would really think a great deal about the effect of what they are going to be doing.*
> *—Bridget Potter*

Industry "track-through narratives" attempt to illustrate how content can become increasingly charged with exploitative edges through the development process, sometimes taking on a life of its own. These sections also represent the briefest of forays into the business side of the ethical decision-making question.

These were, in part, inspired by my own experiences in developing mate-rial for the screen. At times, I have developed projects, believing them to have a certain ethical integrity, and the production process has diluted or distorted them to create a rather different animal. This happened to some extent on a film I produced entitled *Vig*.[2] Certain of the powerful ethical mainstays present in the script were lost in production through creative disagreements and other reasons. Without these elements, the final story felt rather different than the way it had begun.

The point is that I fully understand the business "realities" that surround our work, and the difficulties these can pose. We are suggesting striving for ideals here, not implying that you can always reach them.

Also of note are a series of companion essays by noted filmmakers, commentators, and journalists following various chapters that illuminate certain themes. Featured throughout is a running commentary from noted industry professionals—producers, writers, directors, special effects directors, composers, and casting directors—who discuss ethics in relation to their area of expertise. These quotes were collected in a series of personal one on one interviews conducted by journalist and writer Laura Blum during the spring and summer of 1998.

> *I don't know how, in good conscience, people in the film business or television or music can say that what they do has no measurable influence on the way people think. If that's so, then why make the product at all? Or if you make the product, then why not make a complex story that challenges the intellect? Because, after all, if you have no influence on how people think then basically it's one and the same—the banal and the intelligent.*
> *—Paul Hapenny*

Although the book is for a general audience interested in the media, in various places I have taken special care to attempt to illuminate issues for those in the beginnings of media careers, in an attempt to help them navigate turbulent ethical waters. One of the primary reasons for the creation of this volume is that many schools do not offer an ethical component to their film and television production curricula as yet. This is intended as a first step toward changing that situation.

For filmmakers, this book is an attempt to nurture an "ethical choice reflex" to help keep them on whatever track they may choose, while not losing sight of the broader issues. I am attempting to show that there are ethical choices to be made in every aspect of what we do, and we should recognize and deal with them as such. The book is designed to start people thinking, not to tell them how or what to think.

We attempt to shed light upon where ethical choice may fall in the creation of film and television, and to present a tool or two and certain ideas with which to illuminate the ethical choices that creators* of programming make constantly, and sometimes inadvertently. If used correctly, these ideas will help creators be better, more informed creators. Information is power. The more knowledgeably used, the greater the power.

More than a few directors defend Hollywood's penchant for violence as a reflection of mankind's violent nature. Shakespeare recognized that too, they point out—so why lie about it? Others place the blame with the moviegoing public, saying if they stop going to see violent films we'll stop making them, as if the issue were one of supply and demand. One can make the same argument for dealing in drugs. There is clearly an appetite for sex and violence, but the issue is how to deal with them responsibly. Shakespeare did not exploit them for their own sake.

—Les Brown

Finally, this book is merely a first step. If it gets the ball rolling in the direction of creating in the minds of all of us in the industry—and all who consume the output of our industry—the idea that we must recognize the ethical choices around us, for good or for ill, then it will have accomplished its goal.

---

* Please note that, throughout this book, I use the term "creator" to condense the unwieldy phrase "filmmakers and creators of television" into a single appropriate term that takes into account creators of both film and television.

The Skeptic Speaks: Arguments for (and Against) Considering Ethics in Entertainment Content

Filmmakers today are coming of age in a business reality that represents a real challenge, especially to their ethical faculties. They are breaking in at a time when to be "edgy" (virtually always the desired moniker for the neophyte in the industry and for many veterans as well) translates into being violent, graphic and almost ridiculously direct. Cleverness is brutality, presented "in your face" (a phrase we should all despise by now). Gone are the days of subtlety and cleverness that Peter Bogdanovich longs for in his Foreword to this book.

The film business is 100 years old, give or take a few years, and television is just passing its fiftieth birthday as a mass medium. Perhaps now the time has come (some would say it is long overdue) for the entertainment industry as a whole to look at itself critically, as many other professions and occupations have in the past, and to develop a set of principles or a system of ethics. Please note that this is most definitely *not* a First Amendment Issue, but a responsibility issue. It is also just plain good sense.

> *The American public has an insatiable appetite for film. Anything to do with what they're about, who's sleeping with whom—film personnel transcend just being movie stars, they become icons of pop culture. You're saying something about that culture.*
> —*Stu Zakim*

> *I wish for no more incredibly dumb comedies, and I wish for no more extraordinarily bad shoot-em-up action movies. There's a reason this is called a fantasy: it will not happen. But wouldn't it be lovely?*
> —*Mark Gill*

But why would the study of ethics be important to a creator of film and television? Isn't ethics just a set of rules invented by dead white males? In this case, very, very *long* dead. The First Amendment to the Constitution guarantees that we, as creators, do not have to abide by any restrictions that attempt to curb our freedom of artistic expression. Why should we, blessed by the founding fathers with a unique freedom to create unfettered, voluntarily embrace a system of beliefs that might, directly or indirectly, subvert that freedom? Why should we pay any attention at all?

To answer these questions, I have constructed a hypothetical argument, based upon actual discussions with former University of Southern California students. One voice is dissenting—"The Skeptic"—who might be a film student; a filmmaker already long in the business; a general reader or anyone who believes in the unfettered creative expression of the artist, and that considerations of ethics will hinder that freedom. An answering voice—"Response"—represents this volume's mission, argues for ethical choice, and posits that this book *is* worth the reader's time. If we can convince "The Skeptic," perhaps we can convince you. Here goes:

The Skeptic: Why "ethics?" Ethics stifle creativity, and have no place in the world of art. They keep creators from pushing the edge of the envelope, and developing into unique voices. They hew off the rough edges of new creation, so necessary for growth.

Response: Ethics in and of themselves do not stifle creativity. If you know an ethical choice when you see one, it can vastly increase your power to develop your art. If "the unexamined life is not worth living," arguably, the unexamined creation may not be worth creating. Artistic creation is most often enhanced through understanding. Ethics provide a frame of reference, freeing the artist to focus his or her creative energies. Also, ethics—at least as they are defined in this volume—do not restrict the ability to push the envelope. Rather, they allow artists to judge for themselves why and how *far* they are pushing it. Then the choice is theirs.

Also, arguably, the most dynamic artistic growth comes from an attempt at a true understanding of the human condition and from trying to better that condition, whether by support or criticism, and not from nihilistic negativity.

The Skeptic: I feel a headache coming on. But, the nature of art is a tough one. What if we don't *agree* about the nature of art?

Response: The beauty is, we don't *have* to. The true nature of art is *way* beyond the scope of this book. Yet, whatever art is, the principles we're discussing here should still apply, and more importantly, will still help you.

The Skeptic: I'm glad we're not going to spend hundreds of pages debating insoluble philosophical questions. As an artist—at least under my definition—what I want to know is that you're not trying to stifle my freedom of expression with your ethics.

Response: No. Not in any way. In fact, we're trying to enhance your creativity by giving you a new tool. We're trying to get you to realize that virtually everything you do as a creator of film and television involves some ethical choice, and that when you are comfortable with ethical choice as a tool and use it regularly, it can open up new avenues for you.

The Skeptic: OK. But codes and rules are still restrictive— and dull—like reading insurance policies.

Response: But what if they can help you be better at what you do? Isn't it worth struggling a bit? If you were a gold miner, and I could show you how to get more gold out of the ground, or keep the government or your competitors or critics from restricting your freedom to mine freely, would it be worth the effort? Who knows, you might even enjoy it.

The Skeptic: Let's move on. If we agree to an ethical code, that means content restriction, right? I mean, if we couldn't portray violence, for example, would we have such a powerful film as, say, *Saving Private Ryan*?[3]

Response: We're not suggesting for a moment that you shouldn't be able to portray violence. That's an oversimplified argument that ignores cinema reality, as well as the real world. The argument is that we should think about the *ways* in which we portray violence, and about not portraying it in gratuitous fashion. *Ryan* is extremely violent, yes, but the violence is, for the most part, *not* gratuitous. It is the realistic violence of war. Given the subject matter, the viewer should realize that the movie will be violent, and should go expecting it. "Caveat Emptor."[4] In fact, *Ryan* successfully portrays many of the things we will discuss in later chapters—nonglamorized violence in context, with consequences, rewards, and punishments.

The Skeptic: Well, I want to be able to use violence if I feel it's important to my story. I'm glad you feel it has its place. What do you mean by nonglamorized violence?

Response: Read on. One more thing. I have a question for you about violence and violent images.

The Skeptic: Shoot. Sorry.

Response: Right. Do you agree that in order for violence in the media to have real impact, you have to keep looking for ways to "up the stakes," presenting violence in new and ever "bigger" ways?

The Skeptic: I guess that's true. Otherwise, people get bored. There's nothing new. They've seen it all before.

Response: So at some point, as you keep ratcheting up the violence, it takes over the story, correct? I mean, it becomes the principal thing the audience is waiting and watching for.

The Skeptic: Well, I would hope they're watching my story, but I guess you're right, at least to a degree.

Response: Do you want to be judged for special effects or for your abilities as a storyteller?

The Skeptic: Ouch. I get the point. Please, let's move on. I want to address the whole notion that violence in the media makes people engage in violent behavior. Media images do not "make" viewers "do" anything. The studies aren't conclusive. I know all about Descartes and free will, thank you. Just because I portray or even glorify violence does *not* mean that my audience is going to leave the theater and start murdering innocent bystanders.

Response: Your point that movies and television do not "make" people "do" things is correct, but only as far as it goes. The terminology is imprecise. No, media images do not physically force or compel viewers to commit violent acts. However, if you are suggesting that media images do not encourage violent tendencies or enhance aggressive feelings, your statement is factually wrong. Literally hundreds of studies have supported the conclusion that violent images do, in fact, encourage aggressive and violent behavior (see the "Portrayals of Violence" section). You can disagree with this assertion, but you would be bucking decades of social science research and the consensus of medical scientists and public health officials.

Now, let's say for the sake of your argument that violence in the media encourages aggression in only a few borderline disturbed personalities. If you make a gratuitously violent film, and its nationwide release influences a single person to engage in violent behavior, and that person is an adolescent who goes out—by his own admission motivated specifically by your film—and mows down two dozen of his classmates and teachers by firing on his high school with an automatic rifle, do you hold any responsibility for that action?

The Skeptic: You're trying to pull that old "littering argument" with me.

Response: Excuse me? The who?

The Skeptic: You know, that whole argument "If everybody littered, the streets would be filled with trash." Well, everybody doesn't litter, and the streets aren't filled with trash! And frankly, if I throw one soda can out the window of my car, it adds up to one soda can, not the end of the ecosystem. The world is a harsh place, bad things happen to good people, life is not fair. Why should my films reflect a fake world where the bad guy is always punished, the good guy is always rewarded, "different" people are never ridiculed, and sex and drugs are always a bad experience?

Response: Well, I guess I tapped a vein! OK. Now I understand the littering argument. These are all sentiments I'm sure many readers will be shouting, "YES, YES, YES" over. A partial answer might be in the form of a question. Do you really want to make the situation worse, even by just one soda can, simply because you can? For now, let's just agree to disagree, and move on.

The Skeptic: Alright, how about stereotypes? Just because I make a character a "jive-talking black pimp," doesn't mean that all African Americans are jive-talking pimps. Even if I make *all* my African American characters jive-talking pimps, it doesn't mean all African Americans are jive-talking pimps. Using stereotypes serves a purpose. Stereotypes are easily identifiable by audiences and allow them to infer vast amounts of information about a character without having to use screen time to develop that character.

Response: Some stereotyping can be helpful in pegging characters quickly, I agree (see the "Portrayals of Stereotypes" section). However, stereotypes that play to the viewer's baser instincts and prejudices can be harmful to the individual psyche and to society as a whole.

The Skeptic: That makes sense, but I still seem to be suffering for and taking on all the prejudice in the world.

Response: You just have to think about the choices you make. Now, let's go back to content regulation. Remember that, throughout the history of film and television, there have been many attempts to regulate or censor artistic freedom, some more successful than others. Those who have been at the root of these attempts might well qualify as your critics and competitors in our gold mining analogy....

The Skeptic: Why do they keep trying? Why can't they stop blaming us for society's failures, and leave us alone! First, I'm protected by the First Amendment—even from having to swallow your ethics. Second, don't they believe in free expression?

Response: You might want to rethink this defense somewhat. Maybe in a more perfect (and probably more boring) world, where everyone was of equal intelligence, discernment, opportunity, breeding, and education, you might be able to argue that you could be as much of a renegade, or racist, or violence monger as you like in your programming, and you could comfortably rely on your audience's filtering mechanisms to realize it was merely entertainment and not to be taken seriously. That is *not*, however, the world in which we live. We cannot all defend ourselves against media input equally. In fact, if you're already in or going into a media-related field as your profession, you're probably already better prepared than most to defend yourself against unwanted media messages and influences.

Remember, the Constitution was originally conceived, among other things, to protect all (white male) citizens in society, both the strong and the weak. We are simply advocating that you consider the effect of your work on those not as capable as you of filtering negative, harmful, or persuasive media input.

One answer to your other question might be that our critics believe that to enjoy a freedom, constitutionally protected or not, we should be required to exercise it responsibly. They may well believe that things have gotten way out of hand and that creators are not being responsible at all. The ethical choice reflex we will hopefully be helping you to develop in the following pages should allow you to see both sides of the argument and determine how best to confront it.

The Skeptic: OK. Media can be used to teach, but that's not its only purpose. Media is also there to entertain, spark and spread ideas, and most of all, to sell advertising and make money.

Response: Hold on a minute! I agree when you say that the function of media is not just to teach. Although much learning is transmitted informally through characters' attitudes and actions in the midst of entertainment, let's leave that aside for now. Twenty-four hours a day of "educational" programming would be pretty tough to take. However, your statement that media exists primarily to sell advertising and make money disturbs me. Yes, that's the way the market functions and you're being realistic in acknowledging its nature. However, to quote Katherine Hepburn in *The African Queen*,[5] "Nature, Mr. Olnut, is what we are put in this world to rise above."

Unless you truly believe your artistic integrity is nurtured by this market reality, don't simply accept it. Change the damned reality! Make ethical choices to try and change the system. Media, and all art for that matter, *should* exist to teach, entertain, spark and spread ideas, even anger or enrage, but NOT principally to *sell advertising and make money*. Remember that advertisers and others in charge of that commercial reality do not in most instances care about your artistic vision. They care about what they can sell your viewers.

The Skeptic: Sobering. All right, try this one. To me, it feels like your ethics equate to the responsibility of the creator to reinforce socially acceptable ideals. Why do I have to reinforce these ideals? Who is to say what is socially acceptable?

Response: You're implying that the purpose of ethical choice is to enforce the status quo. This may seem so, but it is not. What we are proposing is that you do what you do by ethical choice. An ethical choice is a process, not a rule. You can even ethically choose to be unethical, if you feel you must. You may not make many friends, but you can do it. However, even you, renegade that you are, have to admit that there are certain behaviors that society cannot sanction if that society is to survive. That's why we have a system of laws.

The Skeptic: Maybe so. I do like the point you make about being able to ethically choose to be unethical. That gives me choice and freedom to do what I want as long as I think about what I'm doing.

Response: Well, that's a start.

The Skeptic: One more thing. Ethics is defined by *The American Heritage Dictionary*[6] (not exactly the *Oxford English Dictionary*, but hey, I'm a poor filmmaker, give me a break) as "The study of the general nature of morals and of the specific moral choices to be made by the individual in his relationship with others." As for morals, if you are a male filmmaker, a female filmmaker, a Jewish filmmaker, a Buddhist filmmaker, a Christian filmmaker or a Satanic filmmaker, you'll follow your own moral judgments according to your group or beliefs.

What I think you're trying to get me to consider is the system of morals of society as a whole. That's exactly the system that filmmaking should be challenging!

Response: Of *course* you should be challenging the system! One gentleman who was largely responsible for *setting up* the system—Thomas Jefferson—suggested that we should have a revolution every 20 years or so, just to challenge that system.

However, you must also remember that it is this selfsame system that allows you the right of free expression. You must realize that this freedom is not yours by Divine Right, and is therefore not unassailable. It is a *privilege* granted you by a document that set up our political system. That document, and a driving reason for the founding of this nation was to create a society where members respect the rights of others.

Many think the media has already gone too far, that we're trampling on the rights of others to too high a degree. Although it's unlikely that anyone will ever seriously propose repealing the First Amendment...

The Skeptic: That's something...

Response: There are other ways that the powers that be can come crashing down on creators and restrict creative freedom. If we as creators abuse that freedom, that's exactly what might happen. It is already beginning—slowly, but beginning—as evidenced by, for example, movie and television ratings, the so-called violence or 'V'-chip, and revised requirements for children's programming. These measures will continue to be instituted to force creators to be more responsible. We may get to a point, during your career, where you no longer have the right to express yourself in any way you please.

It just makes sense to pick and choose where you fight your battles, and not to push the envelope all the time just because you can.

The Skeptic: By analogy, the "squeaky wheel gets the grease." No one is saying don't squeak, just don't squeak all the time.

Response: Not bad. Not bad at all.

In sum, all we are trying to do is get filmmakers to think before they do, not to restrict *what* they do. We are trying to say that everything we do as creators involves ethical choice. Let us be responsible enough not to blunder into things—let us do them because we consciously choose to do them for good reasons, not just because we *can* do them.

Art is art, and for many artists, *one* of its purposes is to make a statement, whatever that statement may be. As media artists, we have the ability to influence a vast number of people, and that's what we should do. However, we have the responsibility to make sure that we do not inadvertently send out statements or moral messages that we don't really advocate. The stakes are far too high to do anything inadvertently. Our purpose is not to limit creators, but to make them aware of the incredible power they wield, whether desired or not, and of the ways in which ethical considerations can help them to portray only what they choose to portray.

The Skeptic: Well, I'm willing to listen, at least for now.

Response: Excellent. Now let's move on to the text.

Notes

1 1996 D: Cameron Crowe, Tri-Star Pictures.

2 a.k.a. Money Kings, The. 1998 D: Graham Theakston, Lions Gate Films.

3 1998 D: Steven Spielberg, DreamWorks SKG.

4 "Let the buyer beware." (Latin).

5 1951 D: John Huston, United Artists.

6 *The American Heritage Dictionary*, Second College Edition, (Boston: Houghton Mifflin Company, 1985.

Does Media Influence Society?

Awash in Media Culture

How much of an impact does the work of film and television creators have on our society and on societies abroad? How important is it to the world?

The entertainment and electronic media (including the Internet, computers, and video games) is arguably the most pervasive force in American society today. Its almost incomprehensible impact continues to grow here at home as our more traditional political, social, civic, and religious institutions degrade and decay.

Compared to the past—even to our relatively recent, pre-Watergate past—we as a society have lost much of our respect for the political system that was once the cornerstone of our nation as well as the envy of the world. Unfortunately, nowadays it has become more important to know with whom the president has had sex than to know about the treaties he signs, the laws he enacts, or the bombs he drops.

Organized religion, meanwhile, long the bedrock of American national life, has lost its once solid hold on many American families.[1]

In an age where, in many cases, both parents work, the divorce rate is extremely high,[2] and the number of single parent families is soaring, the institution of the American family has lost much of its ability to stabilize society.

Our educational system can no longer plug these holes, as it is also deeply flawed, mired in bureaucratic morass and, as a frightening new trend, awash in senseless violence.

Thus, as a society we have arrived at a point where the institutions that gave structure to daily life in times past have eroded severely, leaving a vacuum.

No pressure or anything, but into this vacuum has stepped, you guessed it ... us. Whether we like it or not, the entertainment industry has become *the* new national institution, the common thread. Movie theaters are one of the few places groups of people still gather to focus on the same stimulus. Theaters have, in a sense, replaced the village green.

Television, too, provides societal bonding through common experience. A huge percentage of the population rallies around the tube for such things as the final episode of *Seinfeld*[3] or the season finale of *ER*.[4] What's more, even absent these landmark events, what we see on television factors into our cultural image, again through shared experience.

Many of us are extremely uncomfortable in this role of arbiter of national taste and to some degree, morals. For the most part, we see ourselves as being in the *entertainment* business. However, the reality is that we have become "educators," or at the very least, strong influences, particularly on young people.

Nowadays, we are drowning in a veritable sea of media. With the rampage of multiplex cinema building—and the construction of giant new 40- and 50-plexes being experimented with in several regions;[5] and with statistically very nearly every household in the land having at least one television[6] and most having a VCR;[7] as well as the proliferation of the personal computer and the Internet it brings with it—media is all around us. For many households in the United States and other countries, the TV is a de facto member of the family. On it sits all day, talking, whether anyone is watching or not. It filters into the background of daily life like no influence before it. Children, especially, spend a very large percentage of their time planted in front of it—more time, actually, than they spend in school at certain ages (see the section,"Children: A Higher Standard").

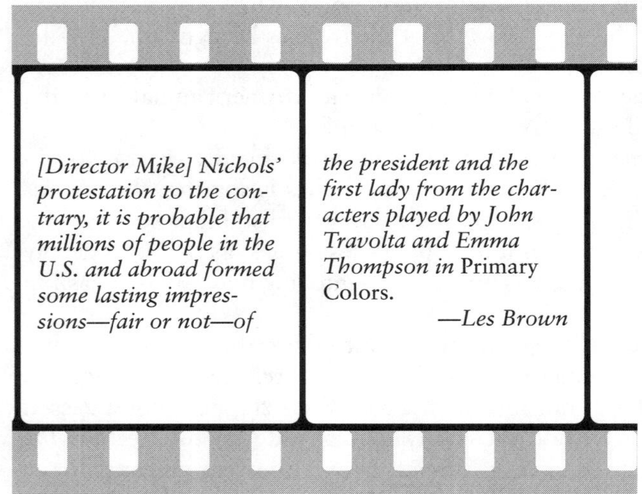

For film, box office receipts in 1998 crested at $7 billion, which means there were more than 1.5 *billion* theatrical admissions.[8] That's right—more than 1.5 *billion* people (obviously many repeat viewers) *paid* to see our product in the United States alone, and that's just at the movies! In addition, home video topped $9 billion for U.S. distributors and $12.6 billion worldwide,[9] thanks, in part, to the release of some major titles. Finally, television advertising revenues topped $25 billion for the year.[10]

As Les Brown forcefully illuminates in his essay "Entertainment in Our Extended World," the first essay at the end of this section, our society has

Entertainment is about diversity. There's no greater community than a movie theater with 500 strangers, all sharing this experience together.
—*Stu Zakim*

The French Minister of Culture was in my office a couple of years ago, and he said, "I have concluded that what Miramax does is take culture and sell it as entertainment." That is very true: In the case of Like Water for Chocolate, *sell the food, sell the sex.*
—*Mark Gill*

I never look at my films as art or entertainment. I look at them as just stories. But I look at them more seriously than as just entertainment. I'm concerned with topics that are accountable and socially redeeming. It costs so much to make a film, so you just can't play around with it. It has such a major impact on audiences that you really have to take what you say seriously.
—*Charles Burnett*

become completely and obsessively "hooked on entertainment." This essay examines the level of this, our national addiction, and describes how we got to this point. Brown focuses on the development of the film and television industries here at home, historical attempts to rate and censor media content, and the overall expansion of entertainment tentacles into our psyches.

And what about the rest of the world? Is this immersion into media culture a uniquely American aberration? Decidedly not. Movies and television produced here are seen in most of the more than 190 separate nations around the globe.[11]

For starters, entertainment has become the leading export industry of the United States, having surpassed the aeronautics and aerospace industry, with no end of growth in sight.[12] As an increasing number of new television stations and other media outlets are established internationally, world hunger for American product will only increase. So too, the current multiplex theater building frenzy taking place throughout Europe and elsewhere will create an enormous need for programming output, much of it originating in the United States. According to Mark Gill, president of Miramax in Los Angeles, it is currently true that "[s]ome 86 percent of tickets sold around the world are to American movies."[13] Entertainment is not only our leading export, but our leading cultural ambassador as well. Globally, more people form their perceptions and opinions of the United States from entertainment product than from any other source.

I hope that people will understand that television has a huge amount of power. More people saw Schindler's List *on NBC in one night than had ever seen that film before. People who didn't believe there had been a Holocaust saw that film on TV. Entertainment on television, in the right hands, can be a really positive social force.*

—*Bridget Potter*

It'd be nice if we could function at a slightly higher level. That doesn't mean that you do things that are not interesting. A lot of interesting stuff is coming out of independent filmmakers. It's good to see that not everyone is brain dead except major studios.

—*Gordon Willis*

Through the media, American culture invades other societies and infiltrates their cultures to an almost ridiculous degree. In an earlier era, this was mostly true of American-manufactured products. Often, even in remote parts of the so-called Third World, one could find the ubiquitous Coca-Cola® sign. Yet this was not nearly as invasive as our worldwide media blitz is today. After all, these were products, not an assaultive and extremely visible stream of values and ideas presented as entertainment.

It is sad to realize that nowadays, for example, the natives inhabiting the jungles surrounding Iquitos, Peru, at the upper reaches of the Amazon River, see *Baywatch*[14] on blaring old televisions when they come to town (by dugout canoe) to pick up supplies. The natives have no electricity or running water except the river. Iquitos can only be reached by air or river. There are no roads. Yet there is *Baywatch*.

There is a new sense that anyone can make a movie. The medium is accessible to all and if you have a story to tell, get yourself a movie camera. I think that's really not true. Like any art form there are great filmmakers and lesser ones, and the great ones are few and far between. I find a lot of young filmmakers coming out today don't really know film history, and don't have sense of who came before them, who the great masters were.
—Christine Vachon

I just don't think that people react to something they see on the screen except as a tie-in to their 15 minutes of fame. There is nothing that I—as a normal human being with no inclination to hurt or kill anybody—can see on the screen that can make me want do the opposite.
—Rob Legato

In fact, *Baywatch* is seen in some 144 countries, generating revenues in excess of $100 million per year, with approximately 70 percent of that revenue coming from foreign markets. Not only does this give a rather skewed vision of America, unless you happen to BE an LA County lifeguard, but it also creates a desire for material things and for a life that is not remotely possible where many of these viewers live.

This phenomenon occurs all over the world. So-called cultural "pollution" is one of the principal reasons why many countries resent the United States, and why these sentiments are on the rise. Protectionism in foreign film and television industries all over the world, designed to restrict the import of U.S. programming in the form of quotas and taxes on U.S. product, is a direct result of this sentiment. So too are the numerous international coproduction treaties that exist between various countries for film and television production, most of which specifically exclude the United States. As a result of our dominance of world markets for entertainment product and the cultural sabotage that accompanies that product, we have become the "bad guy" on the block.

We, as creators, are wielding an ever more powerful cultural weapon—a big stick with immense global impact. We are also projecting a picture of America in our programming by which the world judges us.

In his essay entitled "How The World Sees Us," noted journalist Jack Pitman gives an insider's overview of international perspectives on the United States drawn from our media exports. He brings to life the importance of U.S. programming overseas and the way in which that programming projects images of us as a society.

Notes

1 Although traditional religion and religious institutions may be waning to some extent, the interest in spirituality, it seems, is not—note the success of such programming as *Touched by an Angel*, 1994–present, CBS Television, and the growth of such channels as Pax and Odyssey.

2 In 1999, the U.S. divorce rate was approximately 50 percent. Maeder, Libby. "How to Live Happily Ever After," *The Buffalo News*, January 9, 2000, p. 14M.

3 1990–1998, NBC.

4 1994–present, NBC.

5 Actually, there were 34,168 screens as of late 1999. Smith, Samantha Thompson. "Despite Rise in Ticket Sales, Cinema Owners Count Losses," *News & Observer*, December 24, 1999.

6 Currently, approximately 98.5 percent of all households in this country have at least one television set, with a large percentage having multiple sets. "Statistical Abstracts of the United States 1993." *Country Reports,* Walden Publishing, January 30, 1995.

7 "Nationwide, VCR penetration stood at 87% in 1998." "VCR Households," *PRC News*, December 20, 1999, Volume 1, Number 12, p. 3.

8 Mann, Jennifer. "For Cinema Chains, Record Sales Not Balancing Costs of Overbuilding," *The Kansas City Star*, November 9, 1999.

9 Schroder. "Home Video Will Remain Studio Breadwinner," *Video Week*, January 10, 2000, Section: This Week's News.

10 TV advertising revenues were $25.66 billion in 1998. "Cable Television Advertising Bureau Research Update," *Cable Avails*, April 1999, Volume 9, Number 3, p. 17.

11 *World Almanac & Book of Facts 1999,* (Primedia Reference Inc., March 1999).

12 Stern, Christopher. "U.S. Ideas Top Export Biz," *Variety*, May 11–17, 1998, p. 50.

13 Interview with Laura Blum, Summer 1998.

14 1989–present, The Baywatch Company, Syndicated.

Entertainment in Our Extended World

Les Brown

As a veteran television reporter for *The New York Times* and author of *The New York Times Encyclopedia of Television,* Les Brown specializes in thinking and writing about the electronic media. He founded *Channels* and *Television Business International* magazines and has written articles for *Harper's, The Saturday Review,* and *The American Educator,* among others. He is an associate professor at Fordham University Graduate School of Business and Administration.

Twentieth-century technology has made us the greatest consumers of entertainment since the beginning of civilization. With so much available 24 hours a day in one or another of its myriad forms, both inside and outside our homes, for many of us the world of entertainment has become our extended world. Our obsession with stars, filmmakers, new movies, and television shows, moreover, has served to elevate entertainment to prime news status, much to the despair of serious journalists. As a public we seem to have as great a desire to know what's happening in Hollywood as in Washington or other world capitals.

Whatever succeeds commercially in entertainment tends in some way to reflect the social and moral tides and helps to define the national mood, which, in a backward look, seems to change by the decade. We learn something about ourselves and our times from what dominates the television charts and the movie box office in any year, and these trends, tied as they are to the Zeitgeist, even have a certain political dimension. It was no mere coincidence, for example, that *Dallas*[1] and *Dynasty*,[2] prime time serials about the super-rich, were the reigning TV shows in the probusiness Ronald Reagan era, or that a decade earlier such working-class comedies as *All In the Family*[3] and *Sanford and Son*[4] dominated during the more liberal Jimmy Carter presidency.

So entertainment in the mass media is more than a frivolity that provides affordable escape from the workaday world; it is our popular culture and to a large degree our social glue. The sign-off of *Seinfeld*[5] on NBC, watched by nearly half the nation in the spring of 1998, was a bonding experience in the tradition of the *Cheers*[6] and *M*A*S*H*[7] finales, rivaling the annual male bonding of the Super Bowl. Far more socially significant than the immense box office of the movie *Titanic*[8] was the universal chord its love story struck with teenage girls. The film and the idolization of Leonardo DiCaprio became the common denominator for schoolgirls not just in the United States, but around the world.

One of the reasons entertainment is so popular is that it demands so little of us for its rewards. It seldom taxes our brains beyond asking us to get the joke, comprehend the lyrics to a song, or follow the plot of a film and the motivation of the characters. The aim of entertainment is to engage our emotions rather than our minds, and this may be how it essentially differs from art. Successful entertainment makes us feel something that results in some kind of pleasure for the moment: the enjoyment of a good laugh, or a good cry, or of having been scared out of our wits.

When you think about it, there's no perfect synonym for entertainment. Diversion and amusement fall way short—for what is diverting about a great ship sinking with more than 1500 people aboard, and what is amusing about a couple of natural born killers murdering people wantonly? The emotional gamut of entertainment ranges from heaven to hell, from inspiration to horror, from love to hate. In the arc between are such feelings as awe, amazement, delight, hilarity, sentimentality, sadness, intrigue, suspense, excitement, thrill, fear, fright, anger, shock, and even revulsion. In any well-made film all the creative disciplines, from special effects to sound, conspire to produce or heighten specific visceral responses from the audience. When people say, "Maybe it wasn't a great movie, but I found it entertaining," they usually mean they had a satisfying emotional workout of one kind or another.

Pauline Kael, the noted film critic, observed in a 1998 interview in *Modern Maturity*:

> At a movie house you feel alone with the image and you're affected deeply. The different elements that go into movies—music, cinematography, actors, design—get to you very strongly. That's why so many educated people disapprove of movies; they're not used to giving themselves over to that much emotion.[9]

But if entertainment targets the heart, the spleen and the funny bone rather than the brain, that doesn't mean it leaves no intellectual residue. All stories communicate values and portray styles, so every movie and TV program, however inane, may make some mark on minds, even prompting imitative behavior, especially when the images are cumulative. All those screen images dating to the 1930s of glamorous people puffing on cigarettes conveyed a sense that smoking was sophisticated and sexy and bespoke maturity, as if to validate the extensive tobacco ad campaigns. The effect was to influence several generations of moviegoers and TV viewers to take up the habit.[10]

Today when an impressionable teenage boy sees scores of movies and TV programs in which all the good guys brandish guns—and who with more admirable flair than Will Smith in *Men in Black*?[11]—he might be forgiven for thinking that guns are standard equipment for grown-ups and that owning one is cool, and using it is a rite of passage. And what should we expect teenage girls to conclude from seeing so many female leads slip easily into bed with men they scarcely made more than eye contact with in the previous scene? Pure entertainment may not mean to teach, but it does inevitably through the myths produced by repeated example.

There is, in fact, one serviceable synonym for entertainment, and that is "show business," a term that immediately summons the commercial imperative and excludes whatever is performed free, for fun, or in the nature of a hobby.

Q: Do audiences go to movies to see their reflections or to project their fantasies?

If there were a referendum, I think the vote would come in that people want to see characters who are more reflective of real people. That was one of the reasons for the long-running success of Roseanne's show. Look at Billy Bob Thornton in Sling Blade. *That film had some real people. But the film and television industry has taken it upon itself to dictate what people want. In other words, we tell you what your dream is.*

—Pat Golden

Most of our entertainment today is driven by the profit motive and usually is well worth the price of admission. The show business industries in the United States are extraordinarily proficient and have produced much that is quite wonderful, including entertainment that has become recognized as true art, dating from the Chaplin movies and the advent of jazz.

Movies and television have become so intertwined over the years that it is hard to think of them any longer as discrete industries. It is not uncommon today for a major Hollywood studio to be headed by a former television executive or for producers and actors to move between the two media. And the crossovers are likely to increase as a result of the vertical integration that occurred during the 1990s, when most of the major Hollywood studios got into the network business one way or another. Following Rupert Murdoch's lead in creating the Fox Network after buying 20th Century-Fox Pictures, the Walt Disney Company acquired ABC, and Warner Bros. and Paramount started their own terrestrial networks, WB and UPN, respectively.[12] And, in the ultimate case of one-upsmanship to date, the first few weeks of the year 2000 saw the creation of the largest media company in history, when Steve Case's Internet provider America Online (AOL) gobbled up media giant Time-Warner for $163.4 billion.[13]

The strategy is to control both production and distribution and thus ensure a market for their programming in the future. Today television is the vital after-market for motion pictures and the financial salvation of many that flopped in the medium for which they were made. A system of release windows has evolved, although it does change periodically: after the theatrical run, most movies go almost simultaneously to cable pay-per-view and home video rentals, then to pay cable channels like HBO and Showtime, then either to the networks or the TV syndication market, and ultimately to cable's vintage and classic movie channels. Movies, then, can thank television for granting them something like eternal life.

> *You can pretend that you're making movies for yourself but you're not. Ultimately you're making movies for an audience. That should be your first concern. Not that you are making decisions for an audience, but that you're making a product for an audience. You have to have some social responsibility.*
> —Gordon Willis

But the relationship was not always so felicitous. The two industries were bitter enemies at first, as television in the 1950s usurped the motion picture's distinction as the most popular form of entertainment and caused thousands of local movie houses to close.[14] In the ensuing years of friction between the two industries, television changed the movies and the movies changed television.

To compete with the new home entertainment medium that was stealing their customers, the film studios began producing pictures on a more ambitious scale than before, often with bolder images and racier themes than television was able to deal with. As a family medium in the service of advertisers and subject to government regulation, television had to be careful in earlier times not to offend the moral sensibilities of anyone in its vast sea of viewers.

Most of the cautions were articulated in the Television Code of the National Association of Broadcasters,[15] to which most stations subscribed. Until it was knocked out by a federal court judge in 1982 on antitrust grounds,[16] the code had set the industry's guidelines for good practices, which included prohibitions against profanity, smut, and representations of sex crimes and sex abnormalities. Illicit sex was never to be presented as commendable nor suicide as justifiable, and in general sex and violence were to be treated without emphasis.[17] The networks' Standards & Practices departments added restrictions of their own, such as barring scenes in which husbands and wives might be thought to share a common bed. Twin beds were the rule.

For the motion picture business, these puritanical limitations on television represented a competitive opportunity. Having freed themselves from their own industry's self-regulating structure, the MPAA (Motion Picture Association of America) Production Code,[18] the studios promptly took advantage of their new creative liberties. Movies began flouting the old taboos against sexual candor, coarse language, and brutal violence, making television look very bland in contrast. The box office began perking again,[19] especially with young adults.

As it happened, television advertisers were just then becoming obsessed with demographics, and the age group they prized most was the very one that was the core audience for cinema—18 to 35.[20] Advertising spots in programs whose viewers were predominantly in the 18 to 49 age group brought twice the price of those reaching an older audience, and even more if the concentration was 18 to 35.[21] The surest way for the networks to capture that target group was obviously with motion pictures, and NBC started a prime time wave in 1966 by buying films of fairly recent vintage and launching a showcase called *Saturday Night at the Movies*.[22] It was so successful that soon all three networks established two or three such showcases, leaving no night of the week without at least one.

This raised some problems, however. Many of the films had to be edited to clean them up for television, but since the essential "adult" themes remained—as in films like *The Graduate*[23] and *Love Story*[24]—the networks had to loosen their rules for content in the prime time movie slots. Moreover, the movies were drubbing all competition in the ratings, leaving the networks puzzling over how to program against them. The solution, they decided, was to upgrade production standards for TV programs to achieve the look of a motion picture, which meant increasing the budgets, and also to eliminate the double standard for acceptable content.[25]

In the general liberalizing of restrictions, whatever was allowable in the movies being aired became approximately the standard for TV programs as well. This naturally brought a blast of criticism from many sectors of the viewership and from government officials, but network executives maintained that they were only keeping up with the changing morality in the country, and insisted that they were following the trend of the times, not leading it.[26]

As the supply of movies worthy of prime time began to dwindle, the networks commissioned made-for-TV movies to help feed the showcases, but eventually—largely as a result of overkill and diminishing quality—the feature films started losing their ratings luster. By the late 1970s, cable's pay channels—HBO, Cinemax, Showtime, and The Movie Channel—were able to outbid the networks for the top titles, and the trend ended, but not before the two industries became irrevocably linked.[27]

There has since been a certain shifting of roles. Today, the studios have a greater dependency on television as an advertising medium than the networks have on movies as program fare. Television has become absolutely vital to the marketing of motion pictures, especially the big-budget Hollywood films. In the bizarre way the movie business works today, these have to enter the public consciousness at least six months before they are actually released. Most pictures created by the major studios cost upwards of $50 million to produce[28] and almost half as much to promote,[29] mainly with television spots and in-theater trailers. The marketing needs to begin months before the film's release—*Independence Day*[30] was given eight months—to create anticipation for the opening. And this is so important because a film has to prove its drawing power in the first weekend of its release or be doomed, as theaters will then start canceling it and the second tier of picture houses won't book it.

The theaters, most of which are owned by 15 national chains,[31] have an agenda of their own. They don't make their profits off the ticket sales because they usually have to return more than half the receipts to the distributor,[32] and their cut of the box office often just covers operating expenses. Profits come from the sale of popcorn, candy, and soft drinks, for which the margins can be as high as 80 percent.[33] So the theaters are really in a retail business, and the purpose of the pictures on the screens is to produce traffic. Movies that don't draw crowds are quickly cast out for those that will.

The marketing is therefore crucial, and the commercials and trailers have to be somehow titillating. Scarcely a movie introduces itself in these campaigns without promising some sexual excitement or the thrill of violence, if not both, to ensure a strong opening weekend. And there's little doubt that gratuitously racy and turbulent scenes are created for the movies just for the sake of the marketing campaigns. A TV advertising campaign for a single film will generally carry one set of TV spots to run in programs that appeal to young females and another for those that attract young males—one accenting the romance, the other the action.[34]

Disney/Touchstone, which reportedly spent $140 million to make *Armageddon*[35] and $70 million to promote it, spent another $3 million to add some new scenes of explosions and other effects just before the film's release, according to *The Wall Street Journal*.[36] Studio chief Joe Roth explained that this was done to create some "fresh imagery for the last two weeks of the (TV ad) campaign."

Show business is often represented as a cultural democracy in which people vote by the choices they make, but that of course isn't quite the case. Unlike the truly democratic market for products like toothpaste and breakfast cereal in which all age groups participate, mainstream entertainment tends to target teenagers and young adults. They are the main audience for movies, the most desired audience for TV, and the main buyers of pop music recordings that then are aired on radio stations as the nation's top hits.[37] By and large, it's the young who determine our popular culture—and they are the ones in the breaking-away stage, who enjoy irreverence and the styles and behavior that shock their elders.

There's no doubt that television has an enormous influence on the culture. But I don't believe that people copy what they see on TV. Our crime rate is down in New York City, and the amount of violence that you see on television is not getting any less. So I don't think it really has a huge effect. It would be sad to feel restricted as a producer or as a programmer by the idea that everything you see on television could be imitated.

—Bridget Potter

This makes for a most dynamic market, since every new post-teenage wave rejects much of what the previous wave favored—thus the dialectical shift from the crew cuts of the 1950s to the long hair of the 1960s and from the hippies of the 1960s to the yuppies of the 1980s. But in business terms, dynamic can also mean treacherous; it's not easy to tell when a cultural shift is going to happen and what form it will take.

This uncertainty about the youth-ruled market is another reason why movies and television continually resort to the exploitation of sex and violence, since those are cinematic condiments that always seem to work regardless of the temper of the times. Members of a newly arrived generation of youthful trendsetters may jettison the values and styles of the preceding generation but, being human, are subject to the same turn-ons.

To be effective, however, violence must continually be ratcheted up to new levels because audiences become inured over time to seeing people destroyed in the usual gruesome ways.

In Hollywood, the challenge is to innovate with violence, without concern, apparently, for the possible social consequences, such as inspiring imitative behavior. The record of that is extensive and chilling:

Serial killer Nathaniel White traced the ideas for six of his murders to the *RoboCop*[38] movies and told of butchering his first victim the way he saw it done in *RoboCop II*,[39] by slitting her throat and then carving downward through the chest. Killers in Ogden, Utah, who forced five people in a hi-fi shop to drink liquid Drano got the idea from *Magnum Force*.[40] John Hinckley modeled himself on the disturbed Robert de Niro character in *Taxi Driver*[41] and said he shot President Reagan to attract the attention of Jodie Foster, who was in the film. And *The Deer Hunter*[42] was considered responsible for a rash of Russian roulette deaths in 1978.

There are numerous other cases of copycat crime and reckless behavior, but the record-holder for the sheer number of imitated murders is believed to be

Natural Born Killers,[43] an exceptionally violent film whose protagonists are a young drug-happy couple on a capricious murdering spree. The villains are the crazed cop who pursues them and the gluttonous media who turn them into major celebrities.

Movies are about storytelling, and from ancient times storytelling has been a way to teach morality. In the days of the Hays Office,[44] no crime was allowed to go unpunished in a film, so that movies cumulatively sent the message that crime does not pay. Director Oliver Stone sardonically inverts that in *Natural Born Killers*,[45] which ends with the evil lovers raising a family and living happily ever after. Stone characterizes his film as a satire, but some would dispute that in light of the many murders committed by people who took the film seriously and romanticized themselves as natural born killers.

By Stone's ethical standards, apparently, it is more important to show how things happen in real life than to pretend the ideal. Fair enough. But I think it is fair to surmise that many other directors would have had serious qualms about making such a morally squalid picture in the first place.

Fortunately, a great many filmmakers, perhaps the majority of them, resist the temptation of pandering to the baser delectations of youth and, out of self-respect if not also respect for the society, take on the challenge of creating popular movies that tell a good story well without the cynical creative crutches.

In television, which answers to different rules as a public medium, producers are held in relative check by the networks' Standards & Practices policies and the raised eyebrow of Congress. But still, since the 1970s, there has been a constant pushing of the envelope to extend the parameters of permissibility. Maude has an abortion; James is initiated to sex as a teenager; Murphy Brown has a child out of wedlock; Roseanne's daughter loses her virginity; Ellen comes out as a lesbian; a woman exposes her nude body (but not to the camera) in *Married, with Children*;[46] and a man's bare bottom appears on camera in *NYPD Blue*.[47] None of these events are truly reprehensible in themselves because they are not salacious and they reflect real life. Indeed, the shock and controversy they created are almost laughable in retrospect, especially in light of the sexual candor of movies that find their way on television through cable.

What we are left to wonder about, however, is why these controversial episodes were made—that is, in what spirit, since none of these shows could presume to pose as art. Was the intent brave, to wake us up to the out-datedness of American Puritanism, perhaps; or to contribute to our greater enlightenment about the trials of young people in today's world? Or was it cynical, purely to gain notoriety for the series in a play for ratings? The difference has everything to do with the public trust; it is the difference between an ethical and unethical approach to program making. When the motive is transparently manipulative, then the message, in the end, is the cynicism.

The word entertainment is deceptively benign because, in its various uses, it connotes leisure-time pleasure and civility. When we entertain guests we extend hospitality and try to show them a good time, and when we entertain a thought it is a good thought, not a troublesome one. Cabaret entertainers present themselves amiably and divert us with their talent, and the rousing anthem, *That's Entertainment!*[48] is high-spirited fun.

But packaged entertainment as a creature of the market in the serious grip of commerce is not about fun and civility. What matters above all else is how well the product sells and what it takes to make it sell in a fiercely competitive marketplace. Corporations, in their daily concern with the price of their stock, and creative practitioners striving to advance their careers in a business community that prizes box office success over artistry, are going to act much of the time from expediency and put conscience aside. When the way of entertainment is a callous disregard for social consequences and the drift is to moral anarchy, entertainment—in a society so immersed in it—can be downright dangerous.

Notes

1 1978–1991, Lorimar Television.

2 1981–1989, ABC Television.

3 1971–1979, CBS Television.

4 1972–1977, NBC Television.

5 1990–1998, NBC Television.

6 1982–1983, NBC Television.

7 1972–1983, CBS Television.

8 1997 D: James Cameron, Paramount Pictures.

9 Kael, Pauline. Interview with Susan Goodman, in *Modern Maturity*, March 1998.

10 "Media portrayals of risky or healthy behaviors may help promote or reinforce the appropriateness of these behaviors through influences on individual values and risk perception and on peer group values. Alternatively, adolescents who engage in many risky behaviors may use more antisocial media to meet otherwise un-met needs for positive self-esteem and identity." Klein, Jonathan D., M.D., MPH; Brown, Jane D., Ph.D.; Walsh Childers, Kim, Ph.D.; Oliveri, Janice, M.D.; Porter, Carol; and Dykers, Carol. "Adolescents' Risky Behavior and Mass Media Use," *Pediatrics* 92 (July 1993): 24–31.

11 1997 D: Barry Sonnenfeld, Columbia Pictures Corp.

12 Howe, Peter J. "Massive Media: Viacom CBS Merger Plan Raises Questions over Trend of a Few Giant Conglomerates Controlling What We Hear, Read and See," *The Boston Globe*, September 12, 1999.

13 Peltz, James. "Media Mega Merger; It's No Act—Case Is An Ordinary Guy," *Los Angeles Times*, January 11, 2000.

14 "The growing postwar popularity of television was among the factors that led to a wave of movie theater closings in the early 1950s. Grauer, Neil A. "Gone With The Wind: The Movie Houses That Once Dominated Washington Were Elegant, Palatial and, Ultimately, Doomed," *The Washington Post*, July 4, 1999.

15 "Television Code of the National Association of Broadcasters," 1st Edition, 1952; 22nd Edition, 1981. *Encyclopedia Britannica Online*: www.eb.com.

16 *USA vs. National Association of Broadcasters*, Civil Action #79–1549, November 23, 1982.

17 "Television Code of the National Association of Broadcasters."

18 Established in 1930 by the Motion Pictures Producers and Distributors Association (MPPDA), the predecessor to the MPAA, in response to increasing government censorship that arose from public outcry against indecency on the screen and various film celebrity scandals.

19 "Theaters steadily lost admissions until the mid-1970s, then they began to rise again." *Motion Picture Almanac* QP 1999, Stevens, Tracy, ed. (New York: Quigley Publishing Company, 1999).

20 "16–40 year-olds make up 43% of the population but 59% of the movie audiences." *Motion Picture Almanac* QP 1999.

21 Brown, Lester L., *The Business Behind The Box*, (New York: Harcourt Brace Jovanovich, Inc., 1971), pp. 285–287.

22 NBC, 1966.

23 1967 D: Mike Nichols, Embassy Pictures Corp.

24 1970 D: Arthur Hiller, Paramount Pictures.

25 Research files of Lester L. Brown and *Variety*.

26 Research files of Lester L. Brown and *The New York Times*.

27 Research files of Lester L. Brown and *The New York Times*.

28 Natale, Richard. "Company Town: I Know What You Did Last Weekend" *Los Angeles Times*, June 23, 1998, Section D, p. 1.

29 Natale, p. 1.

30 1996 D: Roland Emmerich, 20th Century Fox.

31 *Motion Picture Almanac* QP 1999, p. 10.

32 Passy, Charles. "How Big Are Those Profits From The Tickets And Popcorn?" *Palm Beach Post*, May 18, 1997, p. 4J.

33 Passy, p. 4J.

34 Research files of Lester L. Brown and *The New York Times*.

35 1998 D: Michael Bay, Buena Vista Pictures.

36 Morgenstern, Joe. "Film: Cosmic Crashes, Comic Cons," *Wall Street Journal*, July 1, 1998, Section A, p. 16.

37 "American teenagers listen to an estimated 10,500 hours of rock music between 7th and 12th grades, just 500 fewer hours than they spend in school over twelve years." *Entertainment Monitor*, December 1995.

38 1987 D: Paul Verhoeven, Orion Pictures Corporation.

39 1990 D: Irvin Kershner, Orion Pictures Corporation.

40 1973 D: Ted Post, Warner Bros.
41 1976 D: Martin Scorsese, Columbia Pictures Corporation.
42 1978 D: Michael Cimino, Universal Pictures.
43 1994 D: Oliver Stone, Warner Bros.
44 The MPPDA formed in 1922. The Hays Office refers to the Association's first president Will H. Hays.
45 1994 D: Oliver Stone, Warner Bros.
46 1987–1997, Fox Television Network.
47 1993–present, ABC Television.
48 1974 D: Jack Haley, Jr., MGM Entertainment.

How the World Sees Us: An American in Paris

Jack Pitman

Jack Pitman began his journalism career in Chicago with the *Wall Street Journal* before joining the staff of *Variety*, first in Chicago, then in New York, and finally in London. Pitman is a contributor to *The New York Times Encyclopedia of Television* and is currently a book reviewer and television scriptwriter.

Hard as it may be for the cynical to accept, there actually was a time when Hollywood movies were America's most cost-effective goodwill ambassadors to the world. A generation of foreign filmgoers still nurses affectionate memories of the celluloid America that was—an often eccentric, endearing, and even inspiring America of screwball comedies, madcap romances, and dramas of uplifting idealism that helped see audiences through the dispiriting Great Depression of the 1930s, and which for many still constitute Hollywood's finest hour.

Appealing as it was then, the American cinema has never been more popular with foreign audiences than it is now—nor, paradoxically, more reviled and resented at the same time.

The popularity of our film exports is no surprise. By common consent, no industry anywhere quite matches Hollywood's long-standing populist touch for storytelling of wide appeal, especially those action blockbusters that leave audiences raving over the digital technology much as Broadway audiences are apt to leave a modern musical humming the new-tech score. Even Europe's student radicals, scornful of the American film industry's "mercantile mentality" and what they see as its pretenses at art, avidly attend American movies.

The resentment is also understandable from my experience as an American journalist (with a special interest in popular culture) having been based in Britain for nearly three decades and having traveled widely around Europe.

Foreign critics of our cinema have grown more vocal as it has become more brazen and brutal, more obsessed with the aberrant and the bizarre in its drive for big box office returns. Hollywood product, for all its populist magnetism today, is regarded by many abroad as junk entertainment—"brash, superficial, infantile and inane," to quote Richard Pells, an American historian, and more recently Fulbright professor at Bonn University in Germany, writing in the *International Herald Tribune*.[1]

More to the point, in important markets like Canada, France, Germany, and the UK, our films are most resented for the psychological dangers they are thought to pose, especially for younger folk.[2] Hollywood's obsession with guns and its routinely vicious violence and raunchy up-front sex are worrisome to adults who know their impressionable teenagers will be exposed to them because American movies figure so prominently in the teen culture. What particularly troubles many parents I've spoken with in my travels is that we not only make violence seem an easy option for problem-solving but something of a reflexive norm, even a way of life.

Hollywood producers don't cause movies to be made. They make the movies that their backers, the studios, and the financing entities allow them to make. And yes, they know they have a better chance to succeed with the financiers if they offer subjects of that nature (of violence). But there is nothing new about that. Back in the 1930s, 1940s, and 1950s, excluding World War II, we knew what the foreign market wanted. We knew we couldn't make a musical for the foreign market because we couldn't dub the songs in the various languages. We were always aware of that. And there are a number of small movies that have exported brilliantly. It depends on what the theme is. If the theme is universal, it doesn't need car crashes or burning buildings to export it.

—*David Brown*

A respected German filmmaker once expressed anxiety over *Rambo*[3] and similar American exports out of a fear that such films might excite and instruct the young neo-Nazis and skinheads in a Germany trying hard to go straight since losing World War II. Given all the evidence before us, the fear is not unreasonable.

Another foreign grievance emerged when British health authorities detected a nearly four-fold increase over the period from 1990 to 1995 in the incidence of characters smoking in movies—even as efforts were gathering pace to get young people to kick the noxious habit (or better yet, to not even start).[4]

The health lobby quite naturally believes that it would help the public health cause if films were to kick the killer weed habit.

Consider this in the context of a cinema history rife with examples of film's capacity to influence what we vulnerable humans accept as glamorous, whether it be martinis in the moonlight, the Ginger Rogers look, or the fanciful way Paul Henreid simultaneously lit cigarettes for both himself and Bette Davis in *Now Voyager*.[5]

Because American films are so dominant in the world and are produced in such great quantity, the United States is without a doubt the most visible, the most self-revealing, the most open nation that has ever existed on this planet. People on every continent know us, and who we are, from all they see of American life on the big screen and the small. But to realize this is to find yourself asking if that's really us up there on the screen, in all our depth and diversity, and to start worrying that we may be seriously misapprehended as a people.

It's probable that the world's impression of Americans, for better or worse (and undoubtedly worse), has been formed mainly from the screen stereotypes. During the 1980s, when *Dallas*[6] and *Dynasty*[7] were huge television hits throughout the world, people abroad, especially those who didn't read much, came to think that the characters in those serials typified us—rich, self-centered, greedy, ruthless. Several news correspondents covering the United States for foreign television networks told a magazine writer at the time that their editors were most eager for stories that confirmed the veracity of *Dallas* and presented Americans who really were like the Ewings and their crowd.[8]

Q: Is there ever a worry with a film like Pulp Fiction *that this is how America is seen abroad?*

Absolutely. But you'd have to say that the more pervasive influence comes from television, especially American soap operas where everybody is a millionaire.
—Mark Gill

And what impression of us would have been formed in the 1990s from all those high-energy action movies that traveled so well globally? No doubt that we are brash, materialistic, uncultured, uncouth, and always armed. In a similar vein, movies have a way of creating false impressions of America itself, by typecasting our geographical regions and cities. Chicago, for example, is arguably the first city of American architecture and a major center of culture, with great intellectual and literary traditions, yet it is still thought of by many overseas primarily as the city of Al Capone and criminal anarchy.

Hollywood's long dominance of the world market owes largely to its unrivaled ability to communicate to the masses and to produce on a grand scale for a home market that is large enough and wealthy enough to support it. However, it is also the only motion picture industry with its own international distribution network. No other film industry has Hollywood's economic power, and as a result, over the years, it has reduced most of the others to something like also-rans, even on their home grounds.

More recently, the U.S. movie industry's sway abroad has been enhanced by the boom in multiplexing and the opening of new markets, notably Eastern Europe following the collapse of communism in that region. As a result, Hollywood's foreign revenues in the late 1990s have exceeded for the first time its annual domestic take in gross dollar terms.[9] And of that total, two-thirds comes from Europe, where film attendance has been on a constant climb.[10]

If television and movies were not so rigid in the way they perceived characters and who could be cast in the roles, we would be much further along racially in this country than we are now. If we can get the whole country to know and accept the changes that are going on in the world, like the breakup of the USSR or that now we have Bosnia and Herzegovina, we can certainly make a major impact racially.

—Pat Golden

A further note is that the entertainment industry, led of course by movies and television, is now America's biggest export earner.[11] However reverently the moviemaking community respects such an achievement, for anxiously critical Europeans and others it only confirms Hollywood's obsession with money. And as its imperial grip strengthens, what persistently worries those Europeans are the implications for their own hard-pressed filmmakers and cultural traditions.

Throughout much of the twentieth century, Europe has sought by various protectionist means, including subsidies and formal quota systems,[12] to keep the mighty U.S. movie machine at bay so that their native filmmakers might at least stand a fighting chance in the marketplace. Time and again, though, such measures have failed to do the job as the Hollywood steamroller rolled on.

A declining or moribund national film industry, no longer able to hold its own against Hollywood's superior firepower, is more than a blot on a nation's self-esteem, it deprives a country of an art form, an outlet for indigenous creative expression, for telling its own stories in the styles of its people. It can blur a peoples' sense of themselves, their aspirations, and their ideals.

As in America, the foreign public for current movies is predominantly young and thus open to possibilities, ideas, and values that may differ markedly from those of their elders. No less than those of our own country, the young of Europe, Asia, Latin America, and the Middle East are thus apt to imitate the styles, attitudes, values, and behavior patterns depicted by Hollywood, creating a breach with their own cultural norms and the established domestic order. The Americanization of their youth, down to the wearing of jeans, baseball caps, and printed tee shirts, is of course much resented in countries whose folkways, mores, and manners, some of them based in religion, have been intact for centuries.

In Iran, where Islamic fundamentalism imposes black shroudlike costumes (chadors) as regulation female attire, girls and young women have taken to wearing miniskirts under them—and also, clandestinely, to watching American television shows pulled in by illegal satellite dishes. A friend of mine spent some time in Tunis in the company of three men in their twenties who not only dressed like Americans and used the American vernacular (learned of course from the media) but also frequented a bar in an international hotel to drink alcohol, which is forbidden in their culture. All three spoke often of wishing to live elsewhere, preferably the United States.

The video market for foreign language film has dropped about 50 percent. Some of that results from the consolidation of video stores, and some from the dominance of movies like Independence Day. *It's a shelf-space issue in all video stores. Retailers want depth of copies on the huge titles. The other part of it is that it is getting harder for any small film to get attention at video stores.*

—Mark Gill

In many countries, the fascination of the young with the American way of life, which seems unrestricted compared to their own, has widened the generation gap and led to tensions with their parents and even the vested powers that be. We may be admired and even loved by the rebellious youth of other countries, but that does not endear us to the adult populations, and it especially rankles the cultural orthodoxy.

Government officials in Canada have struggled for years to promote and preserve the indigenous culture, to distinguish their citizens from those of the superpower to the south, but in the English-speaking provinces it has been a losing battle. American movies predominate in the theaters, and the commercial TV networks buy virtually every program produced in Hollywood and usually drub the all-Canadian public service network, the CBC, in the ratings. At an international conference a Canadian broadcast regulator said, with a note of despair, that many of his countrymen not only identify with the United States but often appear to know more about American history than their own.[13]

In a 1998 address at the Banff Television Festival in Canada, Sir Christopher Bland, chairman of the British Broadcasting Corporation, remarked:

> "(W)e Europeans can seem at times to harbour either, at worst, a resentment of American economic success, or, at best, a mild suspicion of things American. And we are eternally neurotic about the pervasive influence of jeans, sneakers, baseball caps and hamburgers, a neuroticism that in France extends to a national debate over whether the word 'hotdog' should make it into the French dictionary."

Europe, because it contains many of Hollywood's principal foreign markets, has often sought to counter Hollywood's economic clout. The most recent protectionist attempt came via the European Union Parliament in the French city of Strasbourg when, after months of debate, only a feeble set of measures emerged. Its highlights were a special fund to assist domestic European Union (EU) film producers, and a quota system obliging EU "general-interest" broadcasters to "devote the majority" of their airtime to material originated within the Union[14]—a meaningless proviso since it was long standard operating practice anyway by those very same broadcasters. America's economic influence had once again prevailed, as everyone knew it would.

> *I enjoyed* Forrest Gump, *where for the sake of the story they put Hanks in these historical situations by accident. It was funny and entertaining. I think it was taken in the right way. When they used Clinton in* Contact *it was different because he's a current world leader and people might not understand all the facts behind it. Foreign countries are going to show it. They might not know that it was digitally manipulated so they might think, "Well, the president is now appearing in movies."*
>
> *—Rob Legato*

Interestingly, one of many proposals dropped from the final package of measures called for something like a European version of the American so-called violence or 'V'-chip in TV sets as a device for protecting the impressionable young from possibly corrupting programs.[15]

Foreign objections to our cinema culture also cite the way Hollywood commonly stereotypes race and gender. Tom Hutchinson, a leading British film critic, says that U.S. movies often "extol racial stereotypes." And black actors, he adds, "do their cause no good by participating in movies which depict them as idiots or riot-stirring morons," for which he says the director Spike Lee and other black filmmakers must share some of the blame. Questionable films in this view include the spate of so-called "Blaxploitation" releases profitably aimed mainly at black urban audiences.

Hutchinson, by the way, also makes the critical point that what he calls America's "imperial nature" tends to sanction the celebration by our filmmakers of "what others may well consider tacky lapses of taste."*The New York Times* film critic Janet Maslin had clearly had it with some of the tacky stuff she had to sit through, including the "gnawing and disemboweling of corpses, the mutilation of a severed head and the aftermath of a killing in which the gun-wielding perpetrator is invited to dip his hand in the victim's blood."[16]

It's Hollywood's seemingly morbid obsession with the violence in our nature that really rings the alarm bells abroad. No other issue so vexes the industry's foreign critics, and what really makes them bristle is the action for actions' sake, the gratuitous mayhem, often rendered in the clinched "slo-mo" that has come to be the self-justifying artistic norm.

Using its permissive license to deal openly with sex and brute force, Hollywood today "has only achieved a more explicit licentiousness without the sophisticated assumptions" of an earlier era, declares film critic Alexander Walker of the *London Evening Standard*.[17] Amen, say those of us who remember when irony and subtlety were more nearly the hallmarks of American films, when directors sensed what to leave to the imagination.

If the America of yesteryear's cinema was often judged to be endearing and inspiring, the image projected nowadays is often perceived abroad as one of "superheros, crime, sleaze and a nation at war with itself," to again quote critic Tom Hutchinson of Britain.[18]

Critical foreigners who claim that our movies are a triumph of commercial instinct over artistic ambition have been gathering adherents lately. The novelist J.G. Ballard has commented:

> Most Hollywood blockbusters such as *Independence Day*,[19] *Con Air*[20] or *Air Force One*,[21] are animated comic strips, driven by the relentless demand for action, the equivalent of a climax every four frames, and with the same crane shots and zooms that energize the static panels in the Batman and Superman strips.... The briefest flicker of an adult relationship seems to come with a built-in fast-forward button.[22]

Along with violence, sex, and torrents of raw language, a preoccupying foreign concern is what is seen as the disturbing effect of America's cultural assault on their traditions. Europeans also fear a threat to "European creativity." In some hierarchic Arabian countries, they declined to air the old *I Love Lucy*[23] TV series because, contrary to local social development and custom, the lippy Lucille Ball character forever talks back to her husband, with impunity. In Japan and other Far East lands, a level of bilingual cultural dilution is evident, and there is wary wonder what American folkways and values, absorbed from movies, may bring next. Within Europe, France has long been the most alarmed over America's cultural penetration, typified by the linguistic corruption known as "Franglais."

As early as 1927, when motion pictures were just beginning to talk, Britain's *Daily Express* was quick to denounce the transformation of British filmgoers by Hollywood into virtual clones who "talk America, think America and dream America."[24] That concern, it's safe to assume, has since become widely shared around the world.

Over the years, almost every national cinema in the developed world has at one time or another tried either to go head-to-head with Hollywood or at least provide a viable domestic cultural alternative. But all were forced to yield to Hollywood's superior financial and technical resources and, as one commentary has put it, to the "superior understanding it demonstrated of contemporary mass tastes."[25]

In decrying the "shrinking diversity" of the world's film industry, German film director Volker Schlondorff blames the commercial imperative to meet American considerations, namely that it's necessary first to gain distribution and exhibitor acceptance in the all-important U.S. market before one can hope to clinch distribution deals in other territories. And the reality is that, in general, the U.S. market isn't highly receptive to foreign films.[26]

In the first years after World War II, what Europe's culture mavens could least abide from Hollywood was the routine way it played up American hedonism and material abundance while their own prostrate economies were struggling to revive. It seemed insensitive of the American industry, but after all the films were not made with overseas markets in mind. Hollywood back then may simply have been innocently unaware of the resentment it was generating. And anyway, the great bulk of its dazzling and mounting revenues was still coming from its own domestic market, so what did it matter that some folks in Europe were displeased?

What matters today, now that Hollywood is consciously producing for the world, is that very insensitivity, that absence of awareness of how we are affecting societies abroad. It is galling to many Europeans that our movie industry has hardly any sense of social concern to go with its worldwide power and influence and that, moreover, it is infecting their cultures with those Tinseltown values that are even deplored in the United States. This seems to bespeak an imperial arrogance and hubris that can only be resented around the world.

That perception has recently contributed to a scary image of America as the new decadent Rome, a society governed "by bread and circuses, with a booming economy and the unprecedentedly invasive and influential entertainment industry distracting the electorate."[27] No, not another jaundiced view from a foreigner, as it happens, but that of an esteemed American pundit, Paris-based William Pfaff, as expressed in one of his syndicated op-ed columns.

As we continue to boggle the folks abroad with our political circuses and other racy shenanigans, with our material gluttony, with our unrestrained popular culture, the more soberly critical Europeans tend to perceive us as a decadent breed spinning out of control.

But I would offer a caveat here. In listening to our foreign critics, and listen we should, we must appreciate that they may often be pushing a more diffuse agenda, by which I mean that their criticism of our popular culture can get mixed up with bruised national egos and other chauvinistic grievances that may or may not have much to do with the United States and its values.

Festering among the French, for instance, is a certain bitterness over the eclipse of their celebrated language by English as the lingua franca of international commerce and diplomacy, and more generally the memory of a different time when France itself, not just its lingo, counted for more in the world. Similarly, the United Kingdom of Great Britain tends to fixate on a time when it ruled the waves and much else besides as the greatest territorial empire the world has yet known. More haunting still for Britain, we shouldn't doubt, is the time it owned what there then was of America, and what might have been, if only.

Those vexations, however, are slight compared to the more complex anti-Americanism that simmers in many parts of the world, fed continually by the distorted images of us projected on the screen by our dazzlingly brilliant creators of motion pictures and television. Those same filmmakers have the power to provide the antidote if they choose to—if they recognized and were moved by the importance of a more positive perception of America abroad. It's not just a matter of wanting to be universally liked, it's a matter of setting an example for the world, especially the developing world.

As the quintessential free society and the standard-bearer for human rights, the United States must inevitably be the role model for the emerging democracies and even for some of the older ones in need of reform. Ideally, the entertainment media, our unofficial ambassadors to the world, should just naturally reflect the virtues of a free and open society—the cultural, intellectual, and moral energy it engenders. I don't mean in a deliberate, heavy-handed way but simply by easing off on all the murder, evil, and blood lust that cumulatively make a poor case for what freedom is about.

Thinking of where we are now in film, I can't help wondering what might have been if only Hollywood had not been so quick to jettison those former social values in its zeal for liberation and unhindered expression.

Notes

1 Research files of Jack Pitman.

2 In addition to Europe; Canada, Australia, and Mexico have laws requiring theaters and broadcasters to reserve a percentage of their schedules for domestic (read non-American) productions. DePalma, Anthony. "Arts Abroad: It Isn't So Simple To Be Canadian," *The New York Times*, July 14, 1999, Section E, p. 1.

3 *First Blood*, a.k.a. *Rambo: First Blood*, 1982 D: Ted Kotcheff, Orion Pictures Corp.

4 Ellis, Rachel. "Rising Use of Tobacco Among Young," *Press Association Newsfile*, September 23, 1997.

5 1942 D: Irving Rapper, Warner Bros.

6 1978–1991, Lorimar Television.

7 1981–1989, ABC Television.

8 Personal recollection of Jack Pitman.

9 For the top 100 films of 1996, domestic: $4.16 billion, foreign: $4.99 billion. "Electric Planet," *Hollywood Reporter*, November 25, 1996, p. 14.

10 "Electric Planet," p. 14.

11 Stern, Christopher "U.S. Ideas Top Export Biz," *Variety*, May 11–17, 1998, p. 50.

12 Bremner, Charles. "French Isolated in Move to Build Culture Barriers," *The Times (London)*, February 15, 1995.

13 Personal recollection of Jack Pitman.

14 Tucker, Emma and Rausthorn, Alice. "EU Loan Scheme for Filming Unveiled," *The Financial Times (London)*, October 7, 1998, p. 3.

15 "'V'-Chip: Empowerment or Placebo?" A panel discussion held October 2, 1996. Moderator: Margaret Warner. From the personal files of Jack Pitman.

16 Maslin, Janet. "Film View: G, PG, R and X: Make the Letter Reflect the Spirit," *The New York Times*, April 29, 1990, Section 2, p. 19.

17 Personal recollection of Jack Pitman.

18 Personal recollection of Jack Pitman.

19 1996 D: Roland Emmerich, 20th Century Fox.

20 1997 D: Simon West, Touchstone Pictures.

21 1997 D: Wolfgang Peterson, Columbia Pictures.

22 Research files of Jack Pitman. Interview excerpt from a London publication.

23 1951–1957, Paramount Television.

24 Research files of Jack Pitman, from the *Daily Express*, 1927.

25 Personal recollection of Jack Pitman.

26 In 1998, the top foreign film was *The Full Monty*, 1997 D: Peter Cattaneo, 20th Century Fox. It still, however, made only $11 million domestically and was ranked #40. Klady, Leonard, Compiler. *Variety*, January 25–31, 1999, p. 36.

27 Personal recollection of Jack Pitman.

Does Influence Imply Responsibility?

But It's Only a Movie ... Or Is It?

For our purposes here, it is enough to question whether the sort of global access and power filmmakers have to influence people's ideas brings with it any ethical responsibility. Because so many people consume Hollywood entertainment product, should Hollywood have to exercise care as to the messages, intended or inadvertent, sent into the world embedded in that product?

This all sounds like more than many film and television creators signed up for when they chose to enter the field: "We are not teachers, we are artists," I hear you cry.

Live with it! Sadly, this is our blessing and our curse. A careful look around will illustrate that our images do in fact teach, even if they are not intended to do so. They can persuade like few other mediums. Argues Les Brown:

> No one ever characterized D.W. Griffith's patently racist *The Birth of a Nation*,[1] with its glorification of the Ku Klux Klan, as only a movie. When a motion picture means to persuade or inspire, or promote hate, it can do that with extraordinary force.[2]

These effects *can* be extremely positive: Scores of children flocked to libraries after "The Fonz" announced that "Library cards are cool" on the TV series *Happy Days*.[3] They can also be market related: Sales of Ray Ban sunglasses surged after Tom Cruise sported them in the film *Risky Business*.[4]

Meanwhile, on the darker side, a growing number of shocking crimes appear to be "inspired" by portrayals of violence on film, television, the Internet, and in music:

- In March 1998, in Japan, a junior high school student stabbed and killed a teacher with a butterfly knife featured by a popular character in a Fuji TV series;
- In January 1998, a 16-year-old Los Angeles boy and his two teenage cousins were arrested for the murder of Gina Castillo, the mother of one of the boys.

According to the police, the boys "admitted to homicide investigators that they killed the mother after getting the idea from the *Scream*[5] movies."

- In December 1997, Michael Carneal, a Kentucky high school student, killed three and wounded eight of his classmates with a semiautomatic weapon in a style he had seen in the film *Basketball Diaries*.[6]

The sordid list goes on. It must be noted that research does *not* point to a direct causal effect between viewing these films and commission of these crimes; however, research *does* reveal that most perpetrators of copycat violence are troubled individuals already predisposed to violent behavior who were perhaps inspired by the graphic violence onscreen.

What about the millions of people who are not predisposed to violence? Are they influenced by blood- and gore-filled scenes, or by a famous actor who seductively injects heroin into his veins while playing a character? Research says these images can and do have an effect, particularly over time.

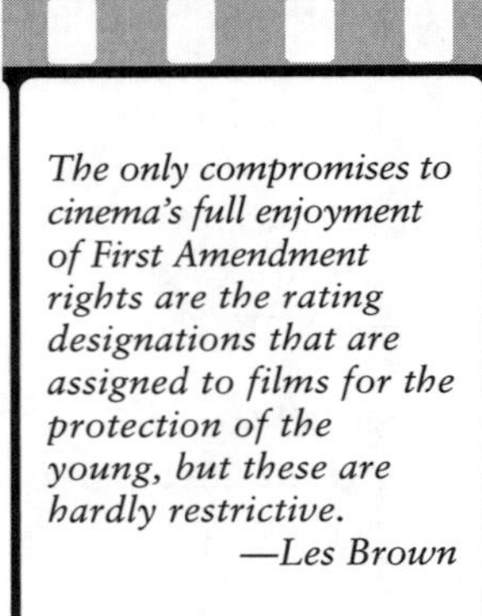

For purposes of discussion here, the message is simply this: do not deny the influence our work has on viewers, particularly young viewers. Realize the power we wield. It's a very big stick.

Filmmakers, when considering the ethical aspects of their work, might ask "What messages do I want to send? To discourage? What behaviors and attitudes am I fostering to society's benefit? To its detriment?"

Most importantly, we must realize that it is *never* "only a movie." The volume of media and the power of images to enter into our psyche have moved us way beyond that, if indeed that statement was *ever* really true. Film and television programming are no longer simply options for whiling away a Saturday afternoon in an air-conditioned palace—air conditioning being one of the primary attractions of cinema in the early days. Then, media was something one had to go out of one's way to find. It was a diversion from the everyday world. Now, to an ever-increasing degree, it *is* the everyday world.

Nowadays, many people the world over paint a good part of their picture of the world from the palette of television and movie content. It can be argued that many people also take much of their self-image from the media. It is a natural process to compare ourselves constantly with what we see portrayed onscreen. We begin to measure ourselves against the ideals in clothes, money, apartments, relationships, and attitudes we are being shown.

There is now really no question that we are helping to shape the world in which we live, not simply entertaining it. It sounds both anticreative freedom and a bit wet-blanket-ish, but we should consider what sort of world we want it to be. Now, this is definitely not to advocate a Magic-Kingdom-esque agenda of social engineering, where we try and gear our messages to creating a nice happy little society. Far from it.

Rather, I am suggesting that with influence comes a certain responsibility to stop and think about what we are doing. Even if we decide not to change anything, the process of examining the underlying meaning and effects of our work will inevitably prove beneficial. It will also make us better and smarter creators.

But "creators only have a responsibility to their own artistic souls, and perhaps at a practical stretch, to the marketplace," I hear you cry.

To spin off from the second responsibility first, it is a matter for debate whether media reflects society or leads it. We would argue that the answer is inordinately complex and is, in fact, a combination of the two.

It is not only what we portray that may be problematic, but what we do *not* portray. In his 1961 address wherein he coined the famous reference to television as "a vast wasteland," former Federal Communications Commission Chairman Newton Minow stated:

> I believe that the public interest is made up of many interests. There are many people in this great country, and you must serve all of us.... You must provide a wider range of choices, more diversity, more alternatives. It is not enough to cater to the nation's whims—you must also serve the nation's needs....[7]

Some 40 years later, many still echo these sentiments.

A number of critics believe that an important example of a large constituency not being properly served is that of some 70 million Christians in the United States. Approximately 56 percent of this demographic, who have been termed the "silent audience,"[8] have stated in various polls that they feel religion and faith do not get enough attention on prime time television. "Why don't we ever see characters with a spiritual side?" they ask.

Outside of the strictly religious realm, according to a 1996 *TV Guide* survey, 82 percent of respondents said they would like to see more references to moral issues on television. Now, one can raise the argument that these respondents, by virtue of being respondents to a survey, are a self-selecting proactive group. You also might disagree with their point of view.

However, regardless of our own beliefs, we, as creators, should realize that these statistics indicate, however crudely, that there is a large audience base that is currently being underserved as a result of the choices we make every day.

Now, in areas such as violence, substance abuse, or even social customs and mores, the process historically seems to be that the media reflects the general state of society at large, then pushes the envelope to the next degree. This next degree, in turn, is absorbed by the mass audience, and society shifts subtly accordingly. This then becomes the new norm reflected by the media, which then pushes the envelope again, and so on in endless cycle.

As to the first point, you might argue that artists are only responsible to their art, and this is, in fact, the way our system is set up.

All right, time to bring out the "800-pound gorilla" of creative freedom, the First Amendment. Now, we all know that the First Amendment guarantees, as a constitutional right, our freedom of speech. The full text of the clause, to begin to put all this in context, is as follows:

> Congress shall make no law respecting an establishment of religion, or prohibiting the free exercise thereof; or abridging the freedom of speech, or of the press, or the right of the people peaceably to assemble, and to petition the Government for a redress of grievances.

Many writers, including noted journalist Ted Pease (who provides a more in-depth discussion of the First Amendment, as well as of the many attempts that have been made to curb this freedom, in the essay that follows this section) have stated that these are 45 of the most powerful words in the history of language, law, and society.

Q: What social responsibility does the film composer bear?

If people's buttons are pressed in completely predictable fashion, you're depriving them of opportunities to have novel and perhaps enlightening experiences. That's not a social obligation. I feel that's my artistic obligation.
—Carter Burwell

[The ethics of a producer?] Don't get involved in something for the wrong reason, which is that it can please the marketing department of the studio.
—David Brown

This sentiment would have puzzled the framers of the Constitution to no end. As evidenced by numerous opinions and debates, early state laws and early drafts, this amendment and particularly freedom of the press and of speech, were not of primary concern as they are today. It was not quite a throwaway, but it was almost an afterthought. The full reasoning behind the question of the amendment's passage is a fascinating morass, having to do with enumerated rights, retained rights of citizens, common law rights, and so on, which we will not dwell on here.

For the framers, as closely as we can tell from the documents that exist,[9] our vaunted freedoms of speech and the press had very different complexions in the eighteenth century than they now enjoy.

First, the amendment's language was intended to prohibit Congress from regulating the content of the press by any means, including direct censorship, taxes on the press, passing a sedition act, or a licensing law of any kind. The only laws the framers wished Congress to be able to pass regarding the press were those affecting copyright.

> *Speaking strictly for me, I refuse to create anything where the violence is gratuitous, the sex exploitative, the prejudice casual. Now I realize these are purely subjective criteria. And I do deal heavily with those themes in my work. But, again, it comes down to consequences.*
> *—Paul Hapenny*

The framers believed that, being a new nation, only once removed from a monarchical society, and supposedly to be governed by the people, the citizenry (white males of voting age) must have the right to comment, by means of publication, on the policies of their government. These rights were firmly grounded in the framers' concern with free flow of opinion in the context of political debate. The press would protect the new nation's freedom by ensuring that the government would not have the ability to repress ideas or criticism.

Fiction and entertainment—particularly, of course, in formats that did not exist in the eighteenth century—were not a part of this equation.

Second, the framers never intended for the rights to free speech and of the press to be absolute. Certain classes of speech, particularly seditious libel against the interests or the government of the United States was not a protected class of speech, for example. Even Thomas Jefferson seems to have agreed with the commonly held theory of the time that it could be a criminal assault to publish certain material critical of the government, the crime manifesting itself in the subversion of that government by lowering its esteem in the eyes of the citizenry.

Third, the rights to freedom of speech and of the press were intended to protect only against prior proscriptive restraint. In other words, the right guaranteed that the government could not prevent you from publishing your material. However, those who published were not to be freed from responsibility for what they wrote. In cases of defamation, for example, the content creators were fully liable for their published statements under the law. It was not enough to simply cry "freedom of speech." A number of people were in fact sued for their published content. Once publication occurred, all bets were off.

Now, we as creators may think that our Constitution gives us the unfettered right to do whatever we wish creatively, so we are safe from censorship or restrictions. We can thumb our collective noses at those who believe we have pushed the envelope of violence, substance abuse, sex, stereotypes, and so on far enough to tear it. We can go on being true to our artistic impulses and indulge ourselves freely. The question is: Where does artistic integrity end, and exploitation begin?

Whenever "they" try to restrict what we wish to say, all we have to do is cry "censorship!" Immediately, we or others will invoke the First Amendment, and although criticisms of our work may remain, we will be able to continue with it. That's the essence of our free society. There's nothing "they" can do about it, right?

Wrong. First, we must focus on the identity of "they" and the true meaning of the word "censorship." The First Amendment was intended to guarantee, among other things, freedom of speech as against *government* meddling.

Putting together a news story is entirely an ethical act, from deciding what details to include or omit, to choosing the adjectives. Making a film is similarly an ethical act, frame by frame, from the selection of images to the use of emotionally manipulative scoring and sound. The difference is that there are well-established ethical guideposts in the journalistic process to minimize the potential for unintended harm, but no such mechanisms exist in filmmaking. There, the responsibility that should be companion to freedom depends on personal standards and conscience. Every moral decision becomes an individual matter, made according to what one believes to be right.

—*Les Brown*

The term censorship, although watered down through usage, refers only to governmental interference. The amendment is intended to protect us only if the government attempts to restrict our speech.

Even this is trickier than it might, at first, seem. Many tentacles of government run through our daily lives, and any of them can bring down the wrath of the First Amendment if they interfere with freedom of speech.

When private individuals, advocacy groups, or companies attempt to restrict speech, this does not rise to the level of censorship by definition. Even though in such cases it may be a restriction of expression, we are most often *not* technically protected by the First Amendment.

This is how "they" can exercise their influence on your rights. This is how "they" can restrict or redirect you.

There is currently a groundswell of those who feel that the media, particularly film and television, must be curtailed in its portrayals of scenes, situations, and stories that are causing or may cause damage to society, and particularly to society's children. Their appeals to Congress, which is listening, and listening hard by the way, are increasing.

Now, it is true that Congress is limited in what it can do because of the First Amendment. If Congress acts to restrict violence in movies through direct regulation of content, for example, whatever law is passed would likely be struck down as unconstitutional. Therefore, members of Congress have been exploring other ways of *indirectly* regulating content.

One recent solution hit upon was the so-called violence or 'V'-chip. The Children's Television Act of 1996 mandated that all television sets manufactured after 1998 contain the chip to screen out unwanted content. A ratings system has been designed and implemented by the film and television industries (not by Congress) that gives viewers information about incoming programming sufficient to program the 'V'-chip, which can then block programs containing violence, sex, nudity, offensive language, and so on. (Alternatively, the 'V'-chip can also block any unwanted programming; for example, you could screen out all programming *except* R-rated films appearing on a premium channel.)

> *Of course, the press has a clearly defined mission and motion pictures do not, beyond seeking to please audiences and to make money. But whether movies are intended as entertainment or cinematic art, they do have a social responsibility because the image on the screen has such great power to influence values, behavior, and human relations. Any movie can either strengthen our moral environment or pollute it.*
>
> —*Les Brown*

In this way, Congress was able to avoid running afoul of the First Amendment, while still giving parents a technological tool with which to restrict the content to which their children are exposed.

Although there are opposing viewpoints on the 'V'-chip, the ratings system has been fraught with controversy since inception; and although the eventual usefulness of the device is a matter of speculation, the chip still represents a look into the future. Perhaps Congress cannot directly regulate content, but are there other 'V'-chips to come?

The necessary conclusion here would seem to be that the First Amendment, which many of us believe is absolute, actually is not. Further, it was never intended to be. It should be treated as a privilege that must be earned with responsible decisionmaking and rediscovered constantly, not as

By summing up all the different parts—the acting, the photography, the directing, the editing, the music, the sound effects—cinema becomes its own art form. The deft use of all these different tools creates a mood or a tone. Some of the more memorable shots of The Godfather *are when you hear the sound effects of somebody walking up the stairs and you see this big long shot of the hospital. It sets a tone. There are no other elements in that scene besides the sound of the footsteps and the wide shot of the hospital. But the image remains in my head. It can't just be the picture. It can't just be the sound effects.*

—Rob Legato

an unassailable Divine Right. Rights have changed in the past and can continue to change over time.

The increasingly vocal section of the public that would like to reign in the media has, of course, other recourse from which the umbrella of the First Amendment offers no defense. It is not against our constitutional rights, nor is it technically censorship for a private company to restrict or even to control content. It happens all the time. From Hollywood studios to independent film producers, from advertisers to television producers, they who write the checks almost always control the content, or have the potential to control it, at least overall.

Now, as a creator, you may be thinking that your ideas are compelling enough, or your personal magnetism *magnetic* enough that you can hold your own in a content dispute with one of these entities. Two points need to be made here. First, it is very likely that you will not emerge unscathed from such a battle, regardless of how confident you feel. The second is that these entities are subject to many outside pressures, particularly economic pressures, which may have nothing to do with the basic quality of your ideas.

Individual viewers, advocacy and church groups, and others are concerned with the levels of what they define as aberrant behavior in film and television. Historically, the inclination of these individuals and groups has been to "defend" society against what they see as the immorality borne of unbridled, unchecked, and excessive free expression. Various forms of restriction have been attempted.

In fact, starting in the early 1900s, some began to believe that media was changing, rather than reflecting, traditional social values.[10] They lobbied for and were able to institute community censoring bodies to monitor and, in effect, license cinema. In Chicago, for example, one such body required both review and an actual permit from the Police Department prior to release of any film.[11] A national censorship body was formed in 1908.[12]

Even those stalwart supporters of the First Amendment, the newspapers, opposed unregulated cinema as immoral at that time. Pressure on lawmakers to regulate creative free expression was intense. Even the U.S. Supreme Court *declined* to grant relief from censorship on First Amendment grounds when licensing and censorship were challenged constitutionally.

"This could never happen today," I hear you cry. However, if we are not careful, it can, and may, happen again.

Some in the film and television industry are beginning to heed the warning signs and, to a greater or lesser degree, to listen to public concerns, at least in certain areas such as stereotypes. As one of many possible examples, Jeffrey Katzenberg solicited feedback about DreamWorks' *The Prince of Egypt*[13] prior to its completion, partly to minimize any damaging statements or perceptions made by the film.

> He did it proactively. He called in anybody who might be interested in the content, Arabs, Jews, and others, and showed us the rough cuts and discussed it and took notes from our input. Very enlightened.[14]

Further, the economics of more wholesome fare bear out as well. In 1999, a group of some of the nation's most influential advertisers announced the formation of "The Family Friendly Programming Forum," a new initiative that would support—both with advertising dollars and indirectly by providing scholarships, awards, and other incentives—family friendly television programs. These programs would be minus what has been described as "the squirm factor" (parents literally and figuratively "squirming" at onscreen content they would rather their children did not see), meaning shows that entire families could comfortably watch together.[15]

Remember, critics and detractors can use economic pressure to influence the entities through which our films or programs are funded, produced, and marketed. That, in turn, influences content. Letter campaigns, petitions, protests, and economic boycotts have all been tried as means to influence the content of the media, with greater or lesser success. In the past, these have been largely isolated efforts spawned by an outcry over a single film or program.

Now, the movement to rein in the media is beginning to reach a pitch such that it is possible to see many such groups banding together to effect change. It is already beginning to happen. Television, as an advertiser-driven medium, is extremely susceptible to economic pressure. So too, is cinema, which more and more is coming to rely on the goodwill of advertisers in the form of commercial support, advertising tie-ins, and now, unfortunately, onscreen pre-feature advertising. Theater owners are sensitive to this pressure as well.

Perhaps the Internet alone is somewhat immune to economic pressures, at least for now. However, I have to believe that a large, targeted boycott of Internet-based business—any business—would raise an eyebrow or two at least.

Is it fair to blame the media for society's problems?

Washington is clearly turning its gaze on the industry as the pressure on our representatives for action to curb the media increases. Many in the industry feel that these criticisms, although perhaps understandable, are not accurate. Screenwriter Paul Hapenny has said, for example:

> Politicians, looking for the easy answer to society's ills have made a convenient scapegoat of the media. It's Washington, acting in the same simplistic manner as it accuses Hollywood of doing, foisting the breakdown of society off on a simple, easy target. Like the mindlessly violent films of American heroes killing untold aliens, while wrapping themselves in the flag, the politicians have reduced a complex issue to black/white, put on the white hat and demonized the film and television industries. Far easier to do that than to really look into the cause of societal unrest. The mirror can be a damned uncomfortable view. Which is why neither Washington nor Hollywood wants to look too closely.[16]

However, it is perhaps true that we sometimes overstep our freedom, use it irresponsibly, and thus jeopardize the freedoms of us all.

It can only help the situation, and is therefore in the creators' best interests, for us to begin exercising our ethical choice reflex more often. Consider the messages we are sending out into the world. Do we really need to use gratuitous violence, prejudice-enhancing stereotypes, and portrayals of smoking and drugs in our work? If we deem one or all of these elements necessary to the telling of the story or the building of the character, then we can and should certainly use them. However, if they are merely backdrop or atmosphere, can we find other ways to accomplish the goals of our story?

Notes

1 1915 D: D.W. Griffith, David W. Griffith Corp.

2 Brown, Les. *The Artist as Citizen*, unpublished.

3 1974–1984, Paramount Television.

4 1983 D: Paul Brickman, Geffen Pictures.

5 *Scream*. 1996 D: Wes Craven, Dimension Films/Miramax Films; *Scream 2*. 1997 D: Wes Craven, Dimension Films/Miramax Films. *Scream 3*. 2000 D: Wes Craven, Dimension Films/Miramax Films.

6 1995 D: Scott Kalvert, New Line Cinema.

7 Minow, Newton. "A Vast Wasteland," *Speech*, 1961.

8 Poland, Larry W., Ph.D. Interview with F. Miguel Valenti, January 26, 2000.

9 For an interesting introduction to this subject, see Levy, Leonard W. *Origins of the Bill of Rights,* (New Haven, Conn.: Yale University Press, 1999).

10 The single most influential voice of this time was Anthony Comstock, who headed the Society for the Suppression of Vice, and is responsible for most of the obscenity laws, both state and federal, known collectively as The Comstock Laws. Ernst, Morris L. and Schwartz, Alan U. *Censorship: The Search For The Obscene.* (New York: The Macmillan Company, 1964), pp. 29–36.

11 Most big cities and states required permits for films. The review boards were eventually struck down, but not until a case went before The Supreme Court in 1961 (*Times Film Corp. vs. Chicago*).

12 *Times Film Corp. vs. Chicago*, p. 148.

13 1998 D: Brenda Chapman/Steve Hickner, DreamWorks SKG.

14 Bustany, Donald S. Interview with Stephanie Carbone, August 8, 1997.

15 "God, Mom, and Apple Pie: Family Friendly Programming Returns to Prime Time," a panel discussion held at the NATPE (National Association of Television Programming Executives) convention in New Orleans on January 27, 2000. Moderator: Laurie A. Trotta, panel included Andrea Alstrup, vice president of Advertising for Johnson & Johnson and cofounder of the Family Friendly Programming Forum.

16 Hapenny, Paul. Interview with F. Miguel Valenti, February 1, 2000.

Free Expression in Hollywood: First Amendment & Censorship

Ted Pease

Ted Pease is a professor and the head of the Communications Department at Utah State University. He is also a columnist on media and society issues for the *Logan (Utah) Herald-Journal*. Pease began his journalism career in 1976 with the *Associated Press*. He has also served as associate director of the Freedom Forum Media Studies Center at Columbia University.

The collision between free expression and what many people see as a growing need to monitor and regulate movies, television, and the Internet is the topic of this reading. More and more Americans, from political leaders to grandmothers, are calling for more "morality," accountability, regulation, and self-restraint from the mass media industries. At issue, ultimately, is not just what my own grandmother would have called "good taste" and decorum, but the question of just who will be licensed to decide what those things are when they appear as programming products.

For both the makers and the consumers of movies, TV, and the wide wealth of self-expression that the Internet represents, the issue is an old one that has been fought before.

On the one hand, here in the land of the free and the home of the brave, we are secure in our tradition of free and open self-expression as defined in what is arguably the most powerful sentence since "Let there be light." In just 45 words, the First Amendment to the Constitution of the United States sets forth a simple but potent recipe for a society that values individual liberty and a reverence for self-expression.

> *The idea that a parent can control what his or her child is seeing and doing has nothing to do with freedom of speech. If the government is telling you what to think or what you may not see, that's one thing. But here it's a question of giving people the choice of to see or not to see. I have a hard time thinking that's censorship.*
>
> *—Bridget Potter*

The First Amendment guarantees four critical freedoms that define a line separating the tyranny of the many as embodied in the government, from the rights of the individual; it is a way of thinking about where a single person's freedoms end when they infringe on someone else, and vice versa. The First Amendment protects our individual rights, telling government regulators to back off. We can (1) think and believe what we like, and observe those beliefs as we wish; (2) express what we believe, in spoken or written word, or in newspapers, film, theater, television, or any other means of communication; (3) get together with other people to talk about those beliefs, or anything else; and (4) complain to government leaders if we have a gripe, without getting in trouble for it, and expect solutions.

But even with those powerful protections, free expression is constantly in jeopardy in the mass media age, as we continue to push the envelope of those freedoms with new kinds of self-expression—words, images, ideas—and new kinds of packages. These result in a recurring reassessment of the wisdom of permitting absolute and completely free self-expression.

Some fear that raunchy excesses by the few put the freedoms of all in danger. Although the constitutional protections and social benefits of free and unfettered self-expression—including everything from political debate to artistic expression—have been defined and reinforced by U.S. courts for more than two centuries as crucial to a free society, some things have always crossed the line. Every time that happens—typically media content involving sex, religion, political beliefs, violence, and other issues offensive to the status quo—everyone's First Amendment freedoms, in ways small or potentially enormous, are endangered.

As the renowned baseball manager and tangle-tongued philosopher Yogi Berra said, "it's deja vu all over again for all of us"—for those who have fought these battles in the past in the face of threats by the public and politicians for legislated "solutions" to the "problem" of free and unfettered expression. Given the crucial importance of free expression to society, complaints about perceived "excesses" in the mass media are nothing to be taken lightly or with arrogance.

As central as the First Amendment is to all of American life, it is also under almost-daily attack in multiple arenas: when lawmakers attempt to legislate "morality" or "family values"; when presidential wannabes attack television and movies for promoting social violence; when legislators hold hearings on song lyrics or actors' political beliefs; when community groups try to ban books or movies as "obscene"; when elected officials censor artwork and photographs, or mandate technological solutions to "protect" TV viewers or Internet users (from what?).

Technology and Free Expression

Every time technology has offered us an opportunity to express ourselves more broadly, it has been burned at the stake by the powers that be. It's not that people don't want to know things, but new things scare us.

In 1456, Johann Gutenberg changed the world: By inventing the printing press he freed legions of ink-stained monks from their tasks of copying manuscripts by hand, and he made ideas and knowledge accessible to the many instead of just to the powerful. Remember that a single upstart priest, Martin Luther, used the new printing technology to challenge the Church of Rome; he was excommunicated in 1520, but Protestantism was on the map.

It's not the technology, of course, but how it's used and what it expresses. And *that* is the challenge for each new generation. In the 1600s, the prolific and politically incorrect poet of his day, John Milton, spat in the eye of the entire power structure of England, and the practice of censorship: "Give me the liberty to know," he wrote, "to utter, and to argue freely according to conscience, above all liberties."[1]

The powers that be have always argued that it is exactly that kind of uppity-ness, about liberty and free thought and individual choice, that has always led to trouble. After all, who is better equipped to decide what kinds of material we see and hear and read: writers, poets, reporters, artists, filmmakers, and the rest, or those who don't like what they say?

The last time we had "new media," before the Internet and multimedia, it was television. That was in the 1930s, although the corner tavern didn't start getting TVs until after World War II. Concerns began to crop up immediately.

In a 1938 article in *Harper's*, the preeminent American essayist E.B. White wrote of the coming new marvel with remarkable prescience:

> Television will enormously enlarge the eye's range, and, like radio, will advertise the Elsewhere. Together with the tabs, the mags, and the movies, it will insist that we forget the primary and the near in favor of the distant and the remote.... When I was a child, people simply looked about them and were moderately happy; today they peer beyond the seven seas, bury themselves waist-deep in tidings, and by and large what they see and hear makes them unutterably sad.... We shall stand or fall by television—of that I am quite sure.[2]

Motion pictures—the "movies"—had already arrived to trouble the peace before television, of course, but White makes a good point that needs considering. You modern-day Miltons and Gutenbergs and D.W. Griffiths can learn from the experiences of your predecessors, who have already fought many of the fights you'll have to fight again.

Do I like going to see a movie in which lesbians are negatively portrayed? I don't always like it, no. But once you start trying to control images you get into dangerous territory. I got a lot of criticism about Valerie Solanis in I Shot Andy Warhol*—on the one hand from people saying, "Why do you have to make a film about a psycho lesbian killer?"—and on the other hand people saying, "You depicted her as far too nice, she was such a bitch!" You can't win. There is no one image that's going to please everybody. There just isn't.*

—Christine Vachon

Free and unrestrained expression is not only a constitutional issue, but (as Thomas Paine argued) a natural right. Although none of us takes kindly to being told what and when and where to express our thoughts, we do accept and even promote the idea that we who have the tools to communicate information and ideas should use them responsibly, with empathy, understanding, and insight.

Struggles within the press over questions of performance, social responsibility, and the importance of free expression and wide-open debate as a cornerstone of democracy have been continuous, robust, often acrimonious, and always vital to keeping freedom of expression and what it means healthy. With that freedom, to which the film and TV industries are just as entitled as newspapers and book publishers, comes a responsibility to the society and the audience that both includes and transcends "art," a responsibility that filmmakers, TV producers and entertainment moguls ignore at their peril. And ours.

History of Censorship

Movie and television creators are different from journalists, of course, but we are relatives who can learn from one another, especially as multimedia technologies blend written, spoken, and visual communication. A look back at movie history and efforts to control the medium indicate that many of the battles fought by film producers have already been waged by their older cousins in print.

The last time the planet turned the page on a new century, the invention of an amazing new technology—the "moving picture"—revolutionized American society. Says film scholar Gregory D. Black, "Entertainment films quickly transcended ethnic, class, religious, and political lines to become the dominant institution of popular culture."[3] In New York City alone, nickelodeons—cheap, silent moving picture shows that cost a nickel—pulled in some 200,000 people a day, and as many as 2 million nationally.[4] *Harper's Weekly* called it a nationwide "nickel delirium."[5]

Sound familiar? The scale is larger today, and the choices are greater, but the delirium is the same. Here at the beginning of the twenty-first century, more American homes have TV sets than indoor plumbing. The final episode of a "television show about nothing"—*Seinfeld*[6]—was touted as *the* cultural event of the year. A movie about the 1912 sinking of the Titanic grossed $1 billion worldwide in the six months after its release.[7] The networks fell all over themselves to bid $18 billion to televise professional football games through 2005.[8] Researchers find that the average four-year-old spends about 70 times as much "quality time" with the boob tube as with Dad (35 hours a week compared to 30 minutes).[9] The Internet has revolutionized communication, information, education, and entertainment. And, as a *Time* writer put it, "it seems pointless to argue with the medium that so dominates our lives and culture."[10]

In the early 1900s, clergy and politicians decried the advent of movies as dangerous—"a new and curious disease," as one child expert put it in 1909; a Philadelphia minister called movies "schools for degenerates and criminals,"[11] and a fellow man of the cloth said they were "schools of vice and crime ... offering trips to hell for a nickel."[12] In 1912, a YMCA official intoned:

> Unless the law steps in and does for moving-picture shows what it has done for meat inspection and pure food, the cinematograph will continue to inject into our social order an element of degrading principle. The only way that the people, and especially the children, can be safeguarded from the influence of evil pictures is by the careful regulation of the places of exhibitions.[13]

So what has changed? In the 1990s, politicians blamed the movies for prompting copycat killing sprees, and Hollywood generally was held responsible for a nationwide decline in "family values" and a growing preoccupation with sex and violence. Researchers counted up the number of acts of violence per hour in "family programming," and (rightly) chastised broadcast executives for their claims that shows like *The Flintstones*,[14] *The Jetsons*[15] and *The Smurfs*[16] were "educational."

"You can't even watch cartoons any more! Why have you let TV go so far?" an angry mother of three told TV executives at a public hearing on TV content in Peoria, Illinois.

As ever, politicians and civic leaders hear the cries. The response to the advent of cinema in the first decade of the 1900s was censorship and regulation; in the last decade of the century, the cry was for technological remedies to "protect" us from TV—the so-called "violence" or 'V'-chip and TV ratings systems—and for legislation to clean up movies.

The inclination—then as now—was to "protect" society from the perceived excesses of unbridled self-expression by imposing various forms of censorship.

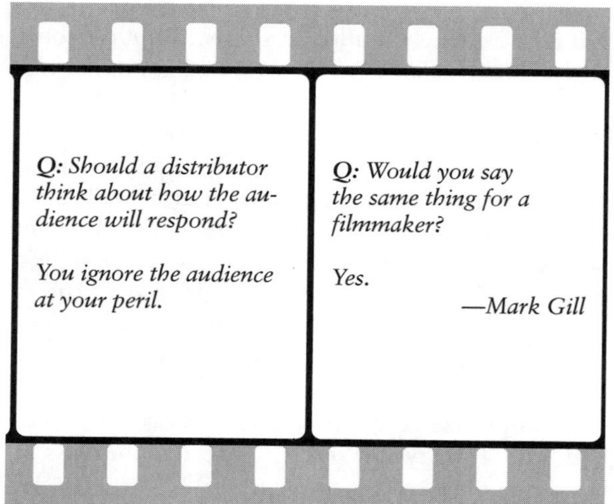

Specifically, social reformers of the early 1900s, who thought cinema was changing America's traditional values, not reflecting them, started first monitoring, then licensing movies. By 1908, a national motion picture censorship board had been formed in New York.[17]

Moviemakers finally challenged the constitutionality of licensing and censorship in 1915, arguing to the U.S. Supreme Court that movies were part of the press and entitled to the same protections. Unbelievably, the Supreme Court, including Justice Oliver Wendell Holmes, unanimously disagreed.[18]

Couldn't happen today, right? In fact, there is plenty of evidence that latter-day "reformers," drawing support from otherwise unlikely partners on both the left and the right, want something to be done to curb a mass media that increasingly is seen as out of control.

"A good part of what has gone wrong in this country is due to our mass media," U.S. Senator John Danforth (R-Mo.), said during Senate hearings on TV violence in 1993.

And this from U.S. Senator Paul Simon, then a liberal Democrat from Illinois, in the same year: "The evidence is just overwhelming that entertainment that glorifies violence adds to violence in our society.... There are a lot of people in the industry who won't acknowledge that."[19]

In 1993, Attorney General Janet Reno, representing the Clinton administration, testified before Senate hearings and sent chills through Hollywood, raising the specter of the infamous House Un-American Activities Committee (HUAC) [20] and, later, the McCarthy hearings of the 1940s and 1950s.[21] "In only half a century, television-brought violence has become a central theme in the lives of our young people, as central as homework and playgrounds," Reno said. "If immediate voluntary steps are not taken and deadlines established, government should respond, and respond immediately."[22]

Government control of TV and movies? In America? Simon wasn't sure he'd go that far, but he agreed that something needs to be done to protect society from the excesses of TV and movies. "I don't want the federal government to control content," he said, "but what I do want to do is to put some pressure on the industry so that they will regulate themselves in an area where clearly harm is being done to our society."[23]

For many of us, these sentiments, coming from the likes of Simon, who as a liberal Democrat is the kind of politician traditionally on the angels' side of First Amendment protections, are horrifying. But they appear to be increasingly widespread as parents worry about whether the mass media, and especially television and movies, are corrupting their kids. Even though the Constitution says clearly and directly that "Congress shall make no law" curbing free expression in any form, pressures on lawmakers to insulate children from the corrupting influences of the mass media age are fierce, and often place politicians in a bind between a reverence for First Amendment guarantees and electoral realities. For many in Washington, it's an uncomfortable place to be.

"Every day, battle lines cross movie lines wherever controversial topics are at odds with local attitudes," points out Jack Perkins of the A&E cable network. "Now Congress is asked to decide how far is too far, how much is too much?"[24]

It's history repeating itself. In Hollywood the first time around, in the early 1900s, the way the issue was resolved was for the motion picture industry to respond to public outcry by agreeing to cooperate with oversight boards, such as the Industry Board Of Censors.[25] Studios hoped that establishing the National Board of Review (NBR) would halt the proliferation of censorship bodies in every community in the land; *cooperation with the NBR and industry self-censorship were seen as the lesser of a variety of greater evils and, thus, good business.*

It didn't work. Movies such as D.W. Griffith's 1915 epic, *The Birth of a Nation*,[26] perhaps the most heavily censored film in history, still outraged critics like the National Federation of Women, which condemned it as "vile and

Q: Does such thinking smack of censorship?

Not at all. For better or for worse, when you're making movies you're not making them for one person. You're making them for a lot of people. There's always a tension between making something you believe in and the audience will be led upward by it, as opposed to pandering and just doing what's absolutely expected. Here's the great news: what we're discovering is that all the pandering that's been done over the last few years is not working nearly as well commercially as it used to. People are bored by having something at the lowest common denominator more so now than they ever have been. Originality and inventiveness seem to be more and more popular with the American public.

—Mark Gill

atrocious."[27] (Audiences obviously disagreed—the film stood, until the 1980s, as the top-grossing movie of all time, earning about $60 million in 1915 dollars, which would amount to about half a billion dollars today.)

The Hays Code

By 1922, the NBR was viewed as too lax and in collusion with Hollywood. Movie producers, fearful of more draconian measures against them, elected to create a trade association, the Motion Picture Producers and Distributors of America (MPPDA), to work at improving Hollywood's image and to lobby against censorship bills at the state and national level. The "squeaky-clean" front man to represent the industry was the chairman of the Republican National Committee and former Postmaster General in the Harding administration, Will Hays from Indiana. Writes film historian Black:

> Hays was an inspired choice. His roots were solidly Midwestern, his politics conservatively Republican, and his religion mainstream Protestant. Teetotaler, elder in the Presbyterian church, Elk, Moose, Rotarian and Mason, Hays brought the respectability of mainstream middle America to a Jewish-dominated film industry. He symbolized the figurative Puritan in Babylon.[28]

Although Hays created rules requiring studios to send him scripts before they were produced, and even though he rejected some 125 of them over six years, pressure was building for federal legislation against what one religious leader called movies' "threat to civilization." When the talkies came in during the late 1920s, the situation—from everyone's perspective—worsened. Now the immoral corrupters could *talk* on the screen, rationalize their behavior, and further flout law, order, and decency.

As one Catholic critic, Father Daniel Lord, S.J., the primary author of the production code that would govern Hollywood for three decades, put it, "Silent smut had been bad. Vocal smut cried to the censors for vengeance."[29] Censors stepped up their work, with the New York State censorship board alone cutting more than 4,000 scenes from 600 movies in 1928.[30]

Although Hays was an unqualified success in the public relations department, he made no headway at all in terms of regulating movie content or reducing the level of public complaints. What was missing was an agreement on rules that would help the studios regulate themselves. In the late 1920s, a group of Chicago Catholics, including Cardinal George Mundelein and Jesuit dramatics professor Father Lord, approached Hays and the MPPDA with "a Catholic movie code ... a fascinating combination of Catholic theology, conservative politics and pop psychology—an amalgam that would control the content of Hollywood films for three decades."[31]

Hays and Lord managed to sell the code to moguls from MGM, Warner, Paramount, and Fox, in part because the studios were jittery about their finances in the wake of the stock market crash, and the threat of a boycott by 20 million Catholic moviegoers. Given the possible alternatives, the studios embraced self-regulation in order to engender goodwill and to prevent more dire repercussions. The code also avoided federal regulation or other outside intervention and censorship; enforcement resided in the Hays office and the MPPDA, as well as a jury of producers, which would make decisions in the case of disagreements between studios and Hays.

"The Code sets up high standards of performance for motion picture producers," Hays said in 1934. "It states the considerations which good taste and community values make necessary in this universal form of entertainment—respect for law, respect for every religion, respect for every race, and respect for every nation."[32]

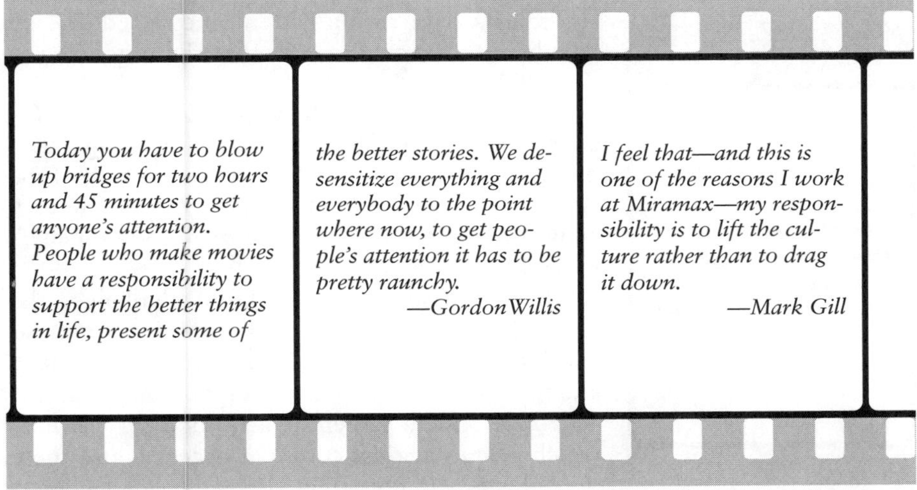

Oversight of the code eventually fell to Joseph L. Breen, a Catholic anti-Semite who had been doing public relations work for Hays in Hollywood. He thought the studios had duped his boss.

He was not, by any means, a fan of Hollywood or its denizens. Breen wrote in a 1932 letter to a Jesuit priest friend: "Here [in Hollywood] we have Paganism rampant and in its most virulent form. Drunkenness and debauchery are commonplace. Sexual perversion is rampant."[33]

Among the Hollywood "sexual perversions" Breen lamented was the blonde bombshell herself, Mae West, whose sultriest and sexiest films, *She Done Him Wrong*[34] and *I'm No Angel*,[35] came out during this period.

Says author and film historian Nat Segalof, "Mae West did three things: She entertained people, she saved Paramount Pictures, and she single-handedly created the Legion of Decency, which was single-handedly created to fight Mae West."[36]

That may be a bit overstated—it wasn't only Mae West—but what is certain is that the increasingly explicit and risqué fare coming out of Hollywood in the 1930–1934 period created yet another crisis for Hays, the studios, and America's forces of "morality."

Though certainly more violent and racist in tone than most Catholic discussion about Hollywood during the early 1930s, Breen's attitudes about Tinseltown as the modern Sodom and Gomorrah were increasingly widespread among American Catholics, who started talking again about a Catholic boycott. Hollywood, "[t]he pesthole that infests the entire country with its obscene and lascivious motion pictures must be cleaned and disinfected," suggested the Catholic magazine *Commonweal* in 1934.[37]

In 1933, clearly disgusted by how poorly the code was protecting American values, the Catholic Church founded the Legion of Decency, which created its own rating system and asked church members to boycott movies that the organization deemed immoral.

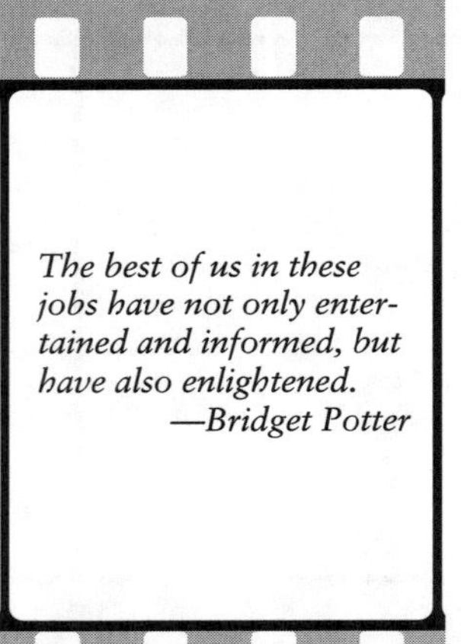

The best of us in these jobs have not only entertained and informed, but have also enlightened.
—Bridget Potter

Monsignor Francis J. Weber served as an officer on the Legion of Decency. "The one thing a producer did not want to do was to get one-fifth of the American public on his back, and they knew they could expect that if the movies were too raunchy," he said in a 1994 interview.[38]

In response to the Catholic challenge, the MPPDA installed Breen as the official protector and interpreter of the code. "The vulgar, the cheap and the tawdry is out," Breen announced. "There is no room on the screen at any time for pictures which offend against common decency, and these the industry will not allow."[39]

It is clear that Hollywood had a serious problem in Breen, but by the end of 1930s, the silver screen genie was starting to escape from its bottle. In 1939, *Gone With the Wind*[40] made various kinds of movie history. One of the reasons that Rhett Butler's one-liner to Scarlett O'Hara is among the all-time most famous movie quotes is not just his delivery, but its content. "Frankly, my dear," actor Clark Gable told Vivien Leigh, "I don't give a damn." He might have been addressing Breen and the do-gooders.

Producer Hal Roach remembers struggling with the script, in the context of the edict of the Production Code banning profanity. "We had a meeting," Roach says, "and we decided that there was just no other word that could do the job that 'damn' would in that situation, so we left the 'damn' in."[41]

Other "subversive" and "immoral" films glorifying sex and drugs slipped through: *Reefer Madness*,[42] and Howard Hughes' production of Jane Russell (and her controversial cleavage) in *The Outlaw*,[43] among others. And then came

Pearl Harbor, and U.S. attention—and Hollywood's—was drawn overseas and to more patriotic fare. World War II provided other grounds for censorship—national security and American morale. Showing American soldiers dead or injured was forbidden; John Huston, who went to work for the military as a filmmaker, often had scenes cut; and footage of the attack on Pearl Harbor was suppressed for 16 months to avoid demoralizing the folks back home.

Black Listing

After World War II, with the beginning of the Cold War, censorship took a new form as Hollywood was scrutinized not so much for immorality and indecency, but on grounds of patriotism. Led by U.S. Rep. J. Parnell Thomas of New Jersey (with colleague Richard M. Nixon at his side), the HUAC went hunting Communist sympathizers in Hollywood in the late 1940s. It was one of the most shameful and painful episodes in American history, a witch-hunt that blacklisted many of the most talented people in Hollywood, and ruined lives. In 1947, Thomas and his HUAC colleagues subpoenaed 41 Hollywood directors, screenwriters, and actors who had joined the Communist Party during the 1930s, when it had been considered rather stylish to do so, or who had contributed funds to its activities during the Depression.

As the focus turned from morality to political ideology, the grip of the Hays Office and the Production Code started to fade. Social change through the late 1950s and into the Civil Rights and Vietnam War eras, along with a more cosmopolitan American population, effectively blunted controls on movie content. Jack Valenti recalls:

> When I became president of the Motion Picture Association of America in May 1966 … the national scene was marked by insurrection on the campus, riots in the street, rise in women's liberation, protest of the young, doubts about the institution of marriage, abandonment of old guiding slogans, and the crumbling of social traditions. It would have been foolish to believe that movies—that most creative of art forms—could have remained unaffected by change and torment in our society.[44]

The MPAA was the successor organization to MPPDA, and, although as Valenti points out, the end of the era of big Hollywood studios had reduced the ability of something like the Hays Office to control content, the Production Code was officially still on the books. "There was about this stern, forbidding catalogue of 'Do's and Don'ts' the odious smell of censorship," Valenti says, "I determined to junk it at the first opportune moment."[45]

The problem of the code was illustrated for Valenti in his first weeks in office, when the script of *Who's Afraid of Virginia Woolf*[46] landed on his desk. He met with studio mogul Jack Warner to discuss some of the language in the script. "We talked for three hours, and the result was deletion of 'screw' and retention of 'hump the hostess,'" he says. "It seemed wrong that grown men should be sitting around discussing such matters. Moreover, I was uncomfortable with the thought that this was just the beginning of an unsettling new era in film, in which we would lurch from crisis to crisis, without any suitable solution in sight."[47]

But it was both more complicated and simpler than that. In the 1960s, movies had slipped, and television had taken over as America's family entertainment option of choice. Hollywood was hemorrhaging as television, not movies, defined American popular culture and, increasingly, defined how American families spent their leisure time. As we had gathered around the new invention of popular radio in the 1930s and 1940s, Americans clustered in their living rooms around the tube in the 1960s. Television's wholesome *Leave It to Beaver*[48] and *Father Knows Best*[49] appealed to entire families, so in order to attract teenagers and young adults in the more permissive 1960s, the studios tried sexier fare—grittier, riskier, more violent—that the TV networks couldn't or wouldn't.

The old Hays Code was abolished in Fall 1968 and replaced with a voluntary film rating system adapted from a similar formula in place in England. This semblance of industry self-regulation eventually evolved into the familiar G-PG-PG/13-R-NC/17 system, providing some minimal guidance about the content of movies and, now, TV programs as well.

As ever, the specter of government stepping into the movie and TV business has been enough to force the industries into self-regulation as the least evil of available bad choices. The transition of MPAA-like ratings systems from movies to TV has been a political battleground in recent years, and also the source of both amusement and consternation among foreign observers.

Claude-Jean Bertrand, a French media scholar, points out a couple of inconsistencies:

> U.S. television and movies are full of violence of the most abhorrent and bizarre kind, from the sci-fi *Jurassic Park*,[50] to the dark *Pulp Fiction*[51] and *LA Confidential*,[52] to Schwarzenegger-esque senseless dismemberments and explosions. But while accepting such violence as entertainment, repressed U.S. attitudes toward sexuality censor most forms of nudity and love-making, even as a 1997 research study finds that the United States is the world's No. 1 producer of pornography.[53]

The dilemma facing producers of all mass media, new and old—newspapers and books, film and TV, Internet content, multimedia, and all the rest—at the beginning of a new century is the same old song: How to balance the free expression of individual artists, writers, filmmakers, and reporters against the perennial complaint of society about "morality"? It is a classic constitutional tension and political struggle, as parents and the politicians who hear them pressure Congress to "protect" children from the depravities of Hollywood. And, of course, the critics are not always wrong about content that is too raunchy or crass or foul-mouthed or otherwise in poor taste.

Where the critics and reformers are wrong, and badly, is in their efforts, however well-intentioned, to control or censor content, whether for reasons of "decency" and "morality," or to promote the "public good" and "family values." The basic fallacy of all such attempts to legislate morality and to control mass media content is the explicit assumption that you can stop people from having dangerous thoughts simply by telling them not to.

> *There are charlatans and mavericks, as well as exceedingly moral men and women producing movies. Their morality is somewhat affected by the immorality or lack of morality of their colleagues.*
>
> *—David Brown*

At best, rating systems and 'V'-chips and other such legislated efforts to protect us from television, movies, and other media content might be tools for viewers, but all such measures are flawed because they depend on someone else—governments or program producers themselves—to make judgments on what is "appropriate." The specter of similar efforts looms to "clean up" cyberspace and the anarchy of free expression that is the Internet.

It's hard work being a responsible consumer of media content in a mass media age of thousands of choices, but for me, I'd rather do the work of filtering and judging myself rather than let either self-appointed or elected censors decide what's appropriate for me and my family in my own home.

Like all media, movies, entertainment television, and all the other new products converging in the age of interactive mass media have the capacity to both educate and inspire, as well as to horrify and degrade. The difference is often in the eye and mind of the beholder, of course. And, for those who produce media as well as for those who consume it, the challenge is to find ways to take advantage of the former traits while not overreacting to the latter. It is a delicate balance.

The answer is not more rules or the threat of regulation, which can lead to a chilling self-censorship that can be more insidious and damaging to the spirit—and to principles of free expression—than legislated censorship may be. A better, more lasting and more responsible solution will involve an understanding both by those who produce media content—TV, movies, Web pages, video games, interactive media, and all the rest—as well as those who are concerned with media effects, of the important balancing act required in a free society between two critical values: individual free expression on the one hand, and larger social good on the other.

For consumers and creators of mass media content alike, this relationship in a society that is truly dedicated to both individual liberties and a larger social responsibility is fragile at best. The First Amendment says nothing about *responsible* free expression, but in a social climate of growing concern about the impact of pervasive mass media, especially as they may influence children, recklessness can pose threats to the freedom and individual liberties of content producers and consumers alike. It is not enough to push the envelope in terms of media content simply because we can, either technologically or legislatively, but because we, as thoughtful, responsible individuals, really think we should.

Notes

1 Milton, John. *Areopagitica*, 1645.
2 White, E.B. *Removal, One Man's Meat* (New York: Harper & Row, 1938), pp. 2–3.
3 Black, Gregory D. *Hollywood Censored: Morality Codes, Catholics, and the Movies* (New York: Cambridge University Press, 1994), pp. 8–9.
4 Fell, John. *Film Before Griffith* (Berkeley: University of California Press, 1983), pp. 162–163.
5 Currie, Barton W. "The Nickel Madness," *Harper's Weekly*, August 24, 1907.
6 1990–1998, NBC Television.
7 "*Titanic*'s Box Office Passes 1 Billion Mark," Associated Press, *Toronto Star*, April 27, 1998, p. E8.
8 Dubow, Josh. "CBS Back in NFL Business," Associated Press Wire, January 13, 1998.
9 "Media Use in America," *Issue Brief Series* (Studio City: Mediascope Press, 1999).
10 Handy, Bruce. "Oh, Behave!" *Time*, February 2, 1998.
11 Jowett, Garth. *Film: The Democratic Art* (Boston: Little, Brown, 1976).
12 Crafts, Wilbur F. *National Perils and Hopes: A Study Based on Current Statistics and the Observations of a Cheerful Reformer* (Cleveland: O.F.M. Barton, 1910), p. 39.
13 Letter to the editor, Darrell O. Hibbard, in *The Outlook*, July 13, 1912.
14 1960–1966, Hanna-Barbera Productions.
15 1962–1963, Hanna-Barbera Productions.
16 1981–1989, Hanna-Barbera Productions.
17 The Industry Board Of Censors. Ernst, Morris L. and Schwartz, Alan U. *Censorship: The Search For The Obscene* (New York: The Macmillan Company, 1964), p. 144.
18 Black, pp. 15–16.
19 Segalof, Nat. *The Hollywood Wars*, Arts & Entertainment Network, 1994.
20 The House Un-American Activities Committee began with the witch-hunts of the 1950s, searching for communists in the film industry. More than 100 witnesses were called. Eight screenwriters and two directors, know as the Hollywood Ten, refused to testify and were jailed. They were subsequently fired and blacklisted. Hundreds more were fired. *Encyclopedia Britannica Online*: www.eb.com.
21 Chaired by Joseph R. McCarthy, the 36-day televised hearings were intended to uncover "card carrying communists" in public office. The hearings, however, did nothing more than allow McCarthy to discredit himself with his own brutal tactics and interrogations. *Encyclopedia Britannica Online*: www.eb.com.
22 "Janet Reno and TV Violence: The Government is Watching," *The Phoenix Gazette*, October 23, 1993, p. B4.

23 Simon, Paul. "Reducing TV Violence," *The Courier-Journal (Louisville, KY)*, August 31, 1989, p. 15A.
24 Personal recollection of Ted Pease.
25 *Censorship: The Search For The Obscene*, p. 144.
26 1915 D: D.W. Griffith, D.W. Griffith Corporation.
27 In addition, even its in own time, the NAACP and Booker T. Washington Clubs tried to have the film outlawed and *The Nation* called it "a deliberate attempt to humiliate 10 million American citizens...." Guthmann, Edward. "Black History Month: Hollywood Racism a Mirror on Society," *The New York Times*, January 31, 1999, p. 30.
28 Black, p. 31.
29 Lord, Daniel A. *S.J. Played By Ear* (Chicago: Loyola University Press, 1955).
30 Black, p. 34.
31 Black, p. 39.
32 Segalof, 1994.
33 Letter from Breen to Wilfrid Parsons, S.J., October 10, 1932; See Black, pp. 70–71.
34 1933 D: Lowell Sherman, Paramount Pictures.
35 1933 D: Wesley Ruggles, Paramount Pictures.
36 Segalof, 1994.
37 *Commonweal*, May 18, 1934.
38 Segalof, 1994.
39 Segalof, 1994.
40 1939 D: Victor Fleming, Selznick International Pictures.
41 Research files of Ted Pease.
42 1936 D: Louis J. Gasnier, G&H Corporation.
43 1943 D: Howard Hughes, United Artists.
44 See Jack Valenti: www.mpaa.org.
45 Valenti: www.mpaa.org.
46 1966 D: Mike Nichols, Warner Bros.
47 Valenti: www.mpaa.org.
48 1957–1963, MCA-TV.
49 1954–1963, Screen Gems TV.
50 1993 D: Steven Spielberg, Universal.
51 1994 D: Quentin Tarantino, Miramax Films.
52 1997 D: Curtis Hanson, Warner Bros.
53 Research files of Ted Pease.

Ethics, A Practical Primer

Dead White Greeks and Why They Matter

The Skeptic: You again. Now what?

Response: Now, we spend some time briefly summarizing the study of ethics, more specifically of Western ethical traditions, trying to figure out what we're talking about.

The Skeptic: Sounds like a barrel of laughs. You know, I really don't believe ethics can be taught. We are programmed from birth. Either we grow up with some sort of ingrained ethics, or we don't. And if we do, that's what we're going to use in any situation, not something taught out of a book. Why waste time?

Response: Alright, we'll start there. Let's be clear on this. We're not trying to teach a code of ethics, rules to live by, or any of that. We are trying to get you to actually use what you probably already know. It's the process of ethical choice that concerns us here, not the underlying ethics of society or you as an individual. For one thing, these are much too broad to be covered here. For another, there *is* an ongoing debate in philosophical circles as to whether such things *can* be taught in any meaningful way.

The Skeptic: So what am I learning?

Response: Ethics provides tools for making so-called moral choices. By the way, we are not saying "good" or "right" choices, but choices based on moral criteria, whatever they may be in your case. Let's go into some background and come back to this.

The Skeptic: If we have to.

Response: In the Western philosophical tradition, "ethics" is a branch of study that is broken into three separate and distinct endeavors. We will not spend time on "metaethics"—the study of the nature of ethics, focusing on such concepts as the meaning of "right," "justice," "good," and so on. We will also not spend time on the second endeavor, "normative ethics," which focuses primarily on the development of general theories of moral behavior. These are well beyond our scope.

The Skeptic: You don't know how happy that makes me.

Response: I thought it might. What we *will* focus on briefly is the third branch of the study of ethics, so-called "applied ethics." Basically, this is the study of what happens when theoretical ethical studies meet real world situations. This is the branch of ethics that gives us problem-solving tools. This is where we live, literally. It is also where prescriptions such as professional codes of conduct are born.

The Skeptic: OK.

Response: But first, do you know where ethics as a serious topic of study originated in Western society?

The Skeptic: Ancient Greece, of course.

Response: Of course. Now by no means will we be talking exclusively about the Greeks, but it did all originate with them—hence the title of this section. The thumbnail sketch is that it essentially all began roughly 2500 years ago with Socrates (c. 470–399 B.C.). He believed that so-called "virtue" existed and that it could be discovered in one's self and practiced. Anyone, through careful thought, could figure out these rules, at least to some degree. This, of course, meant a great deal of sitting around, deep in thought.

> *In the end, the shows that work are the ones that are really smart.* Seinfeld, Frasier, ER—*the hits that last and that you can hang your hat on. These are what I hope the next generation will look to.*
>
> —*Bridget Potter*

The Skeptic: And who has time for that?

Response: Well, for Socrates, it also meant that he wandered around Athens annoying people with constant questioning, much as I'm doing here.

The Skeptic: Is *that* what you're doing?

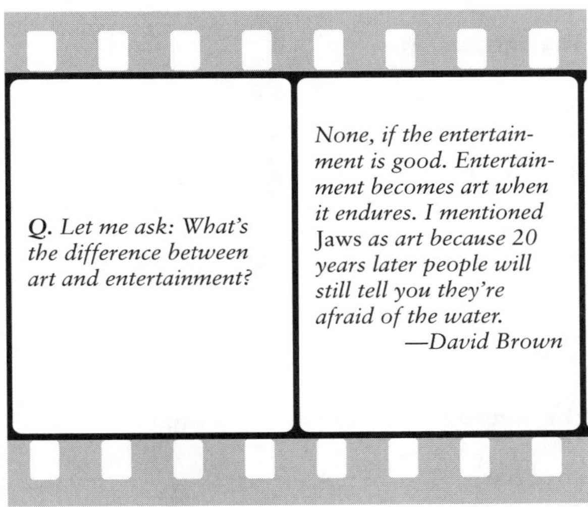

Response: The difference is, his questioning got him condemned to death by the Athenian authorities—no, don't even *think* about it—he asked too many radical questions of all the wrong people and made them *very* uncomfortable. He was nicknamed "The Gadfly" because he would attempt to "sting" people into thinking for themselves with his incessant questions. The other thing you should know is that he left no philosophical system of his own for others to follow, nor did he leave *any* writings.

The Skeptic: Considerate of him, but how do we know he even existed, much less know his nickname or that he annoyed people?

Response: From the accounts of his most famous student, and our next target, Plato (c. 428–348 B.C.). Socrates figured prominently in Plato's dialogues, the primary means by which Plato passed on his teachings. In fact, these dialogues were constructed according to what has come down to us as the "Socratic Method" in honor of you know who—questions and answers on a particular topic in an effort to reveal truth. In the most famous of these, *The Republic*,[1] covering most philosophical questions in existence then or now, Plato argued that moral conduct was to be based on three things: moderate behavior, knowledge of the world/experience, and courage to live up to one's decisions. These would provide the means of making good ethical choices and sticking to them. Plato believed that the "good" existed independent of a particular society or a particular time. If, in the name of the good, you chose to defy society or societal norms, you would most likely be justified in doing so, no matter what the consequences.

The Skeptic: Sounds pretty radical.

Response: It was. It represented another way of looking at ethics and morals that the authorities did not much like. As you know, Plato also had a famous student.

The Skeptic: Aristotle?

Response: Aristotle (384–322 B.C.). He was a student of Plato's for many years—and interestingly enough, the tutor of Alexander the Great—but had a much more pragmatic way of dealing with the world as he found it. His ethical and moral philosophy has been referred to as "virtue ethics." It is based on the "golden mean." For Aristotle, true virtue lay somewhere in between extremes. Between doing too much and doing too little. For example, pride was the mean between humility and vanity. And because virtue ethics is chiefly concerned with the means to an end, Aristotle believed that the ends do not necessarily always justify the means.

The Skeptic: There's that moderation idea again.

Response: You bet. That gets stronger, in fact, as time goes on. But first, more on Aristotle. He did state that not every ethical or moral problem could be decided according to the golden mean. Some actions were just simply wrong under all circumstances. Certain behaviors cannot be permitted in a society if that society is to survive. Aristotle said, in the Second Book of *The Nichomachean Ethics*,[2] one of his most important works, that the "very names of some things imply evil—for example, the emotions of spite, shamelessness, and envy and such actions as adultery, theft, and murder." So, some actions were always wrong.

About three or four years ago there was suddenly a lot of excitement because some previously underserved audiences had been discovered. That was what morphed into so-called gay and lesbian cinema. Really, it was about this idea that if you made a movie that dealt specifically with gay and lesbian concerns it could be marketed specifically to that audience and could actually make some money—there were enough people in that audience who would go and see a movie about themselves.

—Christine Vachon

The Skeptic: What if there were compelling reasons for those acts, or good provocation for those emotions?

Response: It does not seem to have mattered to Aristotle. Wrong was wrong. It is easier to build a stable society that way, rather than having foundations built on slippery slopes. The ancient Greeks were very concerned with citizenship and with man's place in the greater political society. Also, Aristotle's ethics focused on character. He believed that the development over time of the virtuous individual was the ultimate goal, not making the right moral decision in every situation. Aristotle was not as interested in philosophical abstractions as Plato and Socrates before him. He did not focus on concepts such as the true nature of "goodness itself." Rather, he was more concerned with the sort of ordinary, everyday goodness that he believed most people choose naturally most of the time, when left to their own devices.

The Skeptic: Sounds like he was ahead of his time.

Response: You have no idea. However, most germane to our discussions in this book, Aristotle, in his infinite wisdom, believed that virtue and ethical behavior could be achieved by good old-fashioned practice. His idea was that through repetitive ethical decisionmaking and moral behavior, the idea of the good could be inculcated into a person's value system.

The Skeptic: Is that like "act as if you have faith, and faith shall be given unto you?"

Response: Let's stay away from faith and other religious concepts. Again, that is *much* too big a topic to tackle in these pages. Let's oversimplify and say, rather, that "practice makes perfect." OK, now *this* is as close to religion as we will dare to venture. Later in history, we find Judeo-Christian ethics. There are still many Greek holdovers here. For example, perhaps the greatest medieval theologian, St. Thomas Aquinas (A.D. 1224–1274), assimilated Aristotle's idea of exercising personal virtues with moderation as the way to personal fulfillment. But things have definitely changed. The central concepts here translate very well to what we are suggesting you engage in as creators of

What's wrong with popcorn entertainment? In America, we don't have the luxury of … subsidies so we have commercial concerns, and they have to be reflected in the budgets of our movies.
—*Christine Vachon*

The market is there for something really original if you can find a way to crack through all the expectations about unusual subject matter.

As with Sling Blade*—Billy Bob Thornton's performance is so unusual that we were able to overcome all that and create a market.*
—*Mark Gill*

media. In Judeo-Christian ethics, a central concept is respect—respect for others, regardless of their status. Ethical decisions, according to this philosophy, should always be based on respect for the fundamental dignity of the individual as an end, rather than as a means. The goal of any decision must include the preservation of and respect for that fundamental dignity. Really, there is no better summary than "Do unto others as you would have them do unto you."[3]

The Skeptic: That says it, doesn't it?

Response: Pretty clearly. To paraphrase—in the creation and presentation of your work, respect your viewer the way you want to be respected by other creators.

The Skeptic: Anything else? My head hurts.

I would feel really bad about being involved in something that was exploitative and didn't have a driving intelligence behind it or wasn't about something that mattered. The things I've been involved with, at least in their intent, have been about things I thought were important.
—Bridget Potter

Response: Now, you are undoubtedly going to continue to throw the First Amendment up at me periodically (and have) to fend off what you see as interference with your ability to create freely.

The Skeptic: You bet! It is, after all, the foundation of my creative freedom.

Response: Right. Because First Amendment issues, by definition, involve government regulation of individual behavior, we should spend a few words on those philosophers for whom the relationship between private ethics and the state was of paramount concern.

Here, Niccolo Machiavelli (1469–1527), an Italian diplomat born in the City State of Florence, occupies perhaps the key position in relation to the entertainment industry. Interestingly enough, to be known as "Machiavellian" in Hollywood has evolved into a compliment for many. Rightly or wrongly, Machiavelli has come to be thought of as history's master manipulator—hence, to be referred to as Machiavellian in this industry one is perceived as having power as a result of one's ability to negotiate, manipulate, and "play" the system.

The Skeptic: I've certainly heard that term!

Response: It's actually a bit of a misnomer when applied to Machiavelli himself, and does not actually translate all that well into a compliment!

Now, it is true that in his most famous work, *The Prince*,[4] Machiavelli stated his belief that all good rulers (by which he seems to mean primarily successful rulers) need to possess *virtu*, defined as the qualities of courage, inner strength, and self-reliance, among others. In and of themselves, these would seem some decent qualities not only for a prince, but for everyone. It means that one would be strong and would treat individuals fairly, confident in one's own position. It is this confidence and inner strength that would allow one to succeed.

The Skeptic: Yes, but that's *not* Machiavelli's reputation.

Response: The kicker is that Machiavelli also believed that to be successful, the prince needed to be willing and able to engage in "necessary immorality." In other words, a prince must be willing to engage in all kinds of unethical behavior in order to govern the state successfully—lying, cheating, betraying friends, duping enemies, a whole host of unsavory activities. For him, there was a definite difference between public and private ethics and morals. For the good of the state, you understand. In fact, his example of a successful prince, to be admired and emulated, was Cesare Borgia.

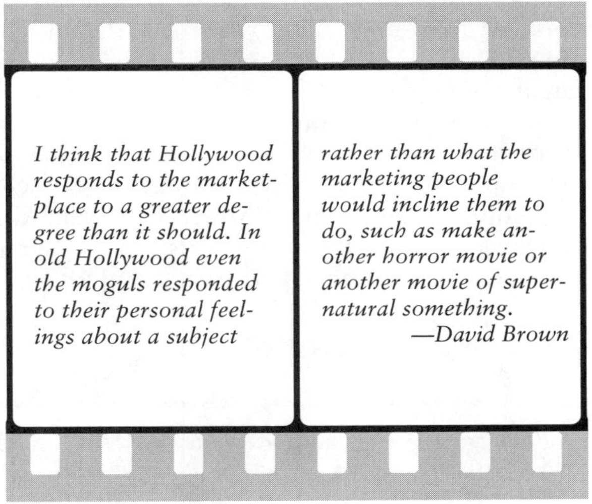
I think that Hollywood responds to the marketplace to a greater degree than it should. In old Hollywood even the moguls responded to their personal feelings about a subject rather than what the marketing people would incline them to do, such as make another horror movie or another movie of supernatural something.
—*David Brown*

Skeptic: Wasn't he a somewhat less than ethical fellow?

Response: You might say that! This guy is the quintessential example of the concept of situational ethics, in the worst sense of the term. He did whatever he needed to do at the time, regardless. He had a nasty habit of breaking agreements, inviting enemies to dinner and having them killed, and so on. This was the prince that Machiavelli most admired, at least if his words are to be taken literally.

Skeptic: What do you mean by that?

Response: Well, there is some controversy about *The Prince*. In fact, one line of argument suggests that the entire piece is a satire, not meant to be taken literally, and that this is why Borgia was chosen as the lofty example to be imitated. Another argument is that it is a technical manual, not to be analyzed for its philosophical content. We are not going to go any further with this discussion, however, and will simply stick with the most traditional interpretation—that the book is a philosophical tract and it is to be taken as representative of Machiavelli's beliefs.

Skeptic: OK.

Response: I'm going to veer *wildly* off the Western philosophical track here for a moment to illustrate a point about our industry. If many a Hollywood dealmaker has perused *The Prince*, the even more popular companion volume on the bookshelf would have to be Sun Tzu's *The Art Of War*.[5] In this work, written some 2,500 years ago, the ancient Chinese master strategist and philosopher laid out a model for successful prosecution of military campaigns. The broader philosophical implications, paralleling in some interesting ways those propounded by Machiavelli, have lifted this work from the realm of military strategy and made it de rigeur for politicians and businessmen, entertainment industry professionals included. Of course, the work was popularized in *Wall Street*,[6] wherein Charlie Sheen and Michael Douglas quoted various statements of its strategy, and increased the level of awareness of this work by leaps and bounds.

All you know is your own personal, your vestigial, your subliminal, your own psychic reaction to a subject. I believe they call them moving pictures—or they used to—because they're intended to move. Not in terms of film action, but in terms of the emotions. So when I tap a subject with Scott Rudin such as Angela's Ashes, *we're preparing it because the book moved us emotionally, not because we want to show a bleak Irish Catholic childhood to see what reaction we'll get to poverty and child abuse.*

—David Brown

You don't want to be connected to a film that is antieverything you believe in just because it's a product you're selling. Film is more than just a product.

—Stu Zakim

The Skeptic: This all brings to mind a broader question, though. Is it possible that creators are simply giving the public what they want, being pragmatic like our friend Machiavelli? Maybe what they want *is* negative. I mean, several important philosophers have believed that man and his desires were not all that lofty to begin with. Look at Hobbes.

Response: Nice segue. A bit obscure perhaps, but nice nonetheless. Thanks. First, this is a complicated argument that will be touched on elsewhere in this book. Second, let's discuss Hobbes for a bit.

The Skeptic: Hoisted on my own petard.

Response: Yup. OK. Thomas Hobbes (A.D. 1588–1679) was a royalist, philosopher, and author. He wrote a book called *Leviathan*[7] that presented a rather dreary philosophy based on the notion that human nature is basically pretty despicable. In what has become known as the doctrine of "psychological egoism," Hobbes says that without society to reign in baser instincts and avoid otherwise inevitable conflict, human beings exist in the "state of nature," where life is "solitary, poor, nasty, brutish, and short."[8]

The Skeptic: Pretty depressing stuff. But for Hobbes, "society" saves all, does it not?

Response: The vital thing was to get man to rise above this state of nature. Hobbes believed that, to rise above, individuals had to band together and become part of "The Social Contract," in which a reciprocal agreement exists to enforce a system of morals and ethics. A further "Governmental Contract" is then formed with a neutral third party, like the state, which is charged with enforcement of The Social Contract. This is how societies should and did begin for Hobbes.

The Skeptic: So, for Hobbes, ethics and morals are in fact a set of rules.

Response: You bet. They are a blueprint for preventing our true natures from allowing us to sink into the mire of perpetual conflict.

The Skeptic: So, what do we do with this guy on our little exploration? I think human nature, although obviously flawed, is basically pretty good. I was just playing devil's advocate with Hobbes.

Response: Good. The truth of the matter is that this whole theory has been pretty strongly discredited. For a bunch of horrible folks who can't be trusted—who will harm or kill each other without the constraint of The Social

Contract, history is replete with examples of selfless, admirable behavior. The whole idea that the state must force us to be good—and by extension, that the state should completely regulate the ethics of content, by the way, ignores the nobler parts of human nature. It ignores the fact that we, as a species, seem to be rather sociable by nature, and that for most of us at least, treating our fellow men as we would like to be treated comes fairly naturally.

I encounter two ethical situations. One has to do with the making of the film, and how composers will deal with the fact that they'll encounter people who are looking for the lowest common denominator. It will take their own determination because no one else will encourage it. It will be up to the composer as an individual to write the music he or she thinks is right, and they shouldn't be expecting a lot of support for it within this very conservative medium.

—*Carter Burwell*

The Skeptic: Right. Glad that's over.

Response: Now, to the opposite end of the spectrum. Jean-Jacques Rousseau (A.D. 1712–1778) stated in *Discourse on the Arts and Sciences*[9] and *Emile*,[10] arguably his greatest works, that he believed that men are born as moral beings with tremendous potential for goodness. Therefore, one of our greatest responsibilities is the education of our children.

The Skeptic: So, what's the problem there? That theory makes some sense, at least.

Response: Well, for Rousseau, the problem is the very civilization that Hobbes was depending upon to save us from ourselves. In this case, we are innately good, but civilization brings with it conflict. We became corrupted by the appetites that civilization engendered in us.

The Skeptic: So, for Hobbes, human beings are bad and society saves us, and for Rousseau, we are good but society corrupts us? I think Rousseau's version is a bit more encouraging, and, I think, realistic.

Response: Yes, except that what he is saying leads to another discredited concept, that of the "Noble Savage."[11] This was the belief that "primitive" people lived morally superior lives to those of contemporary civilized

> *If there's a problem with how to shoot something you think is better, but the director is of a different mind, you have to do what he wants. But you have to sell him on the other way as well, and then hope that in the screening room he'll see that this way is better and the other not so good. Generally speaking, less is better than more. It's all in how you do it. Same thing with violence. There's got to be a certain amount of style.*
>
> —Gordon Willis

man, primarily because they existed apart from the corrupting influence of society. In this case, government should not even exist, Rousseau advocated, except through the expression of "The General Will." Now, who figures out what this will is in any given situation, and who enforces it, pose rather insoluble questions. However, the point for us is that Rousseau would likely advocate that nothing regulate our creation, except the general will of the population—and here is the key—*when* that population is true to its basic, precivilized nature. Once we have civilization, it all becomes corrupted somehow, and we cannot then be trusted to adhere to the finer urgings of our natural selves.

The Skeptic: There's a mouthful. But because we cannot, at this point, separate ourselves from our society, this won't help us much on the idea of artistic freedom. OK. Any other theories to discuss?

Response: Just a few more, to round out the field. Greece is far behind us now. The modern era of ethics study was ushered in during the eighteenth century by a German named Immanuel Kant (A.D. 1724–1804). Not Kant, we hear you cry! He is one of the toughest philosophers, ancient or modern, to wade through. Kant was a deontologist.

The Skeptic: A *what*?

Response: A believer in duties. Higher duties are the basis for ethical decisions, not the consequences actions may bring. Deontological theories are in opposition to teleological theories, which say that correct ethical decisions are those that result in the best consequences. Virtue theories, epitomized by Aristotle's golden mean, form the third branch of ethical theories of moral reasoning.

The Skeptic: Headache's worse ...

Producers as a rule get no control other than what they exert on the set and what they exert in development of the project. I've ended up with films I've thought were compromised by groupthink. Marketing think. Research think. Research screening think. But who knows whether I was right or the groupthink people were right? We'll never know because my movie never came out.

Q: What could you do if you felt a movie was becoming a different beast from what you'd intended?

I wouldn't stay with it if that were the case.
—David Brown

Response: Alright. Back to Kant. His ethics are presented most forcefully in the *Foundations of the Metaphysics of Morals.*[12]

The Skeptic: Even the title is tough.

Response: Agreed. Now, his ethics are based entirely on a belief in duty and the "categorical imperative," as he termed it. A "categorical imperative" is, quite simply, a rule. An unshakable, unalterable rule, like "don't steal." He also believed that moral behavior was to be found in living up to certain codes of conduct, not because of the consequences, good or bad, but because these standards were good in and of themselves. He felt that individuals have a responsibility to live up to these good moral principles. Kant's duty-based ethics mean, for example, that you have an unwavering duty to tell the truth, even if doing so would bring harm to others.

The Skeptic: Sounds pretty harsh, and wouldn't stand up terribly well in the entertainment business.

Response: Thanks for the opening, but I wouldn't touch that with a barge pole! Let's move on. A few more Kant-isms: Hearkening to the Judeo-Christian ethics mentioned above, Kant believed that individuals should always be accorded the respect and dignity to which *all* individuals are always entitled. Individuals were never to be treated as means to your own ends. Now, whenever one acted, the intent was as important to Kant as the act. An individual must be motivated to act by an acceptance of the duty to act, not by a desire to perform the correct or popular act.

The Skeptic: All these rules sound fairly restrictive. It sounds like a recipe for a dreary life, at least from where I sit.

Response: Without question, Kant held a rigid, absolutist view of the ethical universe. This was not likely to be a guy who was fun at parties! In fact, he lived his entire life in one small place, and his habits were so regular, people could apparently set their watches by his routine.

The Skeptic: How could this philosophy still be important in the modern world? It doesn't seem possible for it to work.

Response: Careful, this is not an intellect to be easily dismissed as outmoded or obsolete. What has happened is that modern day deontological philosophers have softened things a bit. For example, they have come to accept that consequences of actions *are* important in ethical decision-making. They now simply maintain that the consequences should not be the *primary* cause of one's ethical behavior.

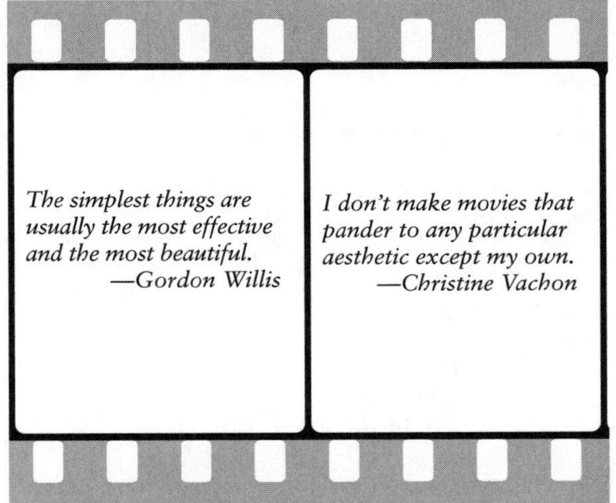

The Skeptic: This has gotten to be fun. As I remember, there are several important philosophers who thought all this was nonsense, right? I mean, those who would laugh at the concept that creativity needs to be hemmed in with any kind of ethical considerations whatsoever, or that grander ethical truths exist at all.

Response: Well, let's start with perhaps the best known of the skeptics, David Hume (A.D. 1711–1776). Hume posed the question of whether there could even be such a thing as certain moral "knowledge." In his book, *A Treatise of Human Nature*,[13] Hume points out that we cannot prove the truth of a moral statement. For him, a statement such as "murder is wrong" is merely an expression of opinion, incapable of empirical proof. It really means, "I disapprove of murder," and nothing more. All knowledge must come through the evidence of the five senses. Hume was a radical empiricist and a radical skeptic, who felt that those philosophers who believed moral truths could be discovered by reason, like Kant or Aristotle, were simply wrong. He further implied that there is really very little of what we call knowledge that we can ever know for sure. So, for our purposes, there are no moral truths, just expressions of opinion, none more right than the other.

The Skeptic: Now that's a philosophy I could get into.

Response: But even Hume acknowledged that this had to be softened a bit to reflect human beings living in a society. He admits that society, in order to function, can be organized to make as many people happy as we can, since human beings generally are "sympathetic" to each other, having similar feelings and

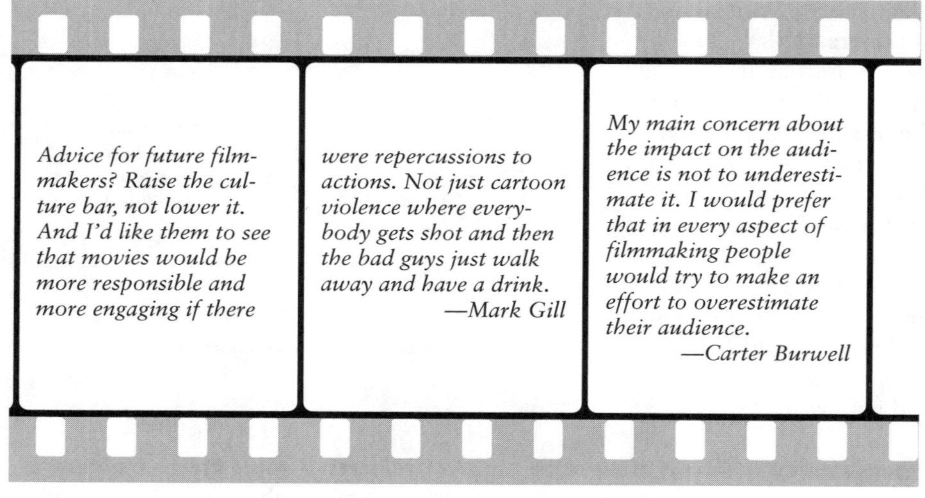

being able to identify with each other. So, the moral opinions of the majority of people could become the basis for that ongoing society.

The Skeptic: Sounds like a pragmatist to me.

Response: Right. Now, there's one last philosophical school I want to throw at you, then we're almost finished with the history lesson. This is utilitarianism, as represented by Jeremy Bentham (A.D. 1748–1832, *Introduction to the*

Principles of Morals and Legislation[14]), and John Stuart Mill (A.D. 1806–1873, *On Liberty*[15] and *Utilitarianism*).[16]

The Skeptic: Utilitarianism. That sounds practical too.

Response: Well, judge for yourself. First, both these men also believed knowledge had to come from use of the five senses, not just be discovered in or invented by the mind. They were radical empiricists as well, differing wildly, from say, Plato or Socrates. They believed that motives did not matter, only consequences. Bentham, a rather interesting character study in himself, tried to reduce moral reasoning to a scientific method, suggesting that for each decision, the decisionmaker should rate various effects of the decision and come up with a "happiness sum." Because human beings were said to be governed by two masters, pleasure and pain, the best decisions were those that produced the greatest happiness for the greatest number, to be determined by finding the highest happiness sum. This he defined as the greatest good.

The Skeptic: Sounds a little loopy. I mean, rating happiness mathematically?

Response: If it's any comfort, this is a man who believed that dead relatives should be stuffed and kept as ornaments in one's house, rather than being buried.

The Skeptic: Well, I suppose there are times …

Response: By his request, his own corpse was dissected in front of his friends and relatives. His straw-padded skeleton currently resides in a case at University College in London, complete with a wax head!

The Skeptic: As I said, loopy.

Response: Anyway, Mill also believed in creating the greatest happiness for the greatest number of people. Consequences to acts were everything. But, whereas Bentham had been primarily concerned with developing an ethical system for lawmakers, who would then govern according to the precepts of that system—a type of elitism, if you will—Mill believed the principles of utilitarianism could be made to serve as a system of ethical behavior for the ordinary citizen. He also thought utilitarianism should emphasize spiritual, cultural, and other intangible types of happiness over the simple physical pleasure Bentham advocated as happiness. So, again, if you follow Bentham, the lawmakers impose rules on your creativity. If you follow Mill, the cultural consensus will provide the precepts you must follow.

The Skeptic: Is that the last one?

Response: Sadly, yes. Twentieth century ethical thought is another vast topic that should and does support a number of books on its own. Unfortunately, unless you want to be reading for a year …

The Skeptic: Uhhh …

Response: We can't cover it here. Suffice it to say that World War II really threw contemporary ethics into a frenzy of confusion, contradiction, and extreme, often diametrically opposed viewpoints. Alternatively, for example, contemporary ethics has been defined as a confused mess, rudderless, business as usual, beholden to the marketplace, impossible to define, meaningless, or absurd in the extreme. Suggestions have ranged from redefining the nature of man in view of the cruelty and atrocities of the war, to going back to the precepts of Aristotle and the Greeks, to abandoning the entire enterprise as inherently worthless. Many of these ideas are both challenging and thought provoking. Some are just plain bizarre. We'll leave all of them to your own studies.

One thought for the twenty-first century—the Dalai Lama, Tenzin Gyatso, summarizes his beliefs for ethics in the future as follows: "The best way to ensure that when we approach death we do so without remorse is to ensure that in the present moment we conduct ourselves responsibly and with compassion for others."[17]

The Skeptic: He certainly seems to embody his own philosophy.

Response: True.

The Skeptic: Well, at least we've covered some basics of "classical" ethical thought.

Response: Basics is right. Remember that this is just the most basic, abbreviated introduction to the almost overwhelming body of Western philosophical thought and construct related to the concept of ethics of content. The reason this primer is relatively short and not mired in detail is precisely because it's intended to set the stage, not analyze how that stage was built. Numerous other texts devote themselves to that and handle it far better than can be managed here. Now, there are elements of each of these philosophies of ethics and ethical decisionmaking

> *More advice for future filmmakers? Try to swim through those choppy waters without being attacked by the sharks of marketing and star actors who don't agree with your vision—and still survive.*
>
> —*David Brown*

that you may find useful in considering the topics dealt with in this book. We seem to have arrived at a kind of situational ethics model in the entertainment business today. Many creators react situation by situation, using each new situation as the new moral context within which to make choices. For many, this creates an inconsistency or ambiguity that can show in their body of work. This is merely an observation, not a point of discussion, but it does raise a question. Are there elements presented in any or all of the philosophies summarized above that you might find useful in working out your own method of ethical decisionmaking?

The Skeptic: Examples?

Response: Do you believe that the consequences of actions are what are most important, as did Bentham and Mill? Do you believe that for you, moral behavior is found in arriving at the greatest good for the greatest number? Do you believe in stuffing your relatives and keeping them around the house? Or, are there certain unalterable truths that you want to abide by, whatever the changing realities around you might be? In this industry, things can change radically every day. The situations you face may be all over the map, sometimes even wildly contradictory. Can you stick to a set of firmly held beliefs? If you have such beliefs, do you believe that following them is a matter of duty, as did Kant? Do you believe you have discovered them within yourself, as Socrates or Plato might have advocated? Does the golden mean make sense? How about the Golden Rule?

The Skeptic: Is this a test? The short answer is that I think there are elements of almost all of these philosophies that make sense to me. I just have to figure out how to weave them into a coherent system that will work for me.

Response: A very worthwhile goal. Now, remember that what we are trying to get you to do in this book is not to decide your life's philosophy, then head happily off into the sunset. All we want to inflict on you is the process of ethical reasoning. Virtually everything you do artistically involves at least some ethical choice. Chances are you, like most creators, do not always recognize such a choice when you see one. But by seeing these ethical choices for what they are and making them based on research or facts wherever possible, the quality of your work might improve, and your sensitivity to the effect your work is having on society will certainly increase.

The Skeptic: So, you're not trying to feed me what you think is moral or ethical, but you're trying to get me to learn and use the power of choice responsibly?

Response: There may be a *little* feeding, as I am only human, but it's the process of choice I am focused on here. Only you can decide what you believe in or think is moral and ethical. Hopefully this book will prompt you to think about that as well. Now, as to the decisionmaking process. First, you must realize that all real-world ethical decisions are made within the context of a given situation. Now, context does not and should not always determine the decision, but it does exert a profound influence. In fact, contextual factors can create real conflict between what we know we ought to do, and what seems to be the more popular or efficacious choice at the time.

The Skeptic: Yes, but what can you do about that conflict?

Response: You should try to filter out the factors that are contextual and separate them from your moral beliefs. For example, someone will buy your screenplay if you change a central element in a way you know will ruin the story. The decision to do this might feel right today because the rent is due, but that does not mean it will sit well with your beliefs. You must realize that the excitement of the offer, coupled with the very real need to pay the rent and your desire to promote your career, are providing powerful contextual factors that may or may not over-balance your beliefs. If they do, fine, but be sure to weigh the situation carefully, recognizing the contextual factors for what they are, lest you not be able to sleep at night afterwards.

The Skeptic: I can see where that might be a problem, especially if the story is important to you, but I'd sure like to be in the position to answer that question for myself.

Response: Me too. Also, once you make an ethical choice, presumably you will act on that choice. When you act, you have a duty to consider the effect that your actions might have on others. A good example of this is the recent adoption of the television ratings system. True, there was a great deal of controversy and political wrangling surrounding the process, but the bottom line for our purposes is that the industry decided it had a duty to warn parents of potentially offensive material it was sending into their homes. "Do unto others ..."

The Skeptic: So everything's an ethical choice?

Response: You bet! From the story you choose to tell to the way in which you tell it, from the casting choices you make to the music you choose, from the props and costumes you want to the way you market the film, everything is a choice. Are you using gratuitous or responsible violence? Are you glamorizing substance abuse? Are you reinforcing stereotypes? Are you inadvertently sending out messages to children or teenagers that you do not ethically choose to send? A great many of these elements rise to the level of ethical choices. Have a look at the "One Person's Method" section, then apply it to the hypotheticals and ethical gymnastics and learn how to apply the method to help you answer these questions. It sounds like a lot of extra work, but as Aristotle implied, "practice makes perfect." If practiced, recognizing an ethical choice when confronted by one, and making that ethical choice according to your own beliefs, will hopefully become second nature. At this point, everyone benefits.

The Skeptic: I feel like I've just been through Philosophy 101, but I'm ready to see what else you have to say.

Response: I'm pleased. Got any aspirin?

Notes

1 Rice, Daryl H. *A Guide to Plato's Republic* (New York: Oxford University Press, 1998).

2 Welldon, J.E.C., Trans., *The Nicomachean Ethics by Aristotle* (Buffalo: Prometheus Books, 1987).

3 Matthew 7:12, "In everything, do to others what you would have them do to you..." Also known as The Golden Rule. The negative form can be found in the second century documents *Didache* and *The Apology Of Aristides*. Also found in Tob. 4:15, the writings of Hillel (first century B.C.), and of Philo of Alexandria (first century B.C. and A.D.) It appears in one form or another in Plato, Aristotle, Socrates, and Seneca. Source: *Encyclopedia Britannica Online*: www.eb.com.

4 Machiavelli, Niccolo. *Il Principe (The Prince)*, 1513. *The Prince* enjoys the distinction of being one of the first books ever to be chosen by the Catholic Church for its inclusion on the *Index of Forbidden Books*.

5 Tzu, Sun. *Ping-Fa* (*The Art of War*), written/compiled sometime between 770–476 B.C.

6 1987 D: Oliver Stone, 20th Century Fox.

7 Flatman, Richard E. and Johnson, David, Eds. *Leviathan: Authoritative Text, Background, Interpreted* (New York: W.W. Norton & Company, 1997).

8 Flatman and Johnson, *Leviathan*.

9 Masters, Roger D. and Kelly, Christopher, Eds. *Discourse on the Arts and Sciences* (Hanover: University Press of New England for Dartmouth College, 1992).

10 Patterson, Sylvia W. *Rousseau's Emile and Early Children's Literature* (Metuchen, N.J.: Scarecrow Press, 1971).

11 Patterson, *Rousseau's Emile*.

12 Kant, Immanuel. *Foundations of the Metaphysics of Morals.* Trans. Beck, Lewis White, (Indianapolis: Bobbs-Merrill, 1969).

13 Hume, David. *A Treatise of Human Nature* (Buffalo: Prometheus Books, 1992).

14 Bentham, Jeremy. *An Introduction to the Principles of Morals and Legislation: An Authoritative Edition.* Burns, J.H. and Hart, H., Eds. (New York: Oxford University Press, 1996).

15 Mill, John Stuart. *Mill On Liberty: Critical Essay.* Dworkin, Gerald, Ed. (Lanham, Md.: Rowman & Littlefield Publishers, 1997).

16 Mill, John Stuart. *Utilitarianism* (Oxford, N.Y.: Oxford University Press, 1998).

17 His Holiness the Dalai Lama. *Ethics for the New Millennium* (New York: Riverhead Books, 1999), p. 233.

Mnemonics for Everybody: "One Person's Method"

Although the purpose of this book is most decidedly NOT to teach the reader how to think, I do want to provide a tool that might come in handy in analyzing the ethical decisionmaking we will discuss.

The following is a mnemonic device representing a formula that the general reader can use as a consumer to confront applied ethics in the entertainment industry. Each film or television program viewed, each video/computer game, each song, or almost any other popular media entertainment can be analyzed with this method. If you're concerned with the issues covered in this book, the "READR" device is a quick way to examine the underpinnings of the entertainment you consume.

Students of film and television can use this device to confront the ethical decisionmaking they will encounter, and in fact should seek out, in order to become better, wiser, and more responsible creators. It represents a way to make an efficient analysis of any project in order to determine and analyze potential ethical issues.

The acronym should be easy enough to remember—"READR." Now, it's true that I skipped a letter there, but a mnemonic device doesn't have to be perfect! It just has to stick in your memory. Like glue. In this case, "READR" stands for: Review; Enumerate; Analyze; Determine; and Reintegrate.

As with many of these devices, it is merely a codification of common sense, but nevertheless, this formula is one way to approach this vast arena.

Now for the explanation. I'll draw illustrations from a film project I helped to develop for ease of discussion, but the method can easily be extrapolated to suit any project.

Step 1: REVIEW the project for general ethical concerns and questions, and to determine the overall context in which your search for ethical issues will be held.

Though we are scarcely aware of it, we confront ethical dilemmas many times each day in mundane ways, starting perhaps with having to decide whether to tell a small fib about why we were late for work. But most often, our ethical principles meet their most severe test when money is involved. And money is not only very much involved in every aspect of moviemaking but is, as we know, the ultimate prize in Hollywood today.
—Les Brown

Illustration: Let us say that you have a screenplay based on the following: A male and a female police officer are charged with bringing down a street gang in an ethnic neighborhood, and they fall in love.

[As an aside, you will notice that we use police stories in several places. These plot lines and characters allow you to infer a vast amount of detailed information about the story, characters, the milieu, and so on, without us having to spend pages painting the entire tapestry. The point here is to make clear a mnemonic device, not to write a screenplay. This is discussed in more depth in the section entitled "Portrayals of Stereotypes."]

In the stated description—(by the way, for those readers who may not be aware, a feature film is most always "pitched" to potential buyers with a one-sentence description called a "log line")—we have all the material we need for the first phase of the READR formula.

In our "Review," we can see, for example, what the broadest ethical concerns and issues involved in the project are: (a) This is ostensibly a story about police versus gang; (b) The gang is probably engaging in some kind of illegal, dangerous or antisocial behavior, or else the police would not be trying to bring them down; (c) There will clearly be some ethnicity issues involved, as the log line tells us this; and, (d) Two people fall in love in the midst of this conflict. So, we have, at the broadest level, good versus evil, illegal conduct that the police are trying to stop, probable violence (which we know to expect from long experience with this American movie genre), ethnic conflict, romance, and possibly, sex (again, a conclusion drawn from experience).

Already, this review tells you that this project will have some hard edges. It will likely not be suitable for family entertainment and you will probably have to struggle with some difficult ethical issues. This is all that needs to be gleaned from this first level of Review under our formula. Now we move on to Step 2.

Step 2: ENUMERATE the component parts of the project, including storyline, subplots, characters, themes, motifs, and milieu.

Illustration: Now, it's time to begin looking beyond the overall ethical issues of the project on its face. Here, we break the project into its component parts by carefully reading the screenplay or the treatment. As a note, it is preferable to list the components on paper, as there may be more of them than you think and it is important to visit them all.

In the case of our hypothetical project, some of the elements we discover include: (a) It's an urban story; (b) It's about the police—that implies other components such as the code by which they do their jobs, their position in society, their being outmanned and outgunned by criminals, and so on; (c) the gang and our two police officers are of different ethnic and social backgrounds—all the gang members are Chinese Americans; (d) The gang's means of income is illegal narcotics sales; (e) The gang commits violent acts routinely and terrorizes its own neighborhood; (f) The gang is heavily financed by Chinese Tongs; (g) The gang is involved in turf wars in its own territory; (h) Our two cops fall in love in the midst of a crises situation; (i) The cops discover that members of their own department are "on the take" from the gang and will attempt to undermine their investigation; (j) The District Attorney is pushing the case for political reasons; (k) The cops attempt to bring the gang down by forcing gang brother to betray gang brother; (l) The cops are forced to kill several gang members; and, (m) The gang leaders go to jail in the end and the Tong connection is exposed.

There's nothing more important in your arsenal than your credibility. Once you lose it you can never get it back. It's a very hard line to walk. Your client wants something from you—meaning, from the studio perspective, the movie—as do the celebrities, as do the media. Successful publicists find some way to make this marriage work. If you blow it you're history. If you're trying to convince somebody that the movie you're working on is the best thing since sliced bread, and they go in and it's not, they won't take your call the next time.

—Stu Zakim

In essence, ethics has to do with respect for fellow man. This underlies the ethical codes of such professions as medicine, law, and journalism, in all of which the potential exists to do unintended harm. But at the very heart of each of these codes is respect for the profession itself and the need to preserve trust in the institution. For if public trust is lost because of rampant ethical breaches, the entire profession suffers, as does society, which is why ethical codes are such a vital part of the curricula for students planning to enter the professions.

—Les Brown

As you can see, there are many elements in a given story—and there are at least as many we did not enumerate for this project. That's why it's useful to list them.

Step 3: ANALYZE each of these components to ascertain ethical issues and to determine where ethical choices should be made. Always try to find at least one possible decision implicit in each component of the project. Evaluate each potential ethical decision in light of what you'll read in this book—which means you'll need to keep coming back to this formula, which is precisely the point, of course.

Illustration: Here we will only indicate the analyses of a few of our components, in the interest of brevity and clarity. Following the above enumeration:

The technology is clearly there to take anybody's life out of context and add your own actors. You can do it with a great degree of fidelity, and people would believe it is the real guy. Too many clues tell you it's probably not correct—and yet it has altered your opinion of him.
—Rob Legato

Every normal person has a conscience. We want to encourage aspiring filmmakers to take a personal pledge not to be freeloaders on the First Amendment, taking its generosity without giving something in return—and that need only be giving thought all along the way to the possible consequences of what they're sending out on the screen.
—Les Brown

(c) "The gang and our two police are of different ethnic and social backgrounds—all the gang members are Chinese Americans"—This point leads immediately to the question of negative stereotyping. You have a situation wherein the cops will inevitably be viewed as the "good" ethnic group and the Chinese Americans will be viewed as the "bad" ethnic group, simply because we know that the cops are the heroes of the story. If you combine the fact that the gang represents the "bad" guys with the facts stated in (d) "narcotics," and (e) "violence," you're going to be forced into making some pretty negative statements about these Chinese Americans unless you are careful.

(d) "The gang's means of income is illegal narcotics sales"—This means that if the picture is to work as a realistic drama that the audience will find believable based on its previous experience with (a) "urban" stories about (b) "police," you'll have to show some of the narcotics trade from the gang's (or the positive) point of view. Will you be glorifying selling and using illegal drugs by showing them in this context?

(e) "The gang commits violent acts routinely and terrorizes its own neighborhood"—Same argument. You'll have to show acts of violence, including those perpetrated on innocent bystanders in the neighborhood as well as those committed on other gang members in the g) "turf wars." Will you be glorifying violence, or can you find a way to present it that will make it appear undesirable.

It's a decision everyone has to make. What's offensive to one person isn't offensive to another. It's what makes this country what it is. We use film because of the power of the medium to promote causes or beliefs that may not be in synch with everyone. It's my choice to say I can't work on that picture, and if it costs me my job, it costs me my job. We can't just follow orders. Advocating a film that might incite a riot or anti-Semitism or intolerance is not a socially responsible thing to do. You have to take film's power to influence pop culture seriously.

—Stu Zakim

(i) "The cops discover that members of their own department are "on the take" from the gang and will attempt to undermine their investigation"—The ethical choice to be made here, of course, is that in order to meet audience expectations, because again they've seen this sort of story before, you'll have to realistically portray cops making unethical and illegal choices. How hard you want to slam those who serve society in this way will be one of your many ethical struggles.

Every now and then there's something about a movie we feel is antithetical to society's best interest. Here's an example: Gummo. *No way. A kid who tortures cats—it just seemed much too sadistic and nihilistic. He's free to make it somewhere else. He did. Good for him. But we weren't interested in promoting that message.*

—Mark Gill

Step 4: DETERMINE whether, in light of your analysis, you are comfortable with the ethical implications of each of your components.

Illustration: Now that you have factored down all the elements of your project, listed the components, and determined what the ethical issues and choices are to be made, you must decide whether you are comfortable with the message(s) each component implies. If you're uncomfortable with specific components, you can always look for ways to change them. Can you change the ethnic mix to alleviate the most negative aspects of racial stereotyping without damaging the story? Can you build in negative consequences for both

Q: Have you ever been associated with a marketing campaign or a visual that you had qualms about?

From time to time I look at something and say, "That seems quite a ways away from the central theme of the movie." Take the example of Dead Poets Society: *if you saw the TV commercials or the trailers, you would never have guessed it was a drama. (I, by the way, didn't work on that movie.) You would never have guessed there was a teen suicide, you would never have guessed a whole lot of things about the movie.*

—Mark Gill

Q: Did the tactic sell?

It worked very well. But there's two parts to that. The other part was to have a window opened up on a culture that, let's face it, most Americans were ignoring at that point.

—Mark Gill

The basic morality of a producer is his or her integrity with respect to the projects that he or she wishes to undertake. By undertake it means to persevere. But a producer must have conviction. There is always that four o'clock in the morning apprehension, often justified, that you are on the wrong track. But you have to have a certain naiveté that underscores your conviction. And that is the morality.

—David Brown

the illegal drug use and the violence, perhaps by showing them in a context that minimizes glorification? Can you make the characters more three-dimensional? The list goes on. Now, for the final step.

Step 5: REINTEGRATE the component parts back into the totality of the project, and review all the ethical implications that have come to light through your detailed factoring and analysis.

Illustration: It's always a good idea, as a final step, to put the whole project back together again and examine it in its totality. Now that you've broken it down into individual components and analyzed each component, it's time to see if the whole is greater than or less than the sum of its parts. In our hypothetical project, you may now feel that overall, it's a study of human conflict that seems quite different from a simple cops versus gangs with a love story.

You may well find that a project reads quite differently to you after engaging in this process. In any case, you now have the context and the detail with which to make overall judgments about the ethical issues the project embodies, as well as about how those decisions should be handled.

That is the "READR" formula. Now, this is not etched in stone from the wisdom of the ancients, nor spawned by a preponderance of great philosophical theory. Clearly, there are many ways in which these problems can be approached. The key, of course, is to begin approaching them! However, that said, habitual use of READR should stand you in good stead until your "ethical choice reflex" is developed to the point where awareness of ethical issues becomes automatic.

All You Need to Make a Movie Is a Girl and a Gun ...*

* Quote by Jean Luc Goddard

The Gun: Portrayals of Violence

Do Unto Others Before They Can Do Unto You

We've all cheered the hero onscreen as he delivers his own brand of "street justice" to the evil villain (who deserves whatever he gets anyway). Beating up the "bad guy" has been a cherished symbol of our cinema history. It's the American way.

No one is going to tell us we can't use violence in our stories, because we all know that—aside from being a ridiculously unrealistic concept—there's something downright satisfying for audiences in seeing the hero beat the bad guy senseless (whether with fists, gun, bazooka, or F-15).

And yet, there is a truly global concern about the issue of violence and how the American film and television industry, a.k.a. "Hollywood," uses, abuses, and drowns audiences with torrents of violence in its entertainment product. Where is the line drawn between the creation of good old American entertainment and the glorification of violence? This section will explore these issues, summarize some of the relevant research findings on the ways in which violence affects viewers, and discuss the ethical issues implicit in violence as entertainment. We will also suggest some ways in which violent content can be used responsibly.

Violence is a pervasive factor in contemporary America. Our world feels increasingly dangerous, and many of us believe we cannot go about our daily lives without keeping at least a metaphorical eye over our shoulder.

The strange thing about this perception is that the reality is somewhat different. Are these violent times? Certainly. No one would deny that fact. However, according to the Federal Bureau of Investigation and police reports across the nation, the number of violent crimes is actually decreasing steadily and has been since the beginning of the 1990s.[1]

So why this discrepancy between perception and reality? As a much deeper question, why *is* our society so violent?

Brooklyn South premiered on CBS and the press was all up in arms about how this was the most violent police drama that had ever been on TV, and that the first seven minutes of the first episode were more violent than anything that had ever been on. I watched and found it to be very inoffensive and very well done. I thought, "What are they talking about?" Turn over to HBO or Showtime or any movie channel and see what's going on there. The things that are made for television are much less provocative and violent than those that are made for theatrical movies.

—Bridget Potter

A *partial* answer to both questions is thought by some to be the rapid rise in film and television violence roughly throughout the last three decades, following the dismantling of the Hays Production Code.[2]

In an earlier era of Hollywood filmmaking, the hero often resorted to violence only when he had been driven to the breaking point or in self-defense. Violence was not completely avoided, per se, it just wasn't the driving essence of the entertainment.

Not so today. Now, a violent response is quite often the *first* solution attempted. It has become relatively rare to see negotiation, compromise, or even simple discussion used to solve problems.

Violence has become very nearly a character in its own right, an end rather than a means to the drama of the piece. What this has created is the *expectation* of violence in response to most any conflict.

At the same time, the realism of the violence has intensified. In a bygone era of Hollywood movies and television, violence stopped short of being gory, obvious, or intense, with few exceptions. Even cowboy, detective, or crime stories of that era used violence that appeared staged or happened offscreen.[3] People died almost magically. That is to say, there was very little realism. When viewed today, many scenes of fistfights, shootings, stabbings, and so on from that period look almost naively comical. The gunshot that sounds like a cap gun, the bullet that strikes leaving no visible damage (save for a tiny hole in a worsted suit), the stab wound with no blood, and the noble, quiet death of the victim—these are all familiar elements to students of movies from the so-called "Golden Age."

Even the legendary "shower scene" from *Psycho*,[4] albeit extremely intense, was so stylized (as a result of being composed of multiple shots),[5] that the audience was manipulated into feeling the terror of the moment without ever seeing the knife enter Janet Leigh's body.

Several years after *Psycho*, films such as *Bonnie & Clyde*[6] and *The Godfather*,[7] although considered tame by today's standards, established a whole new level of violence in film and displayed in strikingly glamorous terms the image of the rebellious antihero. Critic Charles Champlin, writing about *The Godfather* in the *Los Angeles Times*, characterized the film as "incessantly and explicitly violent.... The violence, I had better repeat, is violent and graphic, and it is part of the movie's considered and considerable lure."[8] Many viewers would now consider the mob brutality of the Corleones mild, at least by comparison with the maulings and butcherings that were to come in films such as *GoodFellas* or *The Fight Club*.[9]

In the twenty-first century, filmmakers are in an entirely new ball game, one in which subtlety plays little or no part. Our younger celebrity directors—Quentin Tarantino and John Woo to name two—are noted for "pushing the envelope" in the way they depict violence. Their work is praised as "cutting edge," prompting up-and-comers to pump up the violence in emulation.

Several times on The Godfather, *Francis (Ford Coppola) came up with ideas that were rejected because they were just too dangerous. At one point we were going to do a stunt where someone was going to pull into a gas station, pump gas into the front seat, and throw in a match. You don't want to do things like this on the screen. If you're assuming that people are only looking and saying, "Well, it's only a movie" (laughter). There's a lack of education at a basic level of society today to which you can't show those things. Brutality without style and logic isn't a good thing to do.*

—*Gordon Willis*

One of the inspirations for this book was Woo's statement that he saw himself as a painter and blood red was the most beautiful color he had.[10] Now, aesthetically, no one could argue that red is a very nice color. However, the statement itself gives no indication of concern for its possible underlying meaning or consequences.

Violent acts are direct and graphic in the extreme. If a victim is stabbed or shot, the audience will see, often in slow motion for added emphasis, the weapon or projectile penetrate the victim, blood spurting everywhere.

Further, violence now is often *the point* of contemporary entertainment product, even when it is not necessary to the story being told. As a mental exercise, imagine what a film such as *Casablanca*[11] would look like if made today. What would be the body count? How would this affect the story?

What's more, special effects technology has developed to the point where ultrarealism is a relatively simple and inexpensive matter. Not surprisingly, an often-unrealized competition has developed to "top" the last violent spectacle seen in a film. We seem to be constantly searching for new and ever more hair-raising ways to portray violence. We have, to some degree, become mired in the love of violence for violence's sake. More realism. More gore. More impact.

The Role of Music

We should never underestimate the tremendously potent tools of music and scoring in manipulating the audience. The right music can elicit virtually any desired emotion, often even more viscerally than the images on the screen. Remember *Jaws?* Daaa Dum ... Daaa Dum.... As David Brown, one of the producers of *Jaws,*[12] suggests, "twenty years later people will still tell you they're afraid of the water."[13] Yes, and an important piece of the credit for this goes to the simple yet brilliant base-of-the-spine-rumbling score.

Music can also compensate for weakness in storytelling, as it can guide the audience from scene to scene, emotion to emotion, in ways that the underlying film may not be strong enough to accomplish.

To test this, simply watch an action sequence in a film or television program with the sound off. Try to choose a film that you don't know well, as your mind will fill in the missing music otherwise. Now, it is true that this also means watching without benefit of dialogue and vital sound effects, but this is not meant to be an exacting scientific experiment. It's merely a crude but effective approximation. Now, try watching the same sequence with the music. See how your emotions are peaked, pulled, and prodded to maximize the excitement of the scene—if, of course, the film is well scored.

Carter Burwell, composer for such films as *Fargo*[14] and *The General's Daughter*,[15] describes the powerful role of the score in manipulating audience emotion:

> It plays a subliminal role, but a very powerful emotional one.... The subjective experience of the audience is that they are not often aware of the music or where it is coming from, because human eyes are more powerful sensory organs than ears; sound is more emotionally moving than vision. But I think that's why most people go to the moves—for an emotional experience.[16]

In the specific case of scoring scenes of violence, composers can use their art to heighten the impact of the images. Whether it's pounding, paralyzingly heroic crescendos during violent action scenes or tension-building strains under violent dramatic scenes, music can peak the viewer's emotional state; it can enhance his or her empathy for the victim *or* the perpetrator; it can cause the viewer to fear violence or feel the heady flush of vigilantism. And each effect deepens the influence of the violence.

What the Research Says About Violence in the Media

Does all of this violent imagery have an effect on the viewer? This is one of the most hotly debated questions of our time. For decades, researchers have studied the effects of violence on viewers, especially children. Most social scientists today believe that exposure to media violence is affecting us as a society. Although certainly not the only, or even the most important factor, media violence is contributing to an overall culture of violence in America.

One school of thought historically maintained that violent images, in and of themselves, do not cause violence. This theory held that violence in the media acts as a catharsis[17] for the viewer, draining his or her anger by channeling it vicariously into the situations of the characters engaged in violence onscreen—a harmless venting of emotion, like cheering for a favorite team or band at a concert.

Today, most researchers agree that although violent images do not directly cause violence in most people, viewing these images does have a cumulative negative effect. Hundreds of studies have been conducted on television programming, including made-for-TV movies and theatrical films that air on broadcast or cable outlets, supporting these conclusions. It appears likely that the conclusions would be amplified with regard to theatrical films shown in theaters, where violence is almost entirely unrestrained and filmmakers are free to use the vast arsenal of special effects technology to its fullest gory potential.

The general consensus among scientists and public health researchers is that repeated viewing of violent images has three distinct negative effects on the viewer.[18]

First, viewing violence over time contributes to what media researcher George Gerbner has dubbed the "Mean World Syndrome," which refers to the feelings instilled in viewers that they live in a dangerous environment, a "mean" world. People who are constantly bombarded with images of murder and mayhem can come to believe that the violence they see onscreen is a reflection of society as it actually exists outside their front door. Their distrust is communicated via subtle behavioral cues to those with whom they come into contact. These people, in turn, begin to "strengthen their defenses," both physically (by purchasing guns, pepper spray, dogs, or security systems) and psychologically (by becoming generally mistrustful and misreading situations in the expectation of violence) and so on down the line. In this way, a general sense of fear spreads through society.

This fear of violence, paradoxically, creates a world in which violence, because expected, is more likely to occur. The concept of the self-fulfilling prophecy comes into play. If you believe you will be victimized, you may very well BE victimized, as your fear will be communicated to potential perpetrators. Like bees, they are drawn to fear.

Second, by encountering so much violence onscreen, viewers may simply become desensitized to real-world violence. For example, it has been estimated that the average child in the United States witnesses some 200,000 separate acts of violence, including approximately 16,000 murders on television alone, by his or her eighteenth birthday![19] This averages out to a numbing 2.4 onscreen murders *every day* of their lives. Think about how this numbing process works. By analogy, the first time you watch a movie can be exciting, because everything is new. You don't know what will happen next (at least with a *good* movie). The second time can also be very enjoyable, because there are usually things you missed the first time that keep the movie fresh. After several more viewings, however, most people find themselves snack-trolling even during key scenes. Why? They know that nothing will change and they know what will happen next.

> *The violence in my scripts is not done for the sake of having a big explosion, a car crash, or a mountain of dead bodies. In my picture* VIG *there were only two scenes where people were killed. And that constituted about three minutes of screen time. Yet some people said it was a violent film. And I agree. Why? Because the violence was real and it had consequences.*
>
> —*Paul Hapenny*

It can be argued that viewing violent images is much the same. Essentially, violence takes on a pattern that becomes all too familiar. After a steady diet of violent images, it all becomes "old hat" and is therefore dismissed. There is no revulsion, fear, nor moral outrage, as violence is expected and, in fact, routine. Routine! Should violence *ever* be allowed to become commonplace? The routinization of reprehensible behavior is what has clearly exemplified the bloodiest, most tragic periods of human history.

Third, violent images are believed to be, in effect, a school for violent behavior and aggressive acts. Many people's first exposure to aiming and firing a gun, for example, comes via television or film.[20] The viewer learns that aggression is an appropriate response to many situations. In addition, much as many critics see prisons as places where criminals learn to be better criminals, violence onscreen can inspire and teach specific techniques of real-world violence in the minds of would-be perpetrators. This does not mean that most people will leave their living rooms and amble out to shoot someone after watching *Aliens*,[21] for example. It does mean, however, that among those people who are disenfranchised and isolated and who already exhibit aggressive tendencies, onscreen violence can incite aggression, especially over time.

It should be noted that not all the effects of viewing violent images are negative. If presented responsibly and made to appear wrong, painful, or distasteful, researchers believe that onscreen violence can actually act as a deterrent to real-world violence.

Hot Buttons: How Filmmakers Manipulate Audiences

In 1995, researchers conducting the *National Television Violence Study* isolated nine creative elements that filmmakers use to manipulate viewers' reactions to onscreen violence.[22] The techniques are: choice of perpetrator, choice of victim, presence of consequences, rewards and punishments, the reason for the violence, the presence of weapons, realism, the use of humor, and prolonged exposure. A description of each of these techniques follows.

Choice of Perpetrator

We have all, at one time, consciously or unconsciously, tried to emulate the behavior of characters we like and admire.[23] What young boy, for example, has not tried to act, if only for an instant, like James Bond, one of the innumerable Schwarzenegger characterizations,[24] Will Smith in *Men in Black*,[25] or a Ninja Turtle?[26] What young girl has not copied something from Julia Roberts, Madonna, Jennifer Aniston (remember that dreary haircut *everywhere*?), or *Buffy, the Vampire Slayer*?[27] Whether we like to admit it or not, most of us engage in this sort of emulation at one time or another. Even U.S. presidents have parroted lines and attitudes from contemporary film and television, as when Ronald Reagan dared Libya to attack U.S. interests by quoting Clint Eastwood's classic rejoinder "Make my day."

The perpetrator is of particular importance to young viewers. Many children are not yet capable of analyzing the actual act of violence, thus their feelings about the perpetrator are of primary importance. If the perpetrator is someone they like, they may assume that his course of action is correct without further analysis. They are also much more likely than adults to imitate behaviors they have observed. The result is clear. If children watch a favorite character engage in violent behavior, they are more likely to imitate that behavior.

Therefore, creators must recognize our inherent dilemma. We want heroes to be admirable and likable. It makes good story sense, in that most stories need heroes, or at least sympathetic protagonists. It also makes good business sense, as good heroes sell tickets and promote collateral buying of advertised products. However, we must be aware that if we succeed, this inadvertently carries with it a responsibility, especially where children are concerned. If our hero is popular enough, or the viewer identifies with him closely enough, and the hero engages in violent acts, he *may* be promoting aggressive behavior in the viewer. Does the result—more tickets and products sold—justify the cost in societal terms? Therein lies the ethical dilemma.

In general, villains and disreputable characters do not foster the same emulation as do heroes, and if a villain is violent, it may even *discourage* violence in the viewer. (Although there's always the allure of the antihero.)

This is an extremely potent tool to have been placed at the creator's disposal.

In prior generations, people's heroes were often politicians, especially swashbuckling figures like FDR or JFK (around whom we went so far as to weave the entire Camelot mythology), or those that simply made the country feel confident about its future. Of course, heroes have also always been drawn from the world of sports, and this is still true today (witness Michael Jordan fever during the 1998 NBA Playoffs or the hysteria surrounding Mark McGwire's record-breaking home run(s)). However, it seems that we no longer have enough collective respect for Washington and its denizens to draw other than an occasional hero from the sea of politics. In fact, we seem to believe that our politicians are either "all the same" types of crooks or empty suits, for the most part. A program such as ABC's *Spin City*[28] uses a lovably dimwitted politician as the quiet center around which revolve a more cynical Deputy Mayor and the group that actually governs. Not the stuff political heroes are made from. Adam Sorkin's show for NBC, *West Wing*,[29] goes some small distance in reversing this, as President Bartlett (Martin Sheen) is portrayed as an admirable man with a "good heart" with whom those around him are proud to serve. But this is somewhat of an isolated instance.

No. Our champions are movie and television heroes, and the preponderance of them engage in violent behavior on a regular basis.

Whether it's *Robocop*'s[30] futuristic killing machine, *Rambo*'s[31] sociopathic killing machine, or *Lethal Weapon*'s[32] lovable lethal weapon Mel Gibson, our heroes tend to be violent men. There is, of course, the occasional violent woman thrown into the mix, such as *Terminator 2: Judgment Day*'s[33] Linda Hamilton or the *Alien*[34] series' Sigourney Weaver (see "From 'Boys with Toys' to 'Babes with Bullets.'" Most, however, are male.

The violent "man of action" is also a classic archetype of the American National Character. We tend to identify with this heroic figure in some deep-seated way as a culture. This, of course, stems from our earliest days of pioneers and colonists, followed by cowboys and war heroes. Old archetypes die hard or in some cases, never die; they just metamorphose into action figures more in keeping with their times.

Male or female, our heroes are seen as no-nonsense figures who "get the job done," whatever it takes and whatever the cost, often at the point of a gun. Even against impossible odds, they manage to achieve their goals, be it escaping the "bad guys," rescuing the "good guys," or simply winning the shoot-out. In this context, because we admire the character, we accept and even believe in their methods.

Of course, because this is all television or film *fiction*, we need excitement to sell that fiction to the audience, and violence is nothing if not exciting, at least to the statistical majority of the audience. The viewer ends up embracing violence as standard operating procedure.

We may think, or even hope, that the audience will be able to discriminate and realize that these images are merely entertainment, thus ensuring complete freedom on our part to be as outrageous or as gory as possible. But the reality is that under a constant barrage of violent material, the lines blur and the ability to discriminate degrades rapidly.

In summary, the heroes we choose to portray can and do influence the attitudes and behavior of the audience. If we choose violence as their modus

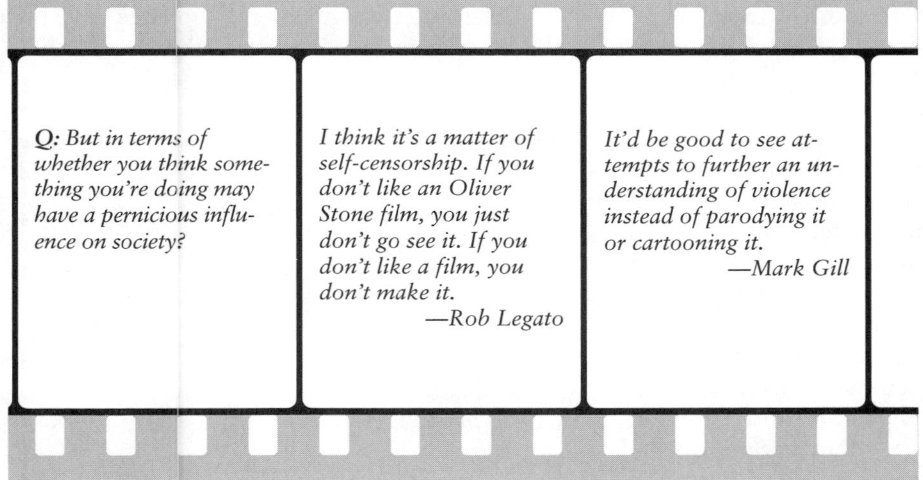
Q: But in terms of whether you think something you're doing may have a pernicious influence on society?

I think it's a matter of self-censorship. If you don't like an Oliver Stone film, you just don't go see it. If you don't like a film, you don't make it.
—*Rob Legato*

It'd be good to see attempts to further an understanding of violence instead of parodying it or cartooning it.
—*Mark Gill*

operandi, either because the story requires it or to appease the marketing gods, we must realize that the choice most probably contributes to the level of violence pervading the world around us. It *is* a choice.

Choice of Victim

The victim of violent acts is also a prime factor in how onscreen violence impacts the viewer.[35] Again, this is especially true with regard to children. If viewers perceive the victim as likable or like themselves, the effect is to increase fear and anxiety. If violence can happen to someone *like* me, it can also happen to me, they reason. This concern can spill over into everyday life, whether consciously or not.

Further, if the victim is not like the viewer, but still likable, the viewer will sympathize with the victim. This sympathy, when translated to the real world, also causes increased anxiety. "If bad things happen to good people," so goes the thought, bad things could happen to "MY people," or worse, to ME. Also, if the victim is sympathetic, it often heightens the viewer's involvement in the dramatic process.

If, however, the victim is dissimilar to the viewer and NOT likable, the viewer can more easily either rationalize the violence or dismiss it because in some way the victim "got what he deserved." This is peculiar ethical reasoning because virtually no one deserves to be the victim of violence. However, such beliefs, whether conscious or subconscious, are common.

Not only should we choose our victims carefully, we should also balance the choice of victim against the choice of perpetrator. If both are sympathetic, it may be that violence will be seen as necessary. "Good people must sometimes do bad things to survive." If both are unsympathetic, violence may be dismissed as belonging to a world apart from the viewer and therefore of little emotional import. If the perpetrator is sympathetic and the victim is not, the violence may be admired, as when our hero gets the villain. Finally, if the perpetrator is unsympathetic and the victim is sympathetic, the violence is likely to be seen as both morally reprehensible and threatening. "Bad people do bad things to good people ... like me!"

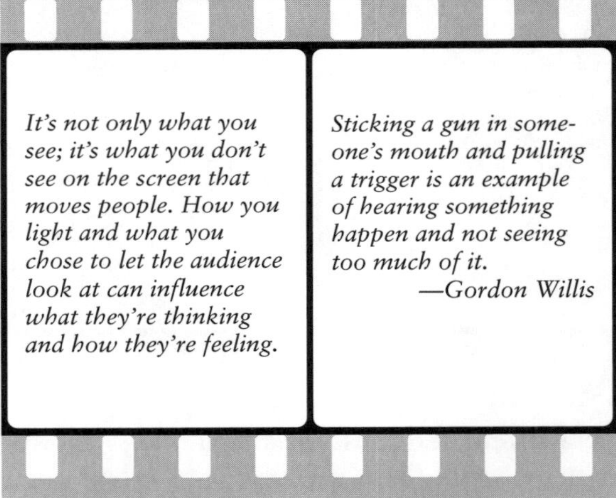

Consequences

Showing the consequences of violent acts provides creators with perhaps their most readily available opportunity to modify possible effects of violence. Social scientists state that when violence is shown in context, complete with depictions of the pain and suffering caused by the violent acts, aggressive behavior in the viewer is inhibited.[36] When no consequences are portrayed and there are no costs in human terms, aggression is increased in the viewer. Unpunished violence sends the message that violence can be fun.

Rewards and Punishments

Does the perpetrator get punished or suffer as a result of the violence he has committed? In instances where the perpetrator is punished overtly for his violent acts, the research suggests that the risk of learning and adopting aggressive behaviors is reduced in the viewer.[37] Again, this has to do with the perceived costs of violence. Onscreen suffering is one such cost. Punishment inflicted on the perpetrator is another. Often, if either factor exists, the viewer sees aggressive tendencies as too costly, and these tendencies are reduced.

In contrast, if a violent act is rewarded—through the perpetrator's attaining his goal or "getting the girl," the likelihood of learning aggressive behavior is increased. The message is: If using violence to solve a problem works, is exciting, and carries no negative consequences, why not indulge yourself?

The violence in Schindler's List *was much more horrific than any special-effects-laden slasher film because it was so real and you knew it really happened. Somebody picks somebody off from a hundred yards for the sport of it. It was so affecting. The film and the reason it was made was to do the opposite of glorifying that—it was to send a message—but it used those tools to help you get it. It's very graphic and very horrible, psychologically more than visually.*

—*Rob Legato*

Given these parameters, it would seem responsible for creators to make a point of giving context to the violence they portray. Consider showing the consequences of violent actions, the suffering, and the costs. Show the perpetrators being punished, or at the very least not being rewarded in the short or the long term as often as possible given the bounds of the narrative. This type of responsible dramatization is executed effectively in the HBO series *OZ*.[38] One of the former producers, Bridget Potter, states: "*OZ* is important because it sheds light on a major issue in this country—what are prisons for? The stories tell about the lives of people in prison, many of whom are redeemed by their (violent) experiences, many of whom are destroyed—but all of it will hopefully provoke thought."[39]

The Reason for the Violence

When a violent act is seen as unjustified, aggressive tendencies are reduced in the viewer.[40] Thus, for example, if a teenager assaults a senior citizen to steal her handbag, or a robber who already has the money from the till shoots the clerk for no apparent reason, or there is a random drive-by shooting, as in the film *Colors*,[41] in which an innocent person is killed, the viewer may well react with indignation and a feeling that aggressive behavior is a terrible thing.

If, however, violence is seen as justified in a particular situation, aggressive behavior is encouraged. So, for example, if the hero must destroy the villain to save the world, rescue the heroine, or protect a child through violent means, the viewer may both sympathize with the hero's plight and admire his actions. This represents a classic ethical choice on the part of the hero, the choice that "the ends justify the means."

The most thought-provoking entertainment, let it be said, does not permit this choice to be so simple. Rather, the more complex story presents a feeling that the "ends," whatever they may be, may be reached in more than one way, and it is the character arc of the hero that will determine which direction is chosen.

Sometimes this gets twisted around on itself. For example, in the otherwise masterful *Saving Private Ryan*,[42] director Steven Spielberg causes Tom Hanks' character to spare the life of a German captive midway through the film. This is clearly noble, showing mercy and restraint. However, that positive lesson is later shattered when this very German shoots Hanks' character in the climax. Now the ironic message seems to become "the only good [enemy] is a dead [enemy]. If you show mercy and restraint, you will pay for it later."

Weapons

Weapons—in most cases firearms of one sort or another—can trigger aggressive feelings in viewers and cause them to interpret a seemingly neutral situation as potentially threatening.[43]

Weapons are used in storytelling for many reasons. Often, of course, they are necessary to service a particular plotline. Sometimes they are just plain fun. From the blasters and elegant light sabers of *Star Wars*[44] to the bizarre but hip weaponry of *Men in Black*, weapons increase tension, raise excitement levels, allow for great sound and special effects, and satisfy a lust for new toys, particularly among

> *The bottom line on* Boyz 'N the Hood *is that it was arguably the most culturally important film of that year. I thought it was most important to get the people in who would respond to the violent message. They were the people who most needed to see that movie, even though they wouldn't come if you told them about the spinach part in the lesson that they'd be getting.*
>
> —*Mark Gill*

How do you sensitively portray mass death? In Titanic, *when you see the lifeboat look for bodies and you see the woman frozen dead with her baby— that detail is what sticks with you. That takes it now from a nameless, faceless group to an emotional experience. This is cemented when you see the little face because it looks like your baby's. What Jim Cameron did in* Titanic *was to take what we have intellectually said was a sad event and personalize it and put people right in the middle of what you only saw from a wide perspective. If one person dies it's a terrible tragedy, but you can't do that for hundreds of people. It takes the person out of it and becomes an event like a news item—50 people died in a bomb explosion—and it doesn't sink in until you knew somebody who was in it.*

—*Rob Legato*

the younger male audience. In addition, weapons help to sell tickets and spin-off products.

Certain ethical issues clearly surround the use of weaponry in film. There are also a few facts to remember. Consider, for example, that until the release of the film *Dirty Harry*[45] in 1971, the Smith & Wesson Model 29 .44 caliber Magnum revolver was relatively unknown in the gun world, and the manufacturer was thinking of discontinuing the model. Then Eastwood's Detective Harry Callahan growled: "This is a .44 Magnum, the most powerful handgun in the world," and suddenly the model became so popular that retailers had trouble keeping it in stock. Gun brands had always received plugs from Hollywood—in movies such as *Dr. No*[46] and TV series such as *Gunsmoke*[47]—but here Eastwood brought home the lesson to gun makers—that getting into a Hollywood movie could be the best form of advertising available.[48] Suddenly, there was a market imperative to promote the use of weaponry, especially guns, in film.

Because weapons influence the viewer's tension level and perception of violence, the choice of whether to include weapons in a scene and which to include is not merely a choice between different levels of firepower. It's ultimately a choice about manipulating the viewer's perception of the world.

Realism

The more realistic the portrayal of a violent act, the more it can generate fear or elicit aggressive behavior.[49] This is not true with young children, as they are not always able to distinguish fantasy from reality, but for the majority of the audience, realism equals impact.

Today's special effects technology certainly makes it possible to create more realistic decapitations, gorings, explosions, crashes, and the like. However, there is a theory that the technology is increasingly being used as a crutch for the weaker and less skilled creator, who must substitute these props for deficiencies in script, characters, or native storytelling ability. Remember, people can get caught up in "fun" special effects at the expense of the story. Rob Legato, special effects expert (*Titanic*[50]) says: "You can further the art form by realizing that you're not in the special effects business—you're in the filmmaking business."[51]

Another, more complex answer to why violence is so prized in entertainment today is that society has changed. Levels of violence that never would have been tolerated, particularly by a World War II generation sick to death of war and bloodshed, are today commonplace. It is possible, ironically, that war made life more precious, whereas today, with no violent global cause in which to engage, violence has become more localized, making the cost of human life cheap in comparison. We expect to see brutal and violent acts portrayed, because the real thing has become part of the normative pattern of our society.

The Use of Humor

Using humor to "sell" violence has become a much-used trend.[52] Violence sold with humor, just like medicine sold with a "spoonful of sugar"[53] can be enjoyed without contemplating the consequences. When Bruce Willis kills one of the "bad guys" (or in his case many of the "bad guys") then cracks a joke, the humor diverts attention from any contemplation of the fact that he just mowed a man down with a machine gun. Humor trivializes and stylizes violence to the point where its effect as a deterrent is lost.

> *I'm appalled that they cut the film* (Brother's Keeper). *It offends me because the footage that didn't make it is essential to understanding everything that happens in the next two and a half hours. They said it was gratuitous. When you watch the film you can understand what it would do to you if it happened to your community, let alone to your own family. In seeing the footage the viewer understands the need to solve the crime.*
>
> —*Joe Berlinger*

In other words, humor strips violence of the moral

outrage the viewer might otherwise feel. And if our hero can joke about the destruction he is causing, surely we can as well.

No one would argue that, for a significant portion of the audience, watching Schwarzenegger, Smith, or Willis blow away a raft of "bad guys" with a snicker here and a joke there, with lots of quick cutaways so the viewer never sees any suffering, is both exciting and fun. The violence is practically comedic, and sometimes, in fact, does make the viewer laugh.

We should perhaps examine the idea of laughing at violence from an ethical standpoint. Do we, as creators, wish to feed this trend? Again, it is a choice.

Prolonged Exposure

The concern here arises from the sheer volume of violent acts surrounding us in the media. The inhibition of sympathy and empathy that are a primary symptom of the desensitization to violence discussed above can result from repeated viewings of violence over a long period of time.[54]

Simply because we as creators *can* continually raise the bar for depicting violence to an ever greater level of impact because of technological developments, does not necessarily mean that we *should.* At the very least, filmmakers should realize that violence in our product is decidedly a choice, with ethical consequences to be considered.

In societal terms, it would seem to make sense to reduce the number and severity of instances of random or gratuitous violence in film and television. It is becoming clear that tolerance for violence in the viewing public may be reaching its limits. Increasingly, one hears grumblings and protests, and increasingly, the government is listening. The requirement that every television set manufactured in the United States after 1998 have a violence screening device or 'V'-chip that allows parents to filter out unwanted material; the new, albeit controversial television ratings system designed to enable the 'V'-chip; and revised guidelines for children's educational programming—these could be just the beginning.

Violence in a film or television program may be random, but the choice on the part of the creator to use violence should *never* be random. If we choose to depict violence, let us do so because the story requires it, and not to compensate for weaknesses in dialogue, character, or design. Let us not use the tool of violence simply because it's there.

Teens and Violence: Rebels Without a Cause

Teens have always been a thorn in society's side, probably since the days of the cavemen—thank goodness! It has been said that the role of teenagers is to shake up their elders and remind them of a time when all did not seem so clear in the world.

As creators, we have especially rich material available to us when portraying teens as they come of age, explore life's glories and failures, and generally deal with the angst of The First Date and The Dreaded Acne. Certainly there is a body of comedic, poignant, and compelling films and TV series that examine such issues on various levels.

There is also a host of more serious social issues surrounding teenagers and the media, issues that tap into some very broad problems. As a general note, creators would be well-advised to realize that, with this particular age group, certain types of rebellious, violent, and "outsider" behavior look pretty appealing to many who see themselves as rebellious outsiders in the first place.

Critics have blamed the media as a contributing factor in the tragic rash of violence in our nation's schools. Some have characterized a "culture of death"[55] in American media, wherein our entertainment products focus on weaponry, the occult, explosive devices, murder, mayhem, drugs, and other so-called negative stimuli. Let's examine some of the leading perceived culprits.

Computer and Video Games

A comparatively recent trend in computer and video games began with roughly the third generation of games in wide circulation in the marketplace. These games, known as "first-person shooters," have come to dominate the game market and are causing some critics concern. These games altered the standard concept of how we relate to and interact with video games.

Traditionally, many computer and video games were based on the player controlling what is referred to as an "avatar" (a character representative of the player) as his way of navigating through the various levels of the game. These games provided a third-person narrative perspective, if you will, wherein the player viewed his character from a distance (usually a side or overhead view).

No matter how much the player attempted to invest the avatar with his personality, it was still a computer-generated character designed by someone other than the player and pictured to look as the designer, not the player, imagined. Later on, a choice of avatars was offered to better fit the imagination (and the gender) of the player. Finally, in certain games, design features were added that would allow the player not only to choose the avatar, but also to have some limited ability to customize it to their liking. However, this was still a crude system that did not fundamentally alter the third-person nature of the game.

However, with the advent of the first-person shooter game, all that changed. Suddenly, the player did not have to watch from a remote position. Now, the entire perspective and point of view of the game was brought around to him or her! Now, the player was inserted directly into the action through the means of "subjective camera." The entire game is designed to appear from the player's point of view as he himself proceeds through the various levels. As stimuli appear, he no longer interprets them from the outside looking in. He can react as if the stimuli were actually placed in his path ... because they are. When the trigger is pulled and the enemy killed, it's the player himself who is doing the shooting. It is no longer a small, one-step-removed, computer-generated figure. And, of course, the player is rewarded for becoming a marksman and killing as many of the "enemy" as possible—in fact, in most games, a certain number of killings must take place before the player can advance to the next level of the game.

I would contend that this change signaled a much greater emotional and psychic involvement for the player. The fact that it's now all happening directly to the player means that the player responds much more as if this were a true-to-life situation. It serves to heighten the emotional state of the player.

As a crude experiment to test this hypothesis, try playing two games in sequence. Try an older game, one I have termed a third-person narrative scenario. Then switch to one of the newer first-person shooter games. You will very likely notice an enormous jump in your level of emotional involvement in the game, as well as, perhaps, in your blood pressure!

In addition, the technological advances in game design and delivery have increased both the level of realism and the level of impact of these games. For those of us who remember such games as "Pong" and "Pac Man," the virtual world has changed to an almost unfathomable degree. This is the world in which many teens now spend much of their lives.

Remember that teens, including those involved in the Columbine High School tragedy in April 1999, spend literally hours a day immersed in this virtual world, taking aim and firing ... taking aim and firing ... taking aim and firing.

The imminent convergence of computer and filmic technologies may only make all this worse, as teens will spend ever more time living their lives in a virtual world that is even more violent than the real world.

The Search for Meaning

Critics suggest that the dangerous combination of onscreen violence, coupled with these "first-person shooter" games—as well as the easy availability of real guns, all contribute to an explosive environment among teens in society.

It is difficult to deny the facts, as painful as they are, that entertainment has influenced young people in the negative: the young perpetrators at Columbine were avid fans of various forms of violent computer games and films, as were those in schools in Kentucky and Arkansas earlier. In each case, the media preferences of the boys involved were cited as being a possible factor in their mindsets prior to the crimes.

After Columbine, the nation's leaders searched frantically for a reason—some*one* or some*thing* to blame for this horrible sequence of events. Some latched on to The Media, broadly defined to include film and television, music, the Internet, news, advertising, and the aforementioned computer and role-playing games. This material is sending out violent, self-destructive, and even demonic messages to teens, these concerned leaders contend, and they are acting upon these messages.

The phrase "overly simplistic" seems fairly to scream for use here. Blaming the media may be an easy excuse to cover up the real problems, but it will certainly not solve those problems. It is absurd to believe that, all other things being equal, music or film or first-person shooter games will drive a teen to kill himself or others. The problem is that all other things are most definitely *not* equal.

There are many arguments to make against the alleged demonizing caused by role-playing games (i.e., the vast majority of players never become violent, the games are really just good escapist fun, and so on). However, as discussed earlier in this book, it can be allowed that to a certain extent entertainment outlets are *contributing to already disenfranchised and isolated youth's* view of the world.

As Mark Gill, president of Miramax Films/LA, has said in the context of film marketing, "[I]gnore the audience at your own peril."[56] In the case of violence and teenagers, this phrase rings ominously true.

Teen Suicide

Another extremely painful issue is teen suicide: every six hours of every day, a child between the ages of 10–19 commits suicide with a gun.[57] Why? Obviously, taking one's life is a complex social, emotional, and psychological act, not to be easily explained away with a pat answer. Research shows, however, that teen suicide portrayals in TV or film often cause a spike in the number of actual teen suicides across the nation, just as gang movies often cause an increase in gang violence following their release. Heeding these statistics, most in the entertainment industry have been extremely responsible in their portrayals, and many creators, especially in television, refrain from depicting suicide at all as a result of this research—and their own ethical decisionmaking.

Teen suicide is not often dealt with in films either. Back during *Saturday Night Fever*,[58] an extremely disturbed teen (or near teen) leaps to his death off the famous bridge. The subject was dealt with in comic fashion in *Better Off Dead*[59] and in a more serious manner in *Dead Poets Society*[60] and in the ultimate of teen suicide movies, *Romeo & Juliet*.[61] The latter engendered some interesting reactions upon its release. As many teens had not read the original masterwork by William Shakespeare, nor seen its previous incarnations (including *West Side Story*[62]), many felt that the death of the two stars was romantic

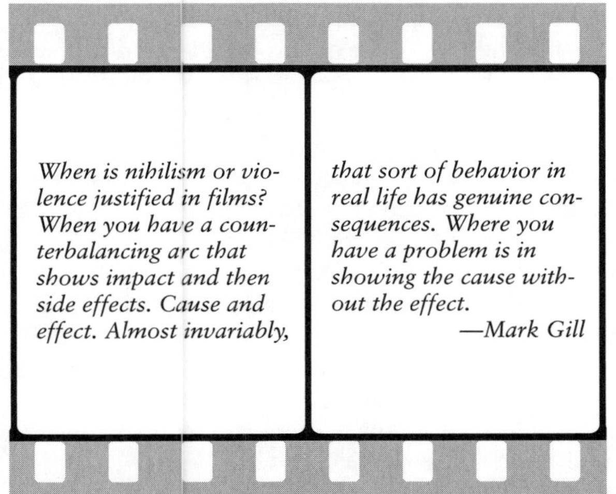

and noble. Some of this was perhaps a result of the fact that Claire Danes and Leonardo DiCaprio made an almost impossibly beautiful and wistful couple, difficult not to empathize with. However, a portion of teen viewers felt that Romeo and Juliet had been fools for throwing away their lives for what was essentially their parents' battle. In a peculiar way, this is a *much* healthier reaction to this timeless story.

Now it might be said that if media messages were consistent, perhaps what we would have is simply a very successful brainwashing technique for raising well-trained drones. However, the only consistent messages are: you can never be too thin or too rich, money makes right, the world is a tremendously violent place, and the like. Everything else conflicts, depending upon the source, as each source has his or her own ax to grind. However, clearly, a teen must be in serious emotional trouble before he becomes susceptible to media influences that bring him to suicide.

Social Attitudes

At the same time teens are being bombarded with dark images of death and destruction, the media often presents a cynical and disrespectful view of the world and authority that feeds in to the disenfranchisement felt by many young people. Now we live in a democratic society and we cherish our rights to go ahead and be just as disrespectful as we'd like toward our leaders, and often they deserve what they get! However, here we are addressing a broad and pervasive general attitude that permeates our entertainment and affects our audience's views of the world over time.

By definition, it is difficult to assess changes in societal attitudes, and by extension, the effects of the media on such attitudes, in snapshot form. In other words, what you grew up learning will be normal for you, and you will use that as your baseline reference. However, if you step back and take the longer view, and examine changes in beliefs over time, the results can be quite startling. The media has played an enormous role in causing many changes over the years.

We as creators have helped to foster a growing disenchantment with our lives on a societal level. Media is not the only cause of this disenchantment, certainly, but we have fueled the fire with our messages: parents know nothing; high school is a waste of time, and so on. Since the Watergate debacle in 1974, we have seen a widespread and increasing cynicism and disrespect for government, politicians, and our country as a whole. In fact, these institutions have become the butt of moronic jokes in movies and television in the past quarter century, not to mention the biting satire of late night TV hosts.

It is certainly true that government and politicians, especially, make great grist for the humor mill, and also make good dramatic material for use in films and television. And it's true that much of our commentary is actually based on truth. However, in our society's case, we seem to exaggerate and focus on the negative, contributing to a general sense of distrust and alienation from our system. This loss of faith is reflected in declining voting rates and a general sense of boredom and disgust with the entire political process.

Another form of disrespect that we as creators have either directly or inadvertently encouraged is a disrespect of authority in general. This hits a bit closer to home, literally, as disrespect of authority has, as elements, disrespect for parents, family authority figures, teachers, and counselors. In fact, this engenders a basic disrespect for institutions in general, from the educational to the religious.

Again, it makes for good drama and an admirable hero to create a character that "bucks the system," rejecting authority and following his or her own course. It is also true, of course, that this country was built by individuals bucking the system and from this, many of our greatest strides have come.

However, there is also something destructive about portraying an endless stream of characters who find nothing of value in the institutions that, like it or

Q: In Pulp Fiction *Tarantino maintained an ironic distance from violence, but Harvey Weinstein's wife walked out of* Reservoir Dogs, *saying that it was too real—that it wasn't cartoon violence.*

[Violence depictions are] definitely in the eye of the beholder. One of the things that Quentin [Tarantino] does brilliantly is ride that line so it's not so immediately obvious that it's a parody. What makes a Tarantino movie so effective is that it's fun and ironic and its own commentary. At the same time, there's something almost realistic enough to buy, too. It's that tension that makes his films so interesting and what makes his commentary a lot more incisive instead of dull and obvious.

—Mark Gill

not, form the glue that holds society together. If we reach the point where we have so thoroughly discredited authority and institutions through endless media ridicule that no one sees any real reason to work together at all, then we have a problem. Society becomes like a European soccer crowd gone berserk, everyone trampling each other in an attempt to get where they want to be. This is not really a productive base upon which to build or maintain a society.

What we seem to be moving toward, both in society itself and in our portrayals thereof, is not the utopian society envisioned in literature and occasionally in the media—for example in Gene Roddenberry's various *Star Trek*[63] series—in which we all work together to achieve common goals. What we are instead moving toward is a society in which everyone thinks of themselves first, and where greed and money seem to be the answer to every question.

Ethical filmmakers might contend that it would not be such a horrible thing for the entertainment industry, which wields such a great influence in society, to consider, from time to time, the long-term effect of constantly reinforcing these ideas through our work. Chaotic, seditious, and generally unproductive attitudes are not likely to help society in any way, and may paralyze it in the long run. We could begin here, as with all these issues, to take the longer view. That is the ethical choice to consider.

Exercise in Violence: Tracking Through the Process

How does ultrarealistic and graphic violence end up on film and television screens? How does an original idea that includes a minimal amount of violence in the service of the storyline get carried through the major departments of a film, being molded and shaped by each department? As a hypothetical exercise, the following section will trace a rather extreme example of exactly that process. Far from being an exhaustive technical education in production, this exercise is merely the briefest look at how the representation of a violent act onscreen can come to be more of a concern than the violent act's role in the story.

Let us assume we have a character-driven screenplay about a "rogue" cop (our hero) tracking a bad guy (our villain) in order to get him before he can murder his next victim in a serial murder spree. It's all about tension and intrigue, with very little action but a great deal of suspense.

1. The writer has come up with a characterization of our hero. Because the hero is a cop, the writer has chosen a signature weapon for him that he believes emphasizes the quirks of his personality. The weapon is a large .45 caliber pistol for "maximum stopping power." In the screenplay of course, the writer has chosen several spots for use of the weapon, including a shoot-out in a liquor store with a robber armed with a Saturday Night Special, just to show he is a good cop; an unsuccessful foot chase with the villain in an alleyway,

with several shots fired; and a final shoot-out with the villain, in which the villain is injured and arrested.

2. A producer now options this script. The producer works with the writer to hone the story and the characters. She is also thinking about casting and marketing. She decides that, to make the film attractive to a studio or financier, she needs to make sure the film will have maximum marketability in overseas territories, because more than 50 percent of a picture's revenue is routinely earned in the foreign markets. Violence travels extremely well. There are no translation problems—violence is not culture specific. Also, she can use a different level and kind of actor to play the cop, thus making casting easier, since the piece will become more action-oriented and less of a character study requiring serious acting chops. Thus, she decides she needs a "bigger" picture, painted on a "bigger" canvas.

   Now, the producer and the studio executives or financiers ask for a rewrite of the screenplay from the writer, and ask him to include the rogue cop's partner, who can join him in the shoot-out with the villain and give him a dramatic foil. He, too, has a signature weapon—a 9-mm handgun. He has a great relationship with the officers at the precinct, which of course our hero, being a rogue cop, does not. This will allow him to bring the cavalry over the hill to save the hero in the last scene, escalating the violence in the process.

   The unsuccessful foot chase with the villain transforms into a shoot-out and is moved from the alley to a crowded main avenue. A homeless man is injured during the battle. The final shoot-out is changed. The villain has somehow acquired a veritable arsenal, most probably in response to our hero's attempt to do him in earlier in the picture, so there is a fierce firefight. In addition, the villain is not injured and captured. Rather, he is killed outright.

   As a side note, even though the writer is still doing the rewrites, he is fast beginning to realize that his small character-driven drama has become something he does not really recognize in the headlong pursuit of action and adventure marketing. He wonders how much worse it can get. He's about to find out.

3. A director is hired. She, too, must have her hand in the creation of this gradually swelling action picture. She brings in a new writer just to "polish" the screenplay for production.

   The shoot-out at the liquor store is moved to a larger venue, to up the stakes. A small market is chosen, with a number of innocent shoppers present to get in the line of fire. The villain's Saturday Night Special is turned in for a shotgun to increase the potential splatter factor.

The stakes of the unsuccessful shoot-out are raised still further with the villain becoming maniacal and cruel, taking a sexy young woman as a human shield during the battle and escaping.

As to the final shoot-out, a car chase is added involving multiple vehicles through crowded city streets. The villain's car crashes, but he leaps out and begins to fire at the cops and the crowd.

Several additional scenes of violence are added. Our villain takes his human shield prisoner between gun battles with the hero, and he holds her prisoner in an old warehouse.

4. The director casts a rough-hewn action hero type, likely without much concern for his native acting ability. What is important is that we believe he can command the action sequences, and look good doing it. As a side note, there are, as rare exceptions, actors who can manage all sides of the equation, such as Mel Gibson, but exceptions are not the rule. The villain is cast as someone rather slight of build, intense and slightly loony, but with a confidence and authority that allow us to believe he is a real threat. The human shield/rescuee is cast as ... well, you know.

   The executives, the producer, and the director are thrilled. They have a large-scale action picture on a citywide canvas with large amounts of violence. The original writer would not recognize his script, except for character and place names, but this doesn't matter, as it's not shown to him anyway.

5. Now the fun really begins. Designers are brought on board. The production designer suggests that the small, dark market for the first shoot-out is too restrictive. The scene can be made bigger and visually more effective if a giant supermarket is chosen as the site of the battle. That way, there can be dozens of brightly lit bystanders to raise the stakes, and thousands of objects to destroy for effect.

6. In addition, working with the props department, the designer determines that the robber should have several hand grenades at his disposal. It seems he was well prepared for this robbery. Explosions add "production value." Also, to raise the stakes yet again, someone should get killed in a way that has not been seen before. The solution hit upon is that the girl/shield/rescuee will escape and kill one of her captors by stabbing him in the eye with the underwire from her bra. Very visual, very gory, very new, and vaguely sexual in suggestion. Perfect.

7. The director of photography now spends many long hours deciding how to best light the exploding cans, bottles, and displays in the supermarket. This battle can be a virtual visual feast, color splashing everywhere. The

grenades really open up possibilities. A brief foray into the use of a rocket launcher is discarded, not because it is insane, but simply because the props department doesn't have one handy.

Also, the lighting of the street for the failed shoot-out is discussed at length to ensure that it is dark enough to suit the mood of the scene, but bright enough to make sure all aspects of the violence are easily showcased.

For the final shoot-out, the car chase lighting is carefully plotted so the villain is never lost in shadow for very long. His reaction to the destruction he leaves in his wake roaring through busy city streets is key to manipulating the audience's excitement level.

8. The special effects department is having a field day, from working out the gunshots and blood pack spurts to planning the explosions and car crashes.

9. The wardrobe and makeup departments struggle with how to make the hero and the girl look more attractive than the average human being could ever hope to be, and the villain more threatening than anyone you would ever meet. They also take account of the fact that blood needs to be seen, as do injuries of all kinds, so clothing, when shot during the night scenes, cannot hide these elements. Finally, the girl must look overtly sexy at all times, regardless of the situation, preferably with ample cleavage.

10. Meanwhile, the sound department is struggling with how they will make all the gunshots, explosions, bodies hitting the floor, cars screeching during the chase, and so on, sound as realistic as humanly possible and then some. Sound design and effects have developed to the point where the sound of bullets striking flesh can be made to sound absolutely realistic, as can the more pyrotechnically inspiring moments of the film. Actually, much of this department's most detailed work will be done in postproduction, but for simplicity's sake, the timeline has been compressed.

    Overall, each department is going to the director with their own ideas as to how to make this or that violent moment more realistic, to give it more impact. Because these people have become extremely proficient at what they do, the level of super-realism that can be achieved is almost beyond belief.

    Finally, the film goes into production, and all departments pull together (so goes the theory) to maximize the "bang for the buck" (literally). The picture is released to great fanfare and makes a quarter of a billion dollars overseas, about three-quarters of that in the domestic markets, and lives forever on video.

    Everyone is happy, except perhaps society as a whole.

Ethical Gymnastics

1. Write a one-page report about a popular movie that you feel glorifies violence or makes it look particularly appealing. Use the READR method to break down and analyze the movie, then discuss the ways in which it presents violence in terms of what you have read in this section.

2. Write a one-page report about the same movie you chose for Question #1, discussing the ways in which you could present the material differently. This does *not* have to result in a nonviolent, or even less violent movie, just one in which imitation is not encouraged, according to the ideas presented in this section.

3. You're writing and filming a scene in which a young woman is brutally raped and murdered. Discuss the ethical choices to be made in this instance. Are there ethically sound ways in which to show this?

4. *Bonnie & Clyde* and *The Godfather*, although tame by today's standards, are widely credited as being the two films that launched the new era of violence in the media. Discuss the ways in which these films changed or did not change the way violence is portrayed.

5. You must write and film a scene in which your hero and a group of terrorists have a firefight in a crowded airport. The terrorists are in possession of a lethal bio-toxin that they plan to release into New York City's water supply that will kill everyone in the city within 24 hours. Your hero's motto is, to quote Mr. Spock, "the lives of the many outweigh the lives of the few ..."[64] Discuss what might happen during the firefight that would make him reconsider his motto.

6. You're immersed in the world of writing for a television sitcom. One of your characters physically attacks anyone who makes fun of his bad haircut, with hilarious results. Discuss ways in which this can be presented that do not encourage violence or aggressive behavior, but also do not dampen the character's comic punch.

7. Discuss the reasons for using violence in your hypothetical film or television program. Consider reasons of dramatic content, economic and market forces, audience reaction, and other factors. Now, consider the reasons for not using violence, based on what you have learned in this section.

8. Discuss the role of humor in the perception of media violence.

9. A serial killer escapes legal prosecution and physical harm at the end of your movie (because there has to be a sequel!). Discuss ways in which you can still show that he has been punished for his actions.

10. Using what you have learned in this section, write a one-page treatment for a responsibly violent movie. For purposes of this exercise, the more violent and the more responsible, the better.

11. Choose three films in which disrespect for authority is promoted in teenagers. In each case, discuss the ethical considerations involved, in light of what you have read in this section. Use the READR method to break down and analyze each example. Also, for each case, discuss ways in which the story would be affected by the removal of this disrespect. Could the story still be told? Is the disrespect integral to the narrative, or is it character texture that may or may not be necessary? Would you make the same choices? Why or why not?

12. You're directing a movie in which a teen dies exotically and under mysterious circumstances. Do you believe it's necessary to point out that this death was *not* a suicide in light of what you've read in this section?

Notes

1 According to *Uniform Crime Report,* issued by the Federal Bureau of Investigations, U.S. Department of Justice, June 1999, the number of Crime Index offenses reported to law enforcement agencies throughout the United States decreased 10 percent during the first six months of 1999 compared to the figures reported during the same period in 1998.

On May 17, 1998, the *Uniform Crime Report: 1997 Preliminary Annual Release* was issued. Among its conclusions was the fact that violent crimes decreased by five percent from 1996–1997. Also, in 1995, the number of violent crimes was 6 percent BELOW that for 1991, although it was 21 percent ABOVE the 1986 number.

Further, in 1994, there were some 1,857,670 violent crimes, whereas in 1995, the number was 1,798,783, a decrease of 3.2 percent. The statistics for murder and willful manslaughter followed a similar trend. In 1995, the number of known murders was 13 percent BELOW the number for 1991, although it was 5 percent ABOVE the 1986 number. Further, in 1994, there were some 23,326 known murders or cases of willful manslaughter, whereas in 1995, the number was 21,597, a decrease of 7.4 percent.

2 The Motion Pictures Producers and Distributors Association was formed in 1922. The Hays Office refers to the association's first president, Will H. Hays. The code

was the restrictive body of rules that content creators had to abide by for motion pictures. *Encyclopedia Britannica Online* (www.eb.com).

3 For example, *The Maltese Falcon*, 1941 D: John Huston, Warner Bros. or *The Public Enemy*, 1931 D: William A. Wellman, Warner Bros.

4 1960 D: Alfred Hitchcock, Paramount Pictures.

5 The number of shots, set-ups, splices, and so on is a matter of some controversy, depending on who is doing the counting. According to *Filmguide to Psycho,* (Naremore, James. London: Indiana University Press, 1973, p. 56), Hitchcock himself said there were 78 cuts and 70 camera set-ups. Naremore counts some 55–65 cuts, depending on where in the scene the counting begins. According to *Alfred Hitchcock and The Making of Psycho*, *(*Rebello, Stephen. New York: Dembner Books, 1990, p. 103), there were 78 cuts and "the camera was in different places all the time." According to *Psycho: Behind the Scenes of the Classic Thriller*, (Leigh, Janet, with Nickens, Christopher. New York: Harmony Books, 1995), Leigh states that she read a dialogue prepared by George Stevens, Jr. "who is meticulous in his research" that said there were 71 set-ups.

6 1967 D: Arthur Penn, Warner Bros.

7 1972 D: Francis Ford Coppola, Paramount Pictures.

8 Champlin, Charles. *Los Angeles Times*, March 19, 1972.

9 For examples of intense or egregious violence, see films such as: *Friday the 13th*, 1980 D: Sean Cunningham, Paramount Pictures or any one of its eight sequels or its television spin-off; *A Nightmare on Elm Street*, 1984 D: Wes Craven, New Line Cinema or any one of its seven sequels or its television spin-off; or, in a genre other than horror, *Taxi Driver*, 1976 D: Martin Scorsese, Columbia Pictures Corporation; *Goodfellas*, 1990 D: Martin Scorsese, Warner Bros.; *Casino*, 1995 D: Martin Scorsese, Universal Pictures; *Natural Born Killers*, 1994 D: Oliver Stone, Warner Bros.; *Saving Private Ryan*, 1998 D: Steven Spielberg, DreamWorks Distribution, LLC with Paramount Pictures or *Fight Club*, 1999 D: David Fincher, 20th Century Fox.

10 Paraphrase of statement made at The Sundance Film Festival; personal recollection of Marcy Kelly, founder of Mediascope.

11 1942 D: Michael Curtiz, Warner Bros.

12 1975 D: Steven Spielberg, MCA/Universal Pictures.

13 Interview with Laura Blum, Summer 1998.

14 1996 D: Joel Coen, Gramercy Pictures.

15 1999 D: Simon West, Paramount Pictures.

16 Interview with Laura Blum, Summer 1998.

17 Feshbach, S. "The Role of Fantasy in the Response to Television," *Journal of Social Issues*, 1976, Volume 32, pp. 71–85.

18 *The National Television Violence Study,* Universities of: California, Santa Barbara; Wisconsin, Madison; North Carolina, Chapel Hill; Texas, Austin. Studio City: Mediascope, 1996.

19 *National Television Violence Study.*

20 Viewers can also learn things such as: how to booby trap their house (*A Nightmare on Elm Street*, 1984 D: Wes Craven, New Line Cinema or more comically in *Home Alone*, 1990 D: Chris Columbus, 20th Century Fox, *Home Alone 2: Lost in New York*, 1992 D: Chris Columbus, 20th Century Fox or *Home Alone 3*, 1997 D: Raja Gosnell, 20th Century Fox); how to build weapons from junk in their garage (*The A-Team*, 1983–1987. Universal Pictures Television, or *MacGyver*, 1985–1992 Paramount Pictures Television); or, in fact, how to garrote your brother-in-law (*The Godfather*, 1972 D: Francis Ford Coppola, Paramount Pictures).

21 1986 D: James Cameron, 20th Century Fox.

22 *National Television Violence Study.*

23 *National Television Violence Study.*

24 Including, for example, Jericho Cane, Adam Gibson, Mr. Freeze, Harry Tasker, Jack Slater, The Terminator, John Matrix, Conan The Barbarian, and U.S. Marshal John Kruger.

25 1997 D: Barry Sonnenfeld, Columbia Pictures Corporation, Sony Pictures Entertainment.

26 *Teenage Mutant Ninja Turtles*, 1990 D: Steve Barron, New Line Cinema; *Teenage Mutant Ninja Turtles II: The Secret of the Ooze*, 1991 D: Michael Pressman, New Line Cinema; *Teenage Mutant Ninja Turtles III*, 1993 D: Stuart Gillard, Golden Harvest Films; *Teenage Mutant Ninja Turtles: The Series* (Animated) 1988–1997 Fox Television; *Teenage Mutant Ninja Turtles: The Series* (Live Action) 1997–1998 Fox Television.

27 1997–present, WB Network/Warner Bros. Television.

28 1996–2000, DreamWorks SKG.

29 1990–present, Warner Bros. Television.

30 1987 D: Paul Verhoeven, Orion Pictures Corp.; *Robocop II*, 1990 D: Irvin Kershner, Orion Pictures Corp.; *Robocop III*, 1994 D: Fred Decker, Orion Pictures Corp.; *Robocop: The Series*, 1994 Rysher Television.

31 *First Blood*, 1982 D: Ted Kotcheff, Carolco Pictures; *Rambo: First Blood, Part II*, 1985 D: George P. Cosmatos, TriStar Pictures; *Rambo III*, 1988 D: Peter MacDonald, Carolco Pictures.

32 *Lethal Weapon*, 1987 D: Richard Donner, Warner Bros.; *Lethal Weapon 2*, 1989 D: Richard Donner, Warner Bros.; *Lethal Weapon 3*, 1992 D: Richard Donner, Warner Bros.; and *Lethal Weapon 4*, 1998 D: Richard Donner, Warner Bros.

33 1991 D: James Cameron, TriStar Pictures.

34 *Alien*, 1979 D: Ridley Scott, 20th Century Fox; *Aliens*, 1986 D: James Cameron, 20th Century Fox; *Alien 3*, 1992 D: David Fincher, 20th Century Fox, and *Alien Resurrection*, 1997 D: Jean-Pierre Jeunet, 20th Century Fox.

35 *National Television Violence Study.*

36 *National Television Violence Study.*

37 *National Television Violence Study.*

38 1997–present, Rysher Entertainment.

39 Interview with Laura Blum, Summer 1998.

40 *National Television Violence Study.*

41 1088 D: Dennis Hopper, Orion Pictures Corp.
42 1998 D: Steven Spielberg, DreamWorks SKG.
43 *National Television Violence Study*.
44 1997 D: George Lucas, 20th Century Fox.
45 1971 D: Don Siegel, Warner Bros.
46 1962 D: Terence Young, United Artists.
47 1055–1975, CBS Television.
48 Hornaday, Ann. "Guns on Film: A Loaded Issue," *The Baltimore Sun*; January 17, 1999, pp. 10F–11F.
49 *National Television Violence Study.*
50 1997 D: James Cameron, Paramount Pictures.
51 Interview with Laura Blum, Summer 1998.
52 *National Television Violence Study.*
53 From *Mary Poppins*, 1964 D: Robert Stevenson, Walt Disney Productions, original music by Richard M. Sherman/Robert B. Sherman.
54 *National Television Violence Study.*
55 Noonan, Peggy. "The Culture of Death," *The New York Times*, April 27, 1999.
56 Interview with Laura Blum, New York, Spring 1998.
57 "Guns and Other Weapons" *Children and Youth Materials: National Crime Prevention Council*: www.ncpc.org/10adu6.htm
58 1977 D: John Badham, Paramount Pictures.
59 1985 D: Savage Steve Holland, CBS Entertainment Production.
60 1989 D: Peter Weir, Touchstone Pictures.
61 1996 D: Baz Luhrmann, 20th Century Fox.
62 1961 D: Jerome Robbins/Robert Wise, United Artists.
63 Star Trek (TV series), Paramount Television, 1966–1969; Star Trek (animated TV series), Paramount Television, 1973–1975; Star Trek: The Next Generation, Paramount Television, 1987–1994; Star Trek: Deep Space Nine, Paramount Television, 1993–1998; Star Trek: Voyager, Paramount Television, 1995–present; and various feature films.
64 *Star Trek: The Wrath of Khan*, 1982 D: Nicholas Meyer, Paramount Pictures.

The Cast: Portrayals of Stereotypes

> Stereotype: "A conventional, formulaic, and usually oversimplified conception, opinion, or belief..."
>
> —*The American Heritage Dictionary*

What is the first thing you notice about someone when you meet them? Are they male, female, blonde, bald? Right there, stereotyping begins.

Now, what do you think of when you hear the word "stereotype?" Exactly. The word stereotype has become a kind of stereotype in and of itself. In general language, it has become a value-laden term with an extremely negative connotation. The idea is that a stereotype negatively and unfairly characterizes an individual according to a particular group of which he or she is a member. "All Xs are Y, A is an X, therefore A is Y" is the general formulation.

However, this is an overly simplistic view of a rather complex process in which we *all* engage. Now, lest the reader begin to contemplate book burning at this juncture, we are referring to a key information processing technique used by the human brain to classify incoming stimuli, not the judgmental "Archie Bunker-esque" stereotyping you may be envisioning.

Stereotyping, as a process per se, is both necessary and natural. It is the extremes of this process that become a problem to society and to creators of film and television product.

It all begins with the structure and function of the human brain. In the science of human perception, one well-established theory concerns the function of an area of memory known as "sensory memory."[1] As information, or stimuli, pours in from each of our five senses, these incoming data stop first in sensory memory.

Incoming information only stays in sensory memory for a half a second in the case of visual input, to around two seconds in the case of auditory input. In that brief time, sensory memory acts as a holding tank or staging area. We selectively filter out the information we do not want and choose the information

> *This country is increasingly mixed racially. And I think movies have yet to catch up to what is actually happening. Whenever I can, I cast against type. You bring in somebody who's black, somebody who's Spanish, somebody who's Asian, and incorporate them into the fabric of the audition just in a natural course of things. Then the director and producer can say, "Hey, that guy's a great actor"; or "That woman's a perfect actor. I hadn't thought of that. Oh, that could work."*
>
> —*Pat Golden*

we do want before any data are allowed to leave sensory memory. As an example, in a crowded, noisy room, this filtering mechanism sifts through the jumble of input that arrives in the sensory memory garage to pick out a single conversation.

All selected information then crosses the bridge to short-term memory, where our filters employ information already contained in long-term storage to engage in the process of "pattern recognition." In other words, in order to instantaneously make sense of incoming data, the mind seeks to match up incoming data with recognizable elements or patterns it has already encountered and processed. Without pattern recognition, we could never process the volume of sensory input we receive on a minute-to-minute basis.

The process of stereotyping is exactly the same. As we move through everyday life, we are constantly bombarded by new information, new stimuli. Just as sensory input is filtered and pattern recognition engaged to determine familiar patterns, so we group information on a larger scale. We use a form of pattern recognition when classifying and grouping all information, including that related to people. We are, in fact, not capable of instantaneous in-depth analysis of every person we encounter. The only way to manage this information is through classifying and grouping by familiar patterns. That's why, for example, the gentleman dressed in black twirling his handlebar moustache is the one we pick as the likely bad guy in a room full of people wearing golf slacks. Although ...

This is obviously a less-than-perfect process, one geared more to the rapid assimilation of data than to the fair and unbiased assessment of every person we see or meet. Is this a necessary process? Absolutely. Without it, we would drown in a mass of unfiltered incoming stimuli, quickly overloading our brains. Does this process result in unfair classifications and so-called "snap judgments?" Absolutely. They are an inevitable, albeit unfortunate side effect of the way we all process information. Because we cannot change the neurons in our brains, nor the way in which pattern recognition works, we must forgive ourselves the "crime" of stereotyping, at least to some degree.

However, this does not relieve us from the responsibility of examining and re-examining the boxes or categories into which we place people. The problem is not really that we assign people instantaneously to a category. The problem is that we often have distorted, unfair, or downright prejudicial information stored in long-term memory about various categories—many times obtained originally from the media.

In other words, it is not the assigning process that is problematic, it's the definition of the categories in the first place. If we assign someone to the category of being Asian or female, that's both fine and necessary. However, if in our minds, we have defined Asians as shifty and women as flighty, then the very act of assigning a new person to one of these categories does them a disservice and attaches to them a negative stigma.

To prevent as many of the negative consequences of stereotyping as possible, we as creators must first realize the potential problems involved in the process itself. We must then understand our unique position, in an effort not to perpetuate or exacerbate these problems.

Although we may not be able to fix things, we are in a unique position to perpetuate and reinforce negative stereotypes or, conversely, to challenge and implode them, so it is something to consider.

In feature films and especially in series television, for example, we use stereotypes continuously. The reasons are fairly simple. First, we are human like everyone else, and we engage in stereotyping on a daily basis, like everyone else. It is not always possible for us, being human, to catch ourselves and correct our definitions before inadvertently building stereotypes into our work.

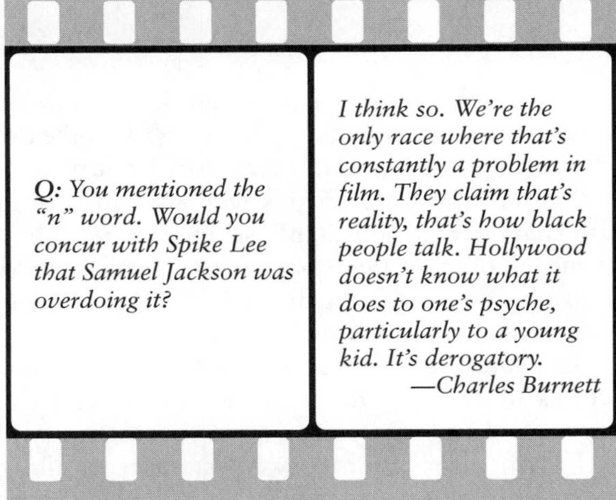

Second, rightly or wrongly, we assume that most people are generally more comfortable if we do not challenge their preconceived ideas. We want them to keep coming back for more, so it often seems the easiest choice to "go with the flow" rather than try to challenge their precepts or attempt to present new ways of defining or thinking. This certainly provokes ethical consideration.

On this point, critics and viewers of Spike Lee's *Do The Right Thing*[2] questioned why the ghetto neighborhoods in the film weren't populated by drug dealers, junkies, pimps, and street people. These critics and viewers were upset that Lee had presented what they believed was a sanitized image of the ghetto—one that did not fit their preconceived notions, or stereotypes, of how a ghetto should appear. Of course, these choices on Lee's part made for provocative discourse on the issue of stereotyping.

Third, we use certain stereotypes because they allow us to save time when introducing a character. Think "shark lawyer" or "dumb blonde." These characters are easy to picture without any further information, aren't they?

In The Killing Fields *it was suggested that if we didn't find a Cambodian man for the role that Haing S. Ngor played we would cast Korean or Hawaiian or Asian. I felt that would be insulting to that community. And since the casting was my responsibility, I felt I should go find the right Cambodian person for that role rather than put someone in it from a different background, especially after all that the Cambodians had been through, the war and everything. It was extremely important to me to do that. I felt very fortunate when we succeeded, though it wasn't in my hands by then.*

—Pat Golden

The simple economics of screen time dictate here. If we can hook into the viewers' pattern recognition process to fill in the details about a type of character from their own long-term memory, we can shorthand the character's introduction into the story. In this way, we can save time, introducing all but the main characters in shorthand, saving that valuable screen time for introducing the more complex (we hope) hero, heroine, or villain and dealing with the major plot points. We let the audience's imagination create detailed characters from the skeletal framework we give them.

Of course, this process is often taken *much* too far, resulting in wooden depictions of dreary, two-dimensional characters. However, the technique has proven tried and true, especially in contemporary film and television.

Fourth, tapping into viewers' stereotypes allows us to create levels of subtext by implication rather than direct inclusion and explanation. Again, we're relying on the viewer to fill in the blanks and use his or her imagination to expand both character traits and plot subtexts so that we don't have to spend time or resources developing these elements.

Fifth, relying on viewers' stereotypes allows those of us who unfortunately might wish to do so to make negative implications about characters without coming out and doing so openly. We may, in fact, not even realize that we're doing this, but it happens. We can cause negative definitions of characters by the groups to which we choose to have them belong. We then let the viewer imagine the worst, and it's unnecessary for us to directly present the worst. This is perhaps the most insidious of our reasons for making use of the stereotyping process.

Considerable public concern has arisen about this type of stereotyping and about issues of media diversity in general. It is commonly accepted in the

I think writers and directors have been shameless in taking the "Vietnam Body Count" mentality to a new low. The message of many of the big budget studio films has been "if it's different and you don't like it, kill it." The bad guys, be they aliens, or fundamentalist Muslims, or South American drug lords, are always presented in simplistic terms, with no redeeming humanity. Our heroes are always wrapped in the flag, mom, and apple pie. It's rare that we see the other side of the conflict with any dimension. And since the enemies tend to be minorities and the heroes white, a subtle, jingoistic racism pervades the movies. It's very easy to kill something that doesn't look, talk, or believe like us.

—Paul Hapenny

realms of social science and the halls of academe (and by this author) that the media has strong social and psychological effects on its audience, so negative stereotyping and lack of diversity is a serious problem to be reckoned with.

Film and television provide many children with their first exposure to people of other ethnicities, religions, and cultures. What they see onscreen can and does impact their attitudes about and treatment of others. In addition, closer to home, it is believed that children who grow up seeing endless negative images of themselves in the media can experience self perception and self esteem problems. "It hurts and has a negative impact when you don't see your own people [onscreen]," says Michael Smith, founder and director of the American Indian Film Institute.[3]

Now, a few sobering facts to set the context: A 1997 study discovered that ethnic minority groups make up 15.7 percent of prime time drama casts, even though these same ethnic minority groups represent 25.4 percent of the population;[4] 26 percent of major film characters are women, although women comprise 51 percent of the population; and people age 65 or older make up 1.9 percent of prime time television characters, although they comprise 12.7 percent of the population.[5]

Jackie Brown was a terrific woman. I loved seeing a movie about a mid-forties woman who really had a big ass. You know? And Tarantino's point is, if I'm trying to make a realistic depiction of this world, I've got to use the language that is used in that world.
—Christine Vachon

Q: Have you encountered pressures to select for or against ethnic stereotypes?

In addition, employment figures released by the Screen Actors Guild (SAG) covering casting for films and prime time television for 1998 showed that the percentage of SAG roles going to Native Americans, Latinos, and African Americans had actually *declined* from the prior year. Of the 56,701 SAG roles in 1998, a total of 10,993 (19 percent) went to members of an ethnic minority. Every ethnic minority (except Asian/Pacific Americans) saw a slight decline in the number of roles, reversing the seven-year trend of slow and steady growth in casting representation. The most underrepresented group relative to population percentage continues to be Latinos, who, although they constitute approximately 10.7 percent of the population, captured only 3.5 percent of the SAG roles available in 1998.[6]

These statistics prompted SAG President Richard Masur to state: "[t]here is clearly room for much improvement in regard to employment.... These performers are simply not receiving the numbers of roles they can and should be playing to accurately reflect American life."[7] To its credit, under Masur, SAG is attempting to heighten awareness by promoting ethnic performers' employment through symposia, and through awards to those who buck the negative trends and lobbying of producers, casting agents, and studio executives.[8]

Activist groups further contend that when people of color, women, seniors, and other social groups *are* portrayed, the images of them are often stereotypical in the worst sense, inaccurate, and not reflective of individual diversity. An American Psychological Association task force agreed that minorities are not only underrepresented on television, but are "segregated in specific types of content, and rarely engage in cross-ethnic interactions."[9]

After it came to light that not one person of color had a starring role in any of the 26 new network shows of the 1999 television season, activist groups—

led by the National Association for the Advancement of Colored People's (NAACP) President Kweisi Mfume—organized and demanded action. As this book goes to print (Winter 2000), Mfume and other minority leaders have reached groundbreaking diversity agreements with ABC and NBC and are closing in on similar pacts with FOX and CBS to bring more people of color into the creative and business sides of the television industry.

The coalition also threatened government intervention. Mfume, a former Maryland congressman, stated during an interview with Connie Chung at the National Association of Television Programming Executives conference in New Orleans: "There is a fine line between dictating content and arguing against perpetuating stereotypes. However ... there is a need now to look at some kind of government regulation that creates ... a content-neutral rule."[10]

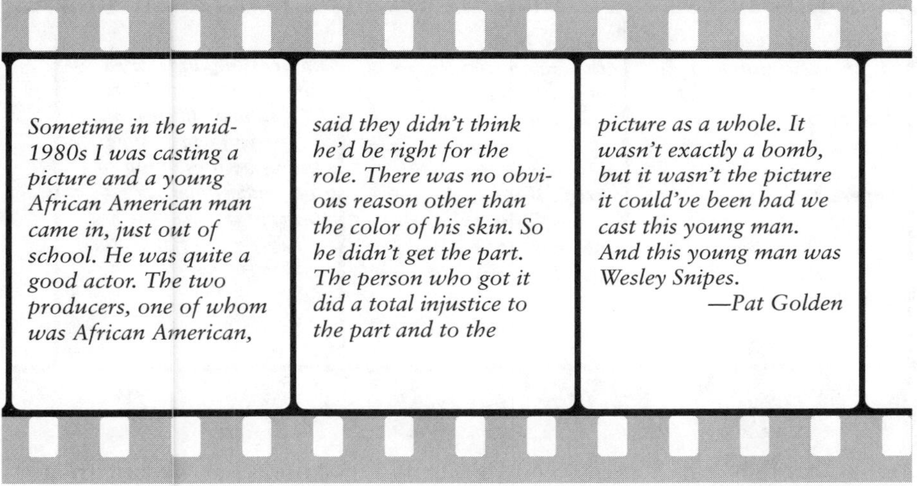

Enter the Stereotypes

The most common stereotypes used in the media, and in society at large, are those of gender, race, age, ethnicity, religion, sexual orientation, and physique. In addition, we have socioeconomic status, political affiliation, occupation, and general personality (i.e., jocks versus nerds), and a myriad of others.

See if these seem familiar ...

As to gender, stereotypes of both sexes persist. For example, men have traditionally either been portrayed as men of action, cold and aloof, or as selfish and dense; women have traditionally either been portrayed as sex objects or as mothers and housewives.

When America came out of the beige haze of the 1950s, the tendency to portray women as sex objects increased, especially as it became more permissible to portray sex and to use innuendo without fear of censure. In addition, other elements emerged, some holdovers of earlier times. Women were portrayed as ditzy, driven by emotion rather than intellect, passive in the face of male aggression, and helpless.

Perhaps partially in response to this last, a new trend has emerged in film and television portrayals. As elucidated by Annette Insdorf in this section's essay, we have recently seen a rise in the image of women with guns, or the "tough chick." Insdorf believes this is largely a negative image, but I might add that it has at least shaken male complacency toward the easily dismissed woman. Perhaps "babes with bullets" portrayals have swung the pendulum too far, but they have forced men to sit up and take notice, as women are now often portrayed as dangerous. Ignore them at your peril!

Movies aren't regarded as an institution to change people's social habits, but in reality they create perceptions of differences. Stereotypes are the only means of understanding the diversity. Most people don't interact in this country, so their perceptions come through the media. In my films they're always asking about the nature of the characters, "I never saw black people have homes like that," and "why aren't they involved in drugs?" Even though 1 percent of the population is involved (in drugs).

—Charles Burnett

If a casting director really wants to, and feels a responsibility—which I do—you can change things by presenting a broader diversity onscreen.

—Pat Golden

Striving to create more three-dimensional characters—based on individuals, not stereotypes—is a staple of good storytelling realistically rendered; it also helps writers guard against perpetuating negative aspects of the stereotyping process.

Minorities of all stripes had been unfairly stereotyped long before noted editor and author Walter Lippmann brought the concept of stereotyping to national consciousness in his work *Public Opinion* in 1922.[11] From slavery days right up until the present time, African Americans have been "typecast," assigned characteristics as a group applied to one and all. These characteristics as depicted on film have generally been either demeaning (i.e., lazy and obsequious), designed to cause fear in the mostly white populace (i.e., violent and sexually aggressive), or patronizing (i.e., good athletes and having good rhythm).

Unfortunately, we as creators have enforced and perpetuated all of these portrayals.

It is generally believed that we have made progress in reducing and eliminating racial stereotypes from our media portrayals. Certainly, some persist, but gradually, many of the worst instances are being removed from our product. However, there are those who believe we are still as racist an industry (and as racist a society) as we ever were, and that the stereotypes and prejudice, although perhaps subtler, remain.

African Americans are not the only race that is unfairly stereotyped, of course. Native Americans have faired almost as badly, being characterized first as savages who wantonly raped and killed whites, then as drunks who lie around the reservation all day looking for handouts. This is slowly beginning to change.

Hispanics, whether they are Chicanos, Puerto Ricans, Dominicans, or Spaniards, are often grouped together and stereotyped as lazy, violent, and dull-witted, or, in the alternative, as Latin lovers and sex bombs. According to their portrayals, they often use drugs, detail cars, and hang fuzzy dice from their car mirrors. The list of racial stereotypes is long and *extremely* undistinguished.

There are very nearly as many stereotypes in the area of ethnicity as there are nations in the world. Many of us grew up to portrayals of the dangerous, untrustworthy Soviet or the supremely evil Nazi. Both made great movie villains.

More recently, the generic "Arab" has become the movie villain of choice. In our portrayals, many of us have put all Arabs in the same group, despite the fact that, as with Native Americans, there are a multitude of separate and distinct cultures that fall under the moniker of Arab. This group is shown as bloodthirsty fanatics, willing to indiscriminately kill innocent men, women, and even children to further obscure causes advocated by strange, bearded old men.

Fortunately, the film community has begun, albeit slowly, to become more sensitized to issues surrounding these and other racial stereotypes. Many have dealt with this problem by attempting to create more three-dimensional characters—that include villains as well as leading and supporting characters. For example, *The Siege*[12] with Denzel Washington and Annette Bening featured an Arab terrorist cell (the "bad guys") as well as an Arab American FBI agent who worked closely with the hero (the "good guy"). This provided the audience with a more balanced ethnic portrayal than usual—one man villainous, the other completely upstanding.

Among the most important factors at work here is that of pure cinema commerce. Since the fall of the Soviet Union, we have a vacuum of good movie villains. Nazis are old hat, have been done to death, and date one's product. Also, Germany is currently one of the single largest buyers of

American movie product in the world, and it restricts the efficacy of using Nazis as villains.

The Soviets also made great villains, as they represented a powerful enemy of the United States that it was both universally approved of and fun to hate. Now, we supposedly face no such monolithic threat.

In the absence of a solid "villain culture," we've had to invent one. In fact, we seem to have had to keep fastening on the "villain of the month" to fill the vacuum left by the demise of our über-villains. Our biggest success in this enterprise, aside from the array of colorful aliens from outer space? We have taken our most likely foes—terrorists—and irrevocably linked their activities to the Arab nations of the world. Terrorists in turbans, or the metaphorical equivalent, have become the targets of our scorn, as well as the targets of our heroes. We have endowed them with complete, insane fanaticism. We have also given them, again strictly for our purposes (we hope), unlimited destructive resources and the willingness to use them on the innocents of the world. They may never replace Nazis as the villains *everyone* loves to hate, but with all of these attributes, they fill the villain void reasonably well.

Obviously, members of a number of other cultures are used as villains, or are stereotyped in various ways. This should merely serve as an illustration of the ways in which a culture can be stigmatized, and the reasons, both psychological and commercial, why this occurs.

Religion also offers myriad stereotypes. Catholics are often portrayed as hypocritical, tortured, or woefully out of step with contemporary reality. Those of the Jewish faith are often shown as bookworm-ish, materialistic, and driven by the need to succeed. Evangelical Christians are perceived as wild-eyed, nonthinking proselytizers, or as involved in the crooked dealings of many of the television preachers. The list goes on. Again, it is undistinguished in the extreme.

Age is another area in which stereotypes play a significant role. Young people are portrayed as impetuous and foolish. Older people are portrayed either as feeble, senile, childish, and weak, or as crotchety, pedantic, and cruel. According to Pat Golden, television and film are dominated by the nubile and the beautiful:

> Casting agents are often pressured to cast younger women. Women are unfortunately 'used' up to a certain point at around age 30, maybe 35. If I thought about it I could name 100 women who were used when they were young and perky and then just discarded. Why don't we see more today of Meryl Streep? She's brilliant.[13]

Sexual orientation and gender identity is another area where stereotypes virtually dominate group identification. The effeminate, screeching gay man; the butch, ugly gay woman; and all the other aspects of look and behavior we use to portray these people in films and television help to create a picture of gay culture that much of the world believes.

One would think that, with all the human anatomical variation in the world, it would be difficult to make stereotypes of physique stick. However, this is one of our most stigmatized areas. We can begin with the old adage "blondes have more fun." That creates quite a powerful picture, and has, ever since it became part of the common lexicon.

A great deal more hurtful in the long run, we have portrayed, and the public has come to believe, that overweight people are lazy, slovenly, and not ambitious. Short people are somehow inferior. People who wear glasses are nerds. Unattractive people are, well ... unattractive. Again, the list of physical traits that have been stigmatized, at least partly in response to our portrayals, is long and undistinguished. General personality fits here as well. The jock versus nerd dichotomy is an example of two very distinct stereotypes loaded with pictures, and usually set in opposition to each other.

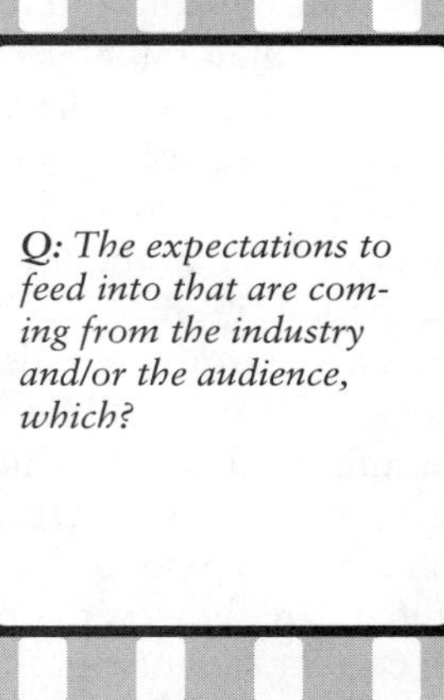

Q: The expectations to feed into that are coming from the industry and/or the audience, which?

From the audience. The industry has this notion that reality is what they created, which is black exploitation films. If you don't want to continue that, and you have ordinary dialogue—which they can't perceive as being real because they're so used to the "n" word being used. They can't believe that people can talk normally. So we present a script with a universal theme and characters who have the same problems as everyone else, but they can't see black people being directed as drama. So it's a continual uphill battle. It's a problem that dates back to the beginning of film, since black faces in vaudeville and D.W. Griffith, and it continues now. There's been a rewriting of history, of the Civil War: Gone With the Wind.

—Charles Burnett

Political affiliation is also rife with stigma. If you close your eyes and imagine a Republican or a Democrat, chances are, if you're like much of the American population, you'll see a very clear picture, not of a specific person necessarily, but of a type with certain attributes. Because we know all people, even politicians, are different, where do these easy pictures come from? Pattern recognition. Stereotypes.

Occupations are also often stigmatized. Blue-collar workers are unintelligent. White-collar workers are often criminals. Journalists are unprincipled sleuths who will stop at nothing to get a story and have no interest in ethics that might slow them down. Again, the list of pictures created by mention of an occupation is just about as long as the list of occupations itself.

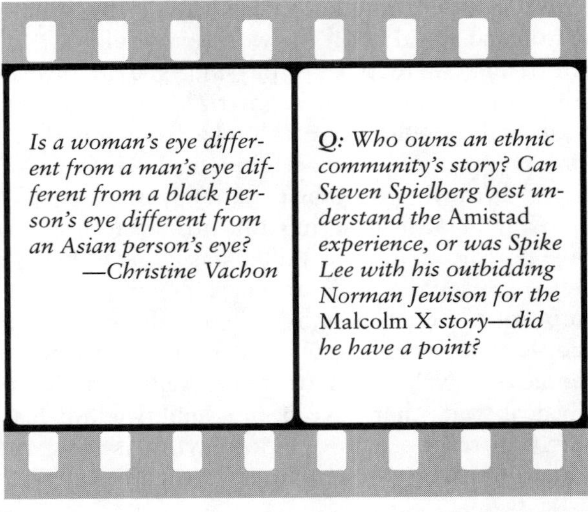

Is a woman's eye different from a man's eye different from a black person's eye different from an Asian person's eye?
—Christine Vachon

Q: Who owns an ethnic community's story? Can Steven Spielberg best understand the Amistad *experience, or was Spike Lee with his outbidding Norman Jewison for the* Malcolm X *story—did he have a point?*

There are obviously many other areas of human life and behavior in which stereotypes play a definitional role. The ones highlighted here, however, form the core of stereotypes that we as creators rely on in turning out our product.

So, what's a filmmaker to do? Be inventive. Be thoughtful. Be imaginative. Be careful. When using the READR method to analyze a project, be certain in Step 2 ("Enumerate component parts"), to list all character and casting concerns and issues, not just those affecting the leads. Examine each leading character, each secondary character, and as many of the subsidiary characters as time allows. Check to see whether you are intentionally using particular characters to communicate negative stereotypical information. If so, is this information necessary to your story? If yes, ask yourself how to make this character more three-dimensional to offset any stereotyping.

Try alternative casting ideas for various roles. Don't be afraid to reach a little. As an example, a young writer brought me a terrific horror action–comedy entitled *Dark Knights*.[14] As we worked through the editing process, we conceived the idea of changing one of the principal characters from a man to a woman. This change was primarily motivated at the time by a wish to create increased variation among the lead characters. What we did not expect was that this simple change altered the entire complexion of the story and added levels that had never even been considered originally.

Now, in the case of the reader or filmmaker, try replicating this casting coup intentionally. Can certain characters be played as members of certain ethnic groups? Can certain of the men be changed to women? Can certain of the younger characters be played older?

In general, filmmakers concerned with using stereotypes should use them only when they have made a choice to do so based on the requirements of character and the unfolding of the story, not simply because they are handy. As we have discussed, negative stereotypes are too powerful be used lightly or unknowingly in film and television.

Filmmaking in Hollywood is not about story. It's about dealmaking, and when the elements come together. If Spielberg makes the film, more people will see it. It's a subject that needs to be told. It needs to be out there. The problem is not so much Steven Spielberg or anyone else, but rather equity and fairness. Can a black person do that story? And the answer is that it would be hard for them (to get a green light). So it shouldn't be reduced to, "He can't do it because he's black or she can't do it because she's white." The issue is rather, "Can anyone have an opportunity to do it?"

—*Charles Burnett*

Exercise in Stereotyping: Tracking Through the Process

We've discussed the fact that stereotyping of information is a natural human process. Yet how does overt stereotyping end up on film and television screens? How does the stereotyping of people get carried through the major departments of a film, being molded and shaped by each department? As a hypothetical exercise, the following section will trace a rather extreme example of exactly that process.

Let's assume we have our rogue cop scenario, presented in the previous section's "Exercise in Violence." It is a character-driven screenplay about a "rogue" cop (our hero) tracking a bad guy (our villain) in order to get him before he can murder his next victim in a serial murder spree. It's all about tension and intrigue, with very little action but a great deal of suspense.

1. The writer has come up with a characterization of our villain. He has chosen a white male yuppie as the villain. Because the villain is actually a brutal killer, the writer has chosen a signature weapon for him that he believes emphasizes the savagery of his personality. The weapon is a large hunting knife with a nasty serrated edge. He also carries a .25 caliber pistol as a backup. In the screenplay of course, the writer has chosen several spots for the villain to use the knife, including to stab an innocent victim in Central Park, just to show how ruthless and cold-blooded he is; a successful escape from the hero on foot in an alleyway with several shots fired; and a final shoot-out with the hero, in which our villain is injured and arrested.

2. A producer now options this script. The producer works with the writer to hone the story and the character. She's also thinking about casting and marketing. She decides she needs a more interesting villain, a worthy adversary for her hero, to make the film attractive to a studio or financier. Although using a nonstereotypical villain has merit as being original, she decides that it's harder to engender the all-out audience hatred that a tried and true (read stereotyped) villain can provide. She needs to make sure the film will have maximum marketability in overseas territories, so she wants a stereotype with proven market value overseas. She also decides more violence is necessary. She believes she needs a "bigger" picture, painted on a "bigger" canvas.

   Now, the producer and the studio executives or financiers ask for a rewrite of the screenplay from the writer, including the improved, more recognizable, villain. He chooses an Italian Mafia hit man as the paradigm for the new villain. The producer and the studio executives or financiers also ask for and get a female sidekick for the villain. She can both cause mayhem on her own and give the villain a dramatic foil. She, too, has a signature weapon—a knot-studded garrote. She's the controlling force in the villain's gang; he, the villain, is the lone criminal genius who might not even be able to raise a gang if it weren't for her.

   The studio executives or financiers have become worried about the casting of the villain, and feel he must be given "more character." They feel that the Italian Mafia hit man, although a serviceable character, is somehow not exotic enough for the film. They want a villain the audience will love to hate. They demand that the script be changed, again. The villain must become a different, yet still recognizable bad guy, like other bad guys the audience has already learned to hate.

   In addition, the villain's sidekick must become as beautiful as she is lethal, injecting both sex and sex appeal into the project. She should be noticeably younger than the villain. This will heighten his mystique. Also, there need to be several sexual exchanges between the two. Although the audience will never see the villain without clothing—he will always wear at least a T-shirt and undress in shadowy darkness—there will likely be a few strategic shots of the sidekick nude. She will be cast accordingly.

   Further, they demand that the final shoot-out be changed. As he makes his escape, the villain will stab a homeless man, just to reinforce that he's a danger to society, with ice water running through his veins. The villain will be given a veritable arsenal, so there is a fierce firefight. In addition, the villain cannot be injured and captured without demystifying him. Rather, he and his sexy sidekick must be killed outright in a hale of bullets, à la *Bonnie & Clyde*.[15]

   The writer chooses to have the villain be a Russian Mafia gangster to add a specific personality. This allows him to be brutal, unprincipled, and hateful. Now, although it's true that this is again a stereotype, the stereotype seems relatively benign because it focuses more on the "gangster" element than the villain's national origin.

3. A director is hired. She, too, must have her hand in the creation of this gradually changing picture. She brings in a new writer just to "polish" the screenplay for production.

   The villain is thought to still be too generic. Yes, being Russian Mafia allows for certain differences from, say, Italian Mafia, but there's not as much to play with as the producer wants. So he's changed to an Arab of unknown national origin. The studio executives or financiers and the producer reason that Arabs are the villains America currently loves to hate—they seem to be causing much of the trouble in the world, and they do things that are unequivocally despicable. Perfect villain material. Here is where the negative stereotypes of Arabs come into play. These stereotypes are being consciously manipulated by those involved to make the movie more successful.

   Once our Arab is in place, the stakes of the entire picture are raised. The villain, maniacal and cruel, is no longer a serial killer. Now, he becomes an international terrorist, seeking to plant a chemical bomb that will poison much of the eastern seaboard and paralyze the government. He is rabidly anti-U.S. This is made worse because his brother was killed in our raids on the terrorist bases in the Sudan. Now, the hero must stop the villain to "save the world." Finally, the producer has her larger canvas.

   During the first shoot-out, our villain takes a woman hostage to use as his human shield. He holds her prisoner in an old warehouse and tortures her. This choice is not to be made at random, of course. The hostage must be young, helpless, and terrified, as well as gorgeous and probably rather underdressed.

4. The director casts a somewhat swarthy, mean-looking type, likely without much concern for his native acting ability. He is cast as someone rather slight of build, intense, and slightly loony, but with a confidence and authority to him that allow us to believe he is a real threat. What's important is that we believe he can command his gang, with his moll's help, and that he is unspeakably cold-blooded. The villain will also be referred to as a westernized Arab, which provides the major benefit of making casting easier, as the "whiter" and more westernized the villain is, the greater the chance of casting a "name" actor. The moll is cast in the James Bond/Faamke Janssen mold—smart, sexy, loony, and absolutely lethal.

   The idea of the stereotype has been used to perfection. The audience will fill in all the negative details of the Arab bad guy from their collective memories and perceptions as they watch the movie. By the end, they'll cheer when he and his moll are destroyed, hopefully by violent means.

The executives, the producer, and the director are thrilled. They have a large-scale good versus evil picture, with very high stakes and clearly defined good guys and bad guys. The original writer would not recognize his script, but this doesn't matter, as it's not shown to him in any case.

5. Designers are brought on board. The production designer suggests that everything connected with our villain be shown as murky and dark, with as much Middle Eastern mystery as possible. He adds a few authentic touches of Arab culture to help this illusion along.

6. The director of photography now decides how to photograph the villain to create maximum villain-ness. He decides on a primarily low angle approach, making him look as imposing and dangerous as possible. Of course, when people view this image, they'll then see the now technically enhanced stereotypical image of an Arab villain. This will heighten the stereotype in their long-term memories.

   Also, the lighting of the villain is discussed. Because he's an Arab, a dirty, somewhat mysterious, yet vaguely unfocused approach is decided upon. Again, this picture, as emphasized by the lighting, will become part of the viewer's memory image.

7. The wardrobe and makeup departments struggle with how to make the villain and his moll look more dangerous, threatening, and evil than the average human being could ever be. The girl must look overtly sexy at all times, preferably with ample cleavage showing; short, tight skirts; and stiletto heels, even when running. They decide to emphasize the "foreignness" of the villain by changing him from his western jeans and polo shirt to a caftan and turban. They also decide to use makeup to make him appear swarthier than the actor playing the role does in real life. Finally, for good measure, they add a large, enigmatic scar on his face, giving him an almost piratical quality. The very clear message is that a villain that looks like this is capable of the most heinous crimes.

8. A dialect coach is brought in to teach the villain certain choice Arabic idioms to add realism. He will mouth sexual comments in English but epithets in the character's supposed native language.

   Overall, each department is presenting the director with ideas as to how to make the villain's character more foreign, more evil, playing on the fact that American audiences will define him as evil and despicable the moment they see him. This will give the movie more impact.

   The picture is released to great fanfare and makes a quarter of a billion dollars overseas, about three-quarters of that in the domestic markets, and lives forever on video.

Everyone is happy, except perhaps anyone of any sort of Arab nationality. In addition, society as a whole is made poorer by the reliance on the cheap parlor tricks of stereotyping in the service of film commerce.

Ethical Gymnastics

1. Name some of the "groups" of which you are a part (i.e., are you a man or a woman, an Italian American or an Asian American, a jock or a geek?), then identify how these segments are generally stereotyped in the media. Are any of these stereotypes true? Discuss.

2. The film *Revenge of the Nerds*[16] and its sequels are comic films entirely based on the idea of stereotypes. Discuss the ways in which these films reinforce, challenge, or break the nerd stereotype.

3. What role, if any, did stereotyping play in Spike Lee's film *Jungle Fever*?[17] How did the film deal with the concept of stereotyping, if at all?

4. Discuss Demi Moore's film *G.I. Jane*[18] in light of what you have read in this section.

5. Choose a secondary character from the *Simpsons*[19] and discuss how this character reinforces or breaks a stereotype. Examples might be: Apu (the Indian Convenience Store Owner), Barney (the Drunk), Reverend Lovejoy (the Faithless Preacher), or Grandpa (the Senior Citizen).

6. You're about to create your first film as a director, a producer, or a writer. You must make a choice between the lead character being a white male, a black male, or a Hispanic female. As you begin to think about what would have to be changed to make the character and the story work in each case, track and examine the stereotypes that surface as you rethink the project.

7. You're making an action film. The villain is a foreigner. Discuss some ways in which to minimize negative stereotyping of that nationality (e.g., Arabs in *Operation Condor*[20] or *Executive Decision*[21]).

8. In the police drama presented in this section, what if the hero were changed to an African American? Discuss ways in which stereotyping could be avoided.

9. Choose and discuss three examples of lead characters in film or entertainment television that successfully avoid the pitfalls of stereotyping.

10. Create an original character for a hypothetical film or television project by choosing a stereotype and adding or subtracting qualities or characteristics to arrive at a successful, nonstereotypical character.

Notes

1 Wade, Carole and Tavris, Carol. *Psychology* (New York: Harper Collins College Publishers, 1993), pp. 244–247.

2 1989 D: Spike Lee, 40 Acres & A Mule Filmworks.

3 Carbone, Stephanie. *Picture This, Diversity in Film and Television* (unpublished), Mediascope interview, July 9, 1997.

4 "Gerbner Tackles 'Fairness,'" *Electronic Media*, February 24, 1997.

5 Gerbner, G. and Ozyegin, N. *Proportional Representation of Diversity Index*, Cultural Indicators Project, Spring 1997.

6 *Screen Actors Guild Press Release*, May 3, 1999: www.sag.org/pressreleases/pr-la990503.html.

7 *Screen Actors Guild Press Release*, 1999.

8 *Screen Actors Guild Press Release*, 1999.

9 Graves, S.B. "Television, the Portrayal of African Americans, and the Development of Children's Attitudes," in Berry and Asamen, *Children & Television: Images In a Changing Sociocultural World* (Newbury Park, Calif.: Sage Publications, 1993).

10 Lorenz, Larry. "NAACP Vigilant to Minorities," *Extra Extra, the NATPE 2000 Newsletter*, January 27, 2000, p. 8.

11 Lippmann, Walter. *Public Opinion* (New York: Macmillan, 1922), pp. 88–89.

12 1998 D: Edward Zwick, 20th Century Fox.

13 Interview with Laura Blum, Spring 1998.

14 1999, written by David Giannovario.

15 1967 D: Arthur Penn, Warner Bros.

16 *Revenge of the Nerds*, 1984 D: Jeff Kanew, 20th Century Fox; *Revenge of the Nerds II: Nerds in Paradise*, 1987 D: Roland Mesa, 20th Century Fox; *Revenge of the Nerds III: The Next Generation*, 1992 D: Joe Roth, 20th Century Fox Television; *Revenge of the Nerds IV!: Nerds in Love*, 1994 D: Steve Zacharias, 20th Century Fox Television.

17 1991 D: Spike Lee, Universal Pictures.

18 1997 D: Ridley Scott, Buena Vista Pictures.

19 1989–present, 20th Century Fox Television.

20 1997 D: Frankie and Jackie Chan, Dimension (Miramax).

21 1996 D: Stuart Baird, Warner Bros.

The Props: Portrayals of Substance Use

We're Not in Kansas Anymore

You're directing your first feature and you want to establish your lead character as a sophisticated lover. So you place him in a chic Manhattan nightclub and watch him sip single malt scotch and light a cigarette—detached, elegant, cool. He inhales deeply, and smiles ... and wouldn't you know it, he attracts the sexiest, most beautiful woman in the room. She takes a drag on his cigarette, and they leave together.

Substances. Interesting problem, aren't they? Also, tried and true grist for the dramatic mill. Is that all they are? Should substance abuse issues really be of concern to the creators of film and television? Many would answer emphatically "yes."

In fact, a certain amount of blame for dramatic increases in substance abuse has, in recent years, been laid at our doorstep. Many media advocates, social scientists, and government leaders believe that our portrayals of smoking, drinking, and drug use contribute to making these problems worse. At play here is the age-old conundrum, "Does art mirror life, or do artists in fact have a hand in creating the reality in which we all live?" It is far-fetched, bordering on the absurd, to believe that all society's ills are the fault of the media, but, that said, it does appear from the research (not to mention common sense) that we bear responsibility for exacerbating certain of them.

The media influences perceptions about many high-risk behaviors. Also affected are people's attitudes, which they learn from onscreen characters. These attitudes include disrespect for authority, family, and religion; our current view that it is "everyone for themselves"; and the materialistic belief that money is always the answer, no matter what the question.

The fact is that, as creators, we sometimes *reflect* reality in our work, and at other times we *create* our own reality. That's the nature of what we do. In the real world, people do smoke, drink, and use drugs. We cannot and should not be blind to this fact. However, we have it in our power to make the ethical choice not to *encourage* the worst of these behaviors by glamorizing them in our characterizations. In the real world, there are generally consequences to actions: unprotected sex can lead to pregnancy or venereal disease, playing with guns can lead to murder, taking drugs can lead to addiction.

A real problem surfaces when our work begins to influence an audience that is not yet capable of dealing with the material we present on an adult level—the young. Many teens, for example, think they are indestructible and immortal, as many of us did at their age. If our stories show them that someone of extraordinary character can survive being a drug addict or an alcoholic and still get that academic scholarship to Yale and go on to lead a wonderful life, many in this audience will feel that they, too, can play this game and win. This is where major ethical issues come into play.

The flaws in the logic are obvious. Stars are paid too much to put them in any danger! Seriously, though, we control the circumstances, and we rarely cross the line and put danger into our hero's path that he cannot ultimately overcome according to the logic of the story. Not so in the real world.

But we are in the business of entertaining, and this is just a movie, you may sigh. A central contention of this book is that it is never "just a movie" or just entertainment. There is virtually *always* more taken from a film or television show than just simply entertainment. Les Brown accurately captures this relationship between film and audience: "Movies are not just seen. They tend to be experienced because they engage so much of our senses; and the films we enjoy most become vicarious life experiences that remain in our memory banks as vividly as some actual happenings."

The following paragraphs will discuss substance use and abuse as an example of high-risk behaviors, as well as certain of the filmmaker's choices when creating characters who engage in them.

A filmmaker's portrayal of substance use and abuse is a complex and controversial issue. A series of studies conducted by researchers at Stanford University and Lewis and Clark College determined that substances—particularly alcohol and tobacco—are ubiquitous in contemporary films popular among teens.[1] Virtually no movies were substance free, the study revealed. Substances are just "there," used in the foreground and background, appearing as an integral part of the fabric of life. Alcohol and tobacco were pervasive, and illicit drugs appeared in approximately one-third of dramas, almost twice as often as in action adventures or comedies; alcohol and tobacco permeated comedies, action adventures, and dramas almost equally. Although substances of any kind were more likely to be used in movies rated PG-13 and R than those rated G or PG, the difference was not significant. A comparison reveals that substance use is substantially less likely to be portrayed in television series than in movies.[2]

To structure a rational discussion of portrayals of substance use and abuse, we must first determine what it is we are talking about. For purposes of discussion here, the "substances" we will examine are tobacco/nicotine (primarily cigarettes, but also cigars, pipes, and smokeless tobacco); alcohol (all normally imbibable types, excluding such exotic variations as Sterno); marijuana; and so-called "hard" drugs.

Tobacco/Nicotine

First, a few facts. Each year, cigarettes kill more than 400,000 Americans, more than AIDS, alcohol, car accidents, murders, illegal drugs, suicides, and fires COMBINED.[3] Every day, 3,000 children and teens become regular smokers.[4] Lastly, the average smoker loses 15 years of life.[5] These are rather startling statistics.

Medical science is no longer confused as to the long-term effects of cigarette smoking. It's not as it was in the 1950s, when doctors were shilling for cigarettes on television. The protests of big tobacco companies notwithstanding, medical science has firmly established that cigarettes KILL people. Smoking also contributes to a raft of ailments and illnesses that, in turn, KILL people.

With this information at our disposal, the logical societal approach, given a perfect world, would be for all smokers to quit and for the big tobacco companies to start making hats. Of course, there are a number of problems with this rather idyllic (and comical) notion.

Cigarettes are both physically and mentally addictive, and quitting is extremely difficult, again despite the manufacturers' protests. Second, big tobacco is not particularly interested in national health, but rather in international profits. Children and teens alone represent a $1 *billion* market for the tobacco industry[6] that they will not easily give up.

In response, the Canadian government took what many consider to be a major step toward combating the spread of smoking. As of January 2000, a law was passed in Canada requiring cigarette companies to plaster at least 50 percent of the surface area of each cigarette pack with pictures of diseased human organs damaged by smoking, or with statistics showing death rates from smoking. Thus far, no such measures are proposed in the United States, but *if* this plan is demonstrably successful in the north, it may just be a matter of time.

Now, even though we know about the ills of smoking, cigarettes are legal for adults and people are passionate about smoking. Many believe they should be allowed to light up in peace if they so choose.

So what does this have to with my housekeeping deal at Paramount, I hear you grumble. Well, the image-glamorizing picture of the cigarette, pipe, and cigar has become deeply ingrained in the national psyche, as well as that of many nations around the globe, primarily through film and television portrayals.

This is where we come in.

The issue that we face as creators is whether we're inadvertently making smoking more attractive by glamorizing it, especially among younger, more impressionable viewers. Historically, cigarette smoking has been portrayed as the very height of sophistication. Is there a sexier, more glamorous, more alluring image than that of Lauren Bacall or Bette Davis with a cigarette perched between their lips?

In the days of black and white movies, cigarettes were an extremely versatile symbol. In detective stories and Westerns, for example, they were a key sign of male virility. The detectives smoked, the cowboys smoked. It was absolutely expected, a badge and privilege of manhood. In comedies and dramas, cigarettes were used to show sophistication and worldliness—after all, where would Fred Astaire and Ginger Rogers have been without their dancing shoes, tails, evening gown, and, yes, their cigarettes, appropriately kept in a silver case? In romances, they were used in a staggeringly inventive array of ways. Smoking was everything from a surrogate for sex, since sex could not yet be shown, to an indicator that sex had just occurred (with each partner lighting up after finishing the business at hand). Smoking was also an aphrodisiac, suggesting future sex. Generally, cigarettes were a sign of mystery and intrigue, or of robust character or behavior.

The negative consequences of smoking were not shown, as medicine had not yet established any link, and cigarettes were too valuable a cinematic tool and too big a business to risk negative implications. In fact, this remained true long after the danger of cigarettes became known, and still exists today to a lesser degree.

A study released by the Office of National Drug Control Policy in January 2000 found that tobacco appeared in one of five television episodes (19 percent) in 1998–1999. To the industry's credit, no characters under the age of 18 were shown smoking. Only eight percent of major adult characters were shown using tobacco. In addition, 23 percent of all episodes showing tobacco use portrayed negative statements or sentiments about smoking.[7] Although this is not a perfect score, it does represent a reinforcement of a positive ethical choice on the part of the television producers and networks.

Given our knowledge of the dangers of smoking, how is it that portrayals continue to creep into our entertainment programming?

One reason is that, for a number of years, producers were paid to put cigarettes into their films through a process called "product placement."

First, the practice of product placement has been around for some time. Through it, a company provides either cash or free products or both in exchange for these products appearing onscreen in a motion picture or television program. This can be a perfectly reputable process and a lifesaver for many a producer.

A little history is in order here. The most famous example of product placement[8] undoubtedly occurs in Steven Spielberg's *ET, The Extra*

Terrestrial.[9] When ET is coaxed out of hiding with a trail of Reese's Pieces, it is both a charming and a profitable moment. The sales of Reese's Pieces soared 65 percent[10] in the weeks following release of the film. The modern era of product placement in films was born.

As an example of the actual process, when we wanted to create a realistic barroom set for *The Money Kings*,[11] product placement was the only way to make it work. Think about it. You want to show a fully stocked and operational bar. Yet, you're not allowed by law to use identifiable products without permission. Not only that, you need many varieties of liquor and many bottles. To stay on budget, we used a time-honored way around this dilemma by enlisting the aid of liquor manufacturers, getting them to provide permission and supply product to fill our shelves, in exchange for featuring their products in a prominent place. This proved beneficial for the companies' marketing, for the producer's bottom line, and for the realistic feel of the film.

However, placement of cigarettes is another matter. Long before *ET*, cigarettes were being "placed" in films, and were routinely given to studio and network executives and producers for use in entertainment programming. The impact of this rather daring, yet brazen hidden advertising was to help create a nation of James Dean wannabes with cigarettes dangling from their lips.

Tobacco giant Philip Morris, for example, provided cigarettes to star Margot Kidder when she portrayed the chain-smoking Lois Lane in *Superman*.[12] Then, in *Superman II*, Philip Morris products appeared again, this time also in the form of billboards and truck logos seen in the background of the film. It has been reported that this form of placement cost Philip Morris $42,000.[13] As time went on and companies began to realize the value of placement, the dollars increased. The same Philip Morris, in 1988, reportedly paid producers $350,000, the highest dollar figure for a placement until that time, to buy placement for Lark cigarettes in *License To Kill*, the then newest installment in the mega-popular James Bond series.[14]

This Lark placement was the straw that broke the camel's back. Once the dollar amount involved became known, certain members of Congress began to take notice.[15] One reason is that in 1971, a law was passed in the United States banning cigarette advertising on television. However, billboard ads and truck logos, not to mention the presence of cigarettes in the hands of glamorous stars in movies that would eventually end up on television, clearly had the result, intended or no, of circumventing this law.[16] As a result of the controversy this stirred, the tobacco companies, in 1990, "voluntarily" agreed to cease the practice of paying producers to display cigarettes in feature films.[17]

Now, there are many critics of the tobacco and the film industries who do not believe that cigarette placement is a thing of the past. They contend that it still goes on in a behind-the-scenes, under-the-table manner. This is a charge that the tobacco industry denies.[18] In a *CBS Sixty Minutes* report[19] producer Rome Hartman searched for and was unable to uncover any contemporary evidence that the tobacco companies were placing cigarettes. Now, the federal government has joined the watch. The Federal Trade Commission began monitoring tobacco product placement in 1990 by examining annual budget reports submitted by the nation's six major tobacco companies. Since that time, none of these companies claims to spend any money on product placement.

Suffice it to say that whatever the reality is here, we must think for ourselves. Placing tobacco products in the hands and mouths of stars presents special ethical concerns that filmmakers should consider very carefully.

There are, of course, other less ominous reasons for the persistence of smoking portrayals. Filmmakers like them. Writers like cigarettes because they *are* such versatile symbols. As such, they are useful tools. Directors like them because, if used correctly, cigarettes can function as very nearly an additional dramatis personae, a tangible presence, a character in many scenes. Actors often gravitate toward their use because smoking gives them something dramatic, yet unobtrusive, to do with their hands. Cigarettes make great props, to be waved and gesticulated with for dramatic emphasis. Also, smoking draws attention to an actor's face and lips (the reason they often may *not* admit).

Directors of photography and cinematographers, gaffers, and designers of all stripes, in turn, can make use of the texture the smoke from cigarettes gives them in the visual creation of a scene.

Finally, the audience has come to consider smoking portrayals second nature, and has come to like both the validation of their own behavior, if smokers, and the sophisticated image they can transfer to themselves. Nonsmokers should arguably not respond well to smoking in the media but they do seem to accept its presence.

Only relatively recently have we begun to show certain of the more sinister aspects of this glamorous symbol, such as the portrayal of Dr. Mark Green's emphysemic father on *ER*,[20] who hacked away painfully whenever onscreen, generally with a cigarette hanging from his mouth. A few creators are finally bypassing image in some attempt, however halting, to portray the results of this behavior.

To consider smoking portrayals from an ethical perspective, we must consider who smokes in our portrayals; why, what, and how much they smoke; and whether there are any positive rewards or negative consequences attached to their smoking.

Who smokes is of vital importance, because the more admirable, sexy, or sympathetic the character, the more positive the viewer will feel about smoking. For a likable role model, such as say Winona Ryder or Julia Roberts,[21] to smoke is a potent endorsement of the habit, particularly if no negative statements or consequences accompany the portrayal.

The reason for the character's smoking is tied in here. If the character smokes because she enjoys it, *that's* an endorsement, whereas, if she lights up to please friends, or in an attempt to "look cool," the viewer may see this as a negative statement.

What is smoked also matters. Many viewers might see pipes as a pretentious holdover from a bygone era. As an alternative, smokeless tobacco has not caught on in films and television like its cloud-spawning cousin, except in Westerns and movies about baseball, where it's generally portrayed as a vaguely disgusting habit worthy of spoofing by the Zucker brothers.

Cigars are a somewhat different story. Cigars have become more of an issue, as their popularity skyrocketed in the 1990s. Once the province of rich, old, white men, cigars have now penetrated much further into the population. This change seems to have been largely spawned from the entertainment industry itself. Many attribute the sudden rise in the popularity of cigars in large part to *Cigar Aficionado*[22] magazine, and more specifically, to its first cover photo of Arnold Schwarzenegger, then the biggest film star on the planet, smoking a stogie. Since that time, the magazine has featured many prominent celebrities. Because they enjoy cigars, it's considered hip, by implication, for the reader to do so as well.

Many cigar smokers believe that because they don't really inhale, per se, and they generally don't smoke more than one or two cigars per sitting, they are safe indulging in their habit. However, cigar smokers have higher death rates from chronic obstructive pulmonary disease and are four to 10 times more likely to die from laryngeal, oral, and esophageal cancers than are nonsmokers.[23] What's more, secondhand smoke from cigars poses the *same* hazard as secondhand cigarette smoke.[24]

For a period of time, the Hollywood establishment was lighting up in ever-greater numbers. The trend among the "young Turk" agents, managers, actors, and studio executives was to sip expensive wine and smoke large cigars (often the elusive and still illegal Cubans) at swanky, elegant private clubs. Fewer and fewer of these people smoke cigarettes.

In the past, cigar-smoking portrayals were often accompanied by an "annoyance factor." You know, the large, balding, badly dressed man with a smug look on his face enjoying his cigar as those around him move away, grumbling about "green smoke."

Nowadays, the cigar has achieved an almost cult-like status. In *Independence Day*,[25] the entire final mission Will Smith and Jeff Goldblum embark upon to save humanity is almost halted because Smith has forgotten his cigars! Lighting up becomes a ritual when Smith and Goldblum think they're about to die later in the film.

The First Wives Club[26] poster featured the three female leads confidently brandishing cigars. The stogies signified the independence of the women, a sign of feminism and liberation from their husbands. Strangely, though, cigars were barely seen in the movie. The idea to make smoking cigars the poster image for these women's liberation was an ethical choice on some marketing executive's part, and could, perhaps, have stood a bit more scrutiny.

How much a character smokes is another important factor. Again, if a sympathetic character chain-smokes, lighting one cigarette off the butt of the last without any stated concerns, this is an even more strongly implied endorsement of the habit.

Finally, as with portrayals of violence in the media, we should consider rewards and consequences. If smoking portrayals provide rewards for the behavior, from achieving sophistication, to cinching a seduction, to closing the big deal, to getting the "bad guy," it is an endorsement of smoking. In the absence of negative consequences, the habit is again supported. These consequences, which will be discussed further below, can be health consequences (coughing, emphysema, cancer); to "hip-quotient"-reducing consequences (dependence and addiction, yellow teeth, bad breath, rubbery face); to plot consequences.

What are the ethical choices?

If creators side with medical science and believe smoking is "bad" and that we do influence behavior by showing role models smoking, we should choose to factor those beliefs into our creative output accordingly. There are a number of ways to accomplish this goal. You can use the READR method, as you can with all the topics discussed in this section, to analyze the ways in which this can be done specifically for each project, but there are a few general ideas to consider.

> *To depict a milieu where substance use is common, sanitized of substances, can hurt your story. However, using alcohol, tobacco, or drugs where there is no such story imperative is gratuitous—and often inadvertent.*
> —*Paul Hapenny*

First, and most obvious, is that characters might simply *not* light up. There are almost always other ways in which to make whatever dramatic point cigarettes were intended to make. Often, other factors come into play, such as the writer's or director's desire to say something about the character by having him smoke, or the actor's desire to use smoking as character activity and motivation. However, ultimately, these are secondary in most cases. Of primary importance is making the ethical choice as to whether the benefit gained by a character's smoking is outweighed by the greater societal good of not further encouraging the habit.

Of course, in some situations, you'll decide smoking is, for whatever reason, necessary. And no one is saying you should *not* make such a choice, at least not in this book. You must, however, realize that it *is* a choice, and weigh it accordingly.

If you determine that smoking is necessary to the drama of a particular scene, or to the make-up of a particular character, or even to the atmosphere of a particular shot or film, is it possible to restrict smoking to the less sympathetic or the minor characters? Can you arrange for the *hero* not to light up, even if other characters do, without compromising your vision?

If the hero must smoke, can you *avoid* rewarding him specifically for smoking (reward him for other things instead) or show the negative consequences of his smoking? Perhaps something as simple as a cough. Perhaps he makes a semi-serious remark about needing to "kick the habit." Perhaps he makes a hackneyed, but still effective joke ("these things will kill you") in a life and death situation. At least some reaction or line of dialogue should be considered so that a direct endorsement of smoking is not perceived. Perhaps other characters can make negative comments about his smoking. Perhaps he doesn't "get the girl" until he quits. Negative consequences are important.

If these sorts of questions seem like interference in the creative process, they are not. You may still make virtually whatever creative choices you like. Our system guarantees that, at least for now. However, first, you should understand that each element of this creative process is always a choice or series of choices. You should never move forward without realizing this anew. Second, there are usually ways to achieve your dramatic goals without sending out messages in tacit endorsement of negative behaviors.

Alcohol

The same sorts of choices rear their ugly heads when we discuss portrayals of drinking in the media, although certain of the details differ rather radically.

Drinking is often depicted as harmless fun, a dis-inhibitor, a prelude to sex, or a good time in and of itself. Again, however, the decision to portray drinking is a choice with ethical implications to be considered.

Because alcohol has been shown to actually be beneficial to health in *small* quantities,[27] portrayals of alcohol consumption should be examined from a different perspective than that for smoking. The elements to consider are primarily *who* is drinking, *how much* in *what settings*, what is their *behavior* while drinking, and *what happens* as a result.

The study sponsored by the Office of National Drug Control Policy in January 2000, found that alcohol appeared in 71 percent of television episodes studied. To our industry's credit, there was only *one* instance of underage drinking portrayed. The study further found that some 66 percent of major adult characters drank onscreen. Nearly half the episodes featuring drinking combined or associated it with humor. In addition, again, 23 percent of all episodes showing alcohol use portrayed negative consequences associated with drinking, and an outright refusal to drink was portrayed in one percent.[28] Perhaps of some concern, though, is the fact that, of the episodes that portrayed alcohol consumption, some 40 percent of these made drinking look like a positive experience, while only 10 percent portrayed it as a negative experience.

The importance of who is drinking can be summed up in one word: *minors*. Underage drinking is a pervasive social problem in this country.

In earlier days of teen comedy, such films as *Porky's*[29] used teenage drinking as a plot and character element. Remember that even when used in this film, the teens got caught and there were consequences to their drinking, albeit none too serious because it was a comedy. In *Animal House*,[30] consequences were laughed off because Dean Vernon Wormer (the man in charge of imposing the consequences) was a complete caricature.

Now, the problem of underage drinking has become severe enough that, whether it is used in a serious vein, or as a comic device, ethically minded filmmakers should carefully consider their portrayals of teenagers and drinking. Teenage drinking should be shown to have definite, direct, and negative consequences.

Some critics would argue that underage drinking should not be portrayed at all, just because the behavior is illegal. However, murder is also illegal, and, according to this logic, perhaps *the* seminal plot point in movie history would disappear. Similarly, there exists a wealth of compelling coming-of-age stories that depict early forays into alcohol, many of these based on true tales of adolescence. To discard them completely as unhealthy would seem awfully like "throwing the baby out with the bath water." I would argue that there is a middle road, to be guided by responsibility and ethical decisionmaking: Does your story illuminate the human condition in any meaningful way? Is it genuinely funny, touching, dramatic, or does it simply glorify the "let's drink till we get sick" mentality?

As far as portrayals of drinking among adults, the issues are not as clear-cut. Drinking is legal for adults, so we have no concern about condoning illegal acts. Many adults enjoy drinking, to one degree or another. Religious convictions aside, the harmfulness of moderate social drinking has not been established, except perhaps to temperance fanatics in their own minds.

However, heavy drinking and *alcoholism* is quite another matter. Here again, the creator should tread *very* carefully, if at all. Alcoholism is considered by many public health experts to be a disease, rather than a weakness or addiction.[31] Whether you personally agree with this or not, just as you would not wish to tread on the feelings of victims, we as creators should be sensitive to the plight of alcoholics. We should think long and hard before using the subject, or a character who is an alcoholic, for any but the most serious purpose. If used for comedy, an insensitive and potentially hurtful choice at best, the comedy should, at the very least, represent such an obvious caricature that there is clearly no negative intent.

Another important element when dealing with portrayals of drinking is behavior *while* drinking and the consequences of that behavior. From domestic problems (as in *When A Man Loves A Woman*[32]) to domestic violence (as in *What's Love Got To Do With It*[33]), behavior and consequences paint the clearest picture of alcohol use versus abuse.

If drinking is painted in a negative light (for example, the drinker is unpleasant, rude, or downright antisocial—when the bad guys drink, they get mean and kill innocent people, or the rum-pot next door makes a pass at his neighbor's wife), this might at a stretch be thought to lessen the viewer's urge to drink. Of more impact, perhaps, would be an attack upon the behaviors resulting from or influenced by drinking. In other words, if a character drinks too much, then drives a car and hits and kills a child, it might provide that vital second thought before a viewer himself drinks and reaches for his car keys.

Marijuana

On to the question of marijuana. This is a tough one—there are so many differing opinions of people of good conscience about whether the substance is in fact harmful and should even be illegal in the first place.

However, the preponderance of researchers and public health officials believe that marijuana is harmful and its use should not be encouraged in the media. For example, a study by Columbia University concluded that children who smoke marijuana are 85 times more likely to use cocaine than their peers who have never tried marijuana.[34] Obviously, there's a lot more at work in this particular statistic than any innate properties of marijuana, including the personalities of the children concerned (e.g., experimental versus nonexperimental). However, the statistic should still not be ignored.

What is clear is that marijuana is a controversial issue, and has been since at least the 1960s.

Portrayals of marijuana use in film and television have fairly uniformly been of two types. Either the weed has been used as a comedic device (as perhaps most famously managed by Cheech and Chong), or it has been used to make characters seem hip, attractive, or "laid back." Either way, these portrayals are virtually always pro rather than antimarijuana. An exception is the film *Clueless*[35], in which the laid-back, pot-smoking slacker Travis gives up marijuana and goes into a 12-step program, delivering his bong to the kitchen appliance section of a disaster relief drive and discussing his new sense of clarity.

When used as a comedic device, the viewer laughs and dismisses marijuana as harmless, if perhaps a bit silly. Its use in a comedic situation sometimes also gives the viewer a chance to laugh at the oppressive establishment that wants to punish nice people for having such harmless fun.

In the other scenario, the use of marijuana is made to look desirable because its users in these portrayals are often powerful or attractive figures.[36] With these scenarios, the conclusion is either harmless dismissal or envy. Rarely is there a negative consequence of any note, as there often is with more serious drugs.

Clearly, whatever the creator's ethical position concerning marijuana, it would seem wise to carefully consider what role the drug is to play in programming in which it is to be used. Once again, as with tobacco and alcohol, an active ethical choice must be made. Does the drug play a necessary or useful role? Is it included just for laughs? Is it necessary, and ultimately, does its use in the programming justify sending the message that may be sent by its inclusion?

"Hard Drugs"

According to one theory, tobacco, alcohol, and marijuana are considered "gateway" substances. The theory is that their use on even a semiregular basis is statistically more likely to lead to the use of so-called "hard drugs" than nonuse. A number of other factors come into play, complicating the issue of course. Myriad social and personality factors are involved. However, it *is* statistically likely that regular use of these substances at a young age is an indication of an addictive tendency on the user's part that could lead to use of hard drugs under certain circumstances.

Obviously, tobacco and alcohol are perfectly legal for anyone over age 18, and marijuana is also legal in some cases in certain parts of the country. But because so-called hard drugs are illegal, an ethical element is added to the mix.

Again, the Office of National Drug Control Policy study released in January 2000 found that illicit drugs were infrequently mentioned and very rarely shown in prime time television. In the few episodes portraying illicit drug use, nearly all showed negative consequences. There were a number of humorous references to drugs, but very little actual use, and even less in the way of glorification.[37]

For purposes of this discussion, hard drugs encompass a wide range of illicit substances, including cocaine, crack cocaine, heroin, LSD, and other hallucinogens, amphetamines, and tranquilizers ... the rainbow of colors. Habitual use of such drugs is considered one of the more virulent plagues of modern society. Drugs pose a serious health threat to the user. In addition, such use often brings with it a raft of problems, including crime, domestic violence, AIDS, and automobile accidents, to name but a few.

One of the very few areas in which the ethical choices seem absolutely clear and the dreaded phrase "social responsibility" fits like a glove (or handcuffs, depending upon your perspective) is with these drugs. Unless the point of the creative process is to create antidrug sentiment, or a particular story is so firmly rooted in a world where drugs play a significant role that the story *cannot* be told without them, creators should consider avoiding hard drug portrayals. If the film or television piece is for children, we should avoid drug portrayals absolutely. Further, there is virtually no justifiable reason for creating prodrug programming.

That said, if hard drugs *must* be used to tell a story, some of the same rules apply as to tobacco, only more stringently. Admirable heroes should not use hard drugs unless the point of the piece is the hero valiantly trying to kick the habit, or the destruction of a character through drugs. Children should not be portrayed as using, again unless that is the point.

A film such as *Trainspotting*[38] is an example of a film in which the violence and degradation (remember that Scottish toilet scene) of heroin addiction is shown with a powerful antidrug slant. Some consider the movie to have a prodrug message, but this seems incorrect, primarily as a result of the consequences of the protagonists' addiction.

Gia[39] is another example of a film with a powerful antidrug message. In it, we watch a beautiful young woman, a supermodel with seemingly everything in the world to live for, gradually disintegrate personally and professionally as the result of drug addiction. Even the film *New Jack City*,[40] which begins by glamorizing the early days of crack, ends in violent death for virtually all of the bad guys who saddled society with the drug (at least in this version).

> *There's no question that in* Trainspotting *the guys had fun for a while, and it was a hell of a fun ride, riding on heroin. Here again, though, once you get to the end of the movie, I don't know too many people who are real eager to walk up to a heroin habit after seeing what Ewan McGregor went through in the last act. If that hadn't been there, I don't think we would have bought the movie. Then it really would have been basically a ride that glorified drugs.*
>
> —*Mark Gill*

The safest course of action is to use drug portrayals only when drug use is the point or drugs are so much a part of the milieu or the character that the story cannot be told without their presence, and then to show that drug use has negative consequences.

Exercise in Substance Abuse: Tracking Through the Process

Back to our now infamous scenario of the "rogue" cop pursuing the bad guy. We've already illustrated both the use of violence and stereotypes with this scenario. Now, we'll examine how substance abuse issues can crop up and be emphasized and re-emphasized throughout the film's development and production process. How does substance use or abuse end up on film and television screens? How does it get carried through the major departments of a film, being molded and shaped by each department? As a hypothetical exercise, the following section will trace a rather extreme example of exactly that process.

Let's assume we have our character-driven screenplay about our "rogue" cop hero tracking our villain in order to get him before he can murder his next victim in a serial murder spree.

1. The writer has come up with a characterization of our villain. He hasn't filled in a lot of detail about his character, preferring to leave that to casting and to the director. For reasons described in the section on "Violence," the writer has included the stabbing of an innocent victim in Central Park; a successful escape from the hero on foot in an alleyway with several shots

fired; and a final shoot-out with the hero, in which our villain is injured and arrested.

2. A producer options this script. The producer works with the writer to hone the story and the character. She decides that to create a really solid, three-dimensional villain, she needs to give him certain quirks or habits. He needs to be a real threat in the audience's eyes. The writer begins to expand on the villain's personality. Of course, he has limited page space in which to accomplish this, as the producer also wants more action, violence, and some sex to ensure overseas sales. Therefore, the writer must shorthand this development. He decides that the villain should smoke thin, black cigarettes, in keeping with the inky mystery of his evil persona.

   Now, the producer and the studio executives or financiers ask for a rewrite, and ask the writer to include a sidekick for the villain, who can both cause mayhem on her own and give the villain a dramatic foil. She, too, has to have a fleshed out characterization, at least to some degree. But, if the writer has little page space to expand the portrayal of the villain, he has virtually none to flesh out the role of the sidekick. Therefore, he decides to give her a visually creepy and "dangerous" habit to help paint a picture of her. Each time she and the villain are about to engage in any illegal or difficult behavior, she breaks a vial of amyl nitrate under her nose to pump up her energy level.

   The studio executives or financiers decide the film needs a villain that the audience will love to hate. They demand that the script be changed, again. Now, among other changes, not only will the villain smoke the black cigarettes, but he will also have the demeaning and ugly habit of blowing smoke rings intentionally in the faces of all his underlings, except the sidekick.

   To preserve some semblance of originality and pride in his work, the writer also explores the hidden past of the villain. He decides that the watershed event of the villain's past must be specified. This is to become our first public health issue (other than the general antisocial behavior of being a violent, murdering villain, of course). He decides the villain was on the straight and narrow, growing up to be normal, when the twin sister he adored committed suicide as a result of depression because she had contracted leukemia. She died when he was 15 and he has never been the same.

   In addition, the villain's sidekick must become as beautiful as she is lethal in order to inject both sex and sex appeal into the project. This will also serve to heighten the hero's allure and sense of mystery. However, the writer now decides to push the sidekick's drug habit in an effort to make her seem volatile and dangerous. In addition to the amyl nitrate ampoules, she is given a mild crack habit, which causes her to have violent fits of rage and scare the crap out of everyone around her periodically. The way this is written, it makes her addiction appear to be the thing that gives her the power to be tough, to be ruthless. It is thus, in a very real way, appealing as a source of empowerment.

Further, the final shoot-out is changed. As the villain is making his escape, he will stab a homeless man, just to reinforce that he is a danger to society, with ice water running through his veins. To increase our pity for the homeless man, he will go down with a half-drunk bottle in his hands, to indicate that he is an alcoholic. This shows the negative consequences of alcohol, so the writer feels somewhat comfortable with it.

The villain will be given a veritable arsenal, so there is a fierce firefight. In addition, the villain cannot be injured and captured without demystifying him. Rather, he and his sexy sidekick must be killed outright in a hale of bullets, à la *Bonnie & Clyde*. The writer adds a brief scene of them *both* using amyl nitrate behind a dumpster just prior to courageously charging out into a hale of bullets, guns blazing.

The writer chooses to have the villain be a Russian Mafia gangster, to add a specific personality. This allows him to be brutal, unprincipled, and hateful. It also allows the writer to quite easily add alcoholism to the list of the villain's problems, as the audience is quite familiar with vodka addiction as a trait they have seen in Russians in the movies on numerous occasions.

3. A director is hired. She, too, must have her hand in the creation of this gradually changing picture. She brings in a new writer just to "polish" the screenplay for production. She decides that the villain should be "an Arab," for reasons discussed at the end of the "Portrayals of Stereotypes" section.

   The villain is still thought to be too generic, and not well-rounded enough (or diseased enough, depending upon one's point of view). However, the studio executives or financiers have come to like the alcoholism element as broadening the character, so that is to be kept. When it's discovered through some quick research on the Internet that alcoholism is not a big public health problem in the Arab world, the studio executives or financiers decide on a compromise. The villain will be a connoisseur of hashish and opium to conform to a problem endemic to his national origins, but he will also be referred to as a somewhat westernized Arab, so he can *also* be an alcoholic.

   Once our villain is in place, the stakes of the entire picture are raised. Maniacal, cruel, and completely unpredictable as a result of mood swings, inner rage, and drug and alcohol addictions, the villain is no longer just a serial killer. Now, he becomes an international terrorist lunatic, seeking to plant a chemical bomb that will poison much of the eastern seaboard and paralyze the government.

   He is rabidly anti-U.S. He was raised and educated in the United States, but has developed a profound hatred for our government by witnessing the disrespect shown by the people for their leaders and institutions on television and in the movies. How can a government be strong, good, and virtuous, he reasons, if the very people it is intended to govern ridicule, mock, and disrespect it at every turn. This hypocrisy would never be allowed in his native country, where the traditional government rules with an iron hand. Similarly, he has come to despise the American family, where the children have no respect and are only trying to get the most for themselves, rather than listening to their elders—these lessons again being learned from the media. He finds western religion to be the greatest hypocrisy of all, preachers seemingly existing merely to ask for money on television and from the pulpit. This is all made worse by the fact that his brother was killed in our raids on the terrorist bases in the Sudan, which he will never forgive.

Now, the hero must stop the villain to "save the world." Finally, the producer has a larger canvas for her movie.

During the first shoot-out, our villain takes a woman hostage to use as his human shield. He holds her prisoner in an old warehouse and tortures her. This choice is not to be made at random, of course. The hostage must be young, helpless, and terrified, as well as gorgeous and probably rather underdressed.

It turns out she is a dead ringer (an unfortunate phrase, perhaps ...) for his dead twin sister. As we learn during a climactic emotional moment for the villain, in a heartfelt confession to his captive, she did not have leukemia, but AIDS, and it killed her. The villain has never forgiven himself for not taking better care of her than he did. It turns out she contracted AIDS while working as a teenage prostitute to support his drug habit. He could have stopped her by quitting, but did not do so. She became pregnant, went to the hospital for tests, and discovered her condition. She could not live with the realization, and that was the end for her.

4. The director casts a somewhat swarthy, mean-looking type as the villain, likely without much concern for his native acting ability. He is cast as someone rather slight of build, intense and slightly loony, but with a confidence and authority that allow us to believe he is a real threat. He is also twitchy, which illustrates the effects of his various addictions. What is important is that we believe he can command his gang, with his moll's help, and that he is unspeakably cold-blooded. The moll is cast in the Faamke Janssen mold, smart, sexy, loony, and absolutely lethal.

   The executives, the producer, and the director are thrilled. They have a large-scale good versus evil picture, with very high stakes and clearly defined good guys and bad guys. The original writer would not recognize his script, but this doesn't matter, as it's not shown to him in any case.

5. Designers are brought on board. The production designer suggests that everything connected with our villain be shown as murky and dark, with as much Middle Eastern mystery as possible. He adds a few authentic touches of Arab culture to help this illusion along. He also adds drug and alcohol paraphernalia as an element in many of the scenes.

   In addition, the designers suggest a cigar for the sidekick, Cuban of course. Giving a cigar habit to a sexy blonde gun moll, they feel, will add an element of sex appeal to the picture. The director agrees, and comes up with the idea that the sidekick cuts her cigars (for the uninitiated, the process of cutting the mouth-end tip off the cigar so air will flow through the cigar) with an oversized switchblade with Arabic symbols carved on the ivory handle. This will make the whole process eccentric, showy, and interesting. It will also draw attention to the smoking.

6. The director of photography now decides how to photograph the villain and sidekick to create maximum villain-ness. He decides on a primarily low angle approach, making them look as imposing and dangerous as possible. The cigar and cigarette smoke will be used to cast an air of mystery over the characters and add visual texture to the scene.

   Overall, each department goes to the director with their own ideas as to how to make these characters more evil, playing on the fact that American audiences will define them as evil and despicable the moment they see them. The various addictions will be used to enhance the evil images. This will give the movie more impact.

   Finally, the film goes into production, and all departments pull together (so goes the theory) to maximize the "bang for the buck."

   The picture is released to great fanfare and makes a quarter of a billion dollars overseas, about three-quarters of that in the domestic markets, and lives forever on video.

   Everyone is happy, except perhaps anyone of any sort of Arab nationality, and society as a whole, as substance abuse has become, in this case, a trick used in the service of film commerce.

Ethical Gymnastics

1. Smoking cigarettes has often been used in movies to add texture or character traits to a given role, such as sophistication and sex appeal to women, or "hipness" and that detached sophistication to men. Discuss other props that can be substituted for cigarettes to provide or strengthen those same traits. Similarly, smoking can also help draw attention to an actor's face. Discuss other ways to accomplish this. Many

cinematographers use smoke from cigarettes to add interesting textures to their work. Discuss alternatives.

2. You're a screenwriter writing a comedy revolving around some hard-drinking "frat" boys. Discuss why you made the choices you did. Also, discuss the ethical questions, if any, you should consider in light of what you have read in this section.

3. There has been much disagreement as to whether the film *Trainspotting* is a prodrug or antidrug film. Discuss the film in light of what you have read in this section.

4. Play the devil's advocate and write a scene in which two characters talk posi tively about hard drug addiction. Can this be done in such a way that it is a compelling argument? If not, why not? Where are the holes in the argument?

5. Now, perform the same exercise substituting marijuana for hard drugs.

6. You're writing or directing a comedy. Discuss humorous ways in which you could build elements into your film to discourage substance abuse. What if your film were a drama? An action picture?

7. Quentin Tarrantino's film *Pulp Fiction*[41] is an example of a contemporary film that provides a gold mine of ethical controversy. Discuss the scene in which the character Vincent "shoots up." Does this scene encourage or discourage drug abuse? If you were remaking the film, could this scene be made more responsible, in light of what you have read in this section, without weakening the plot?

8. Discuss the film *Kids*,[42] in light of what you have read in this section. Does it deliver a prodrinking or antidrinking message?

9. Discuss the film *The People vs. Larry Flynt*[43] in terms of the issues raised in this section.

10. Using what you have learned in this section, write a one-page treatment for a movie that discourages substance abuse, yet gives the audience an interesting film to watch.

Notes

1 *Substance Use in Popular Movies and Music*, Mediascope, December 1998.

2 *Substance Use in Popular Prime Time Television*, Mediascope, January 2000.

3 *The National Center on Addiction and Substance Abuse at Columbia University 1995 Annual Report,* CASA, 1996.

4 *Growing Up Tobacco Free: Preventing Nicotine Addiction in Children and Youths,* Institute of Medicine, 1994.

5 "Cigarette Smoking—Attributable Mortality and Years of Potential Life Lost—United States, 1990," Centers for Disease Control and Prevention. *MMWR* 1993; 42(33): 645–649.

6 *The National Center on Addiction and Substance Abuse at Columbia University 1995 Annual Report.*

7 *Substance Use in Popular Prime Time Television.*

8 Snyder, S. "Movies and Product Placement; Is Hollywood Turning Films Into Commercial Speech?" *University of Illinois Law Review* (Winter 1992): 301–337.

9 1987 D: Steven Spielberg, Universal Pictures.

10 Lackey, W. "Can Lois Lane Smoke Marlboros?: An Example of the Constitutionality of Regulating Product Placement in Movies." *The University of Chicago Legal Forum* (Annual 1993): 275–292.

11 a.k.a. *Vig*, 1998 D: Graham Theakston, Lions Gate Films, Inc.

12 Lackey, 1993.

13 Lackey, 1993.

14 Lackey, 1993.

15 Shapiro, E. "B&W Tobacco Paid to Get Brands In Films, Notes Say," *Wall Street Journal*, May 16, 1994.

16 Hilts, P. "Company Spent $1 Million to Put Cigarettes in Movies, Memos Show," *The New York Times*, May 20, 1994.

17 Shapiro, 1994.

18 Dutka, E. "Force of Habit," *Los Angeles Times*, September 5, 1996.

19 Hartman, Rome, producer. "Smoking Onscreen," *CBS Sixty Minutes*. November 24, 1996.

20 1994–present, Warner Bros. Television.

21 Ms. Ryder and Ms. Roberts have been criticized for persistent smoking in their films, especially because these two stars are extremely popular among young girls. For example, see Ms. Ryder's film *Girl, Interrupted*, 1999 D: James Mangold, Sony Pictures Entertainment, and Ms. Roberts' *My Best Friend's Wedding*, 1997 D: P.J. Hogan, Sony Pictures Entertainment.

22 Published monthly by M. Shanken Communications.

23 Labaton, Stephen, "Gov't Seeks An Ad Ban and Label Warning For Cigars," *The New York Times*, July 22, 1999, p. 14.

24 Labaton, p. 14.

25 1996 D: Roland Emmerich, 20th Century Fox.

26 1996 D: Hugh Wilson, Paramount Pictures.

27 Somerson, Mark. "Growing Evidence Favors Moderate Use Of Alcohol," *The Columbus Dispatch*, November 28, 1999, p. 7B.

28 *Substance Use in Popular Prime Time Television.*

29 1981 D: Bob Clark, 20th Century Fox; *Porky's II: The Next Day*, 1983 D: Bob Clark, 20th Century Fox.

30 1978 D: John Landis, MCA/Universal.

31 *Encyclopedia Britannica Online*: www.eb.com.

32 1994 D: Luis Mandoki, Buena Vista.

33 1993 D: Brian Gibson, Buena Vista.

34 *The National Drug Control Strategy, 1997* (Washington, D.C.: Office of National Drug Control Policy, 1997).

35 1995 D: Amy Heckerling, Paramount Pictures.

36 See, for example, *Romancing the Stone*, 1984 D: Robert Zemeckis, 20th Century Fox.

37 *Substance Use in Popular Prime Time Television.*

38 1996 D: Danny Boyle, Miramax Films.

39 1998 D: Michael Cristofer, Citadel Entertainment.

40 1991 D: Mario Van Peebles, Warner Bros.

41 1994 D: Quentin Tarantino, Miramax Films.

42 1995 D: Larry Clark, Miramax Films.

43 1996 D: Milos Forman, Columbia Pictures.

The Girl: Portrayals of Sex

Now, We're Definitely Not in Kansas Anymore

A word about sex.

Now that I have your attention ... OK, OK, we all know what every creator knows: *Sex sells*! No one can deny the power of sex or sex appeal in entertainment; nor can we deny that viewing beautiful people onscreen in various stages of romantic encounter is, well, pleasurable. Creators use it, audiences love it, so what's all the fuss about onscreen sex?

A number of critics of contemporary media—particularly those with a conservative or religious bent—use as their mantra the elimination of "sex and violence" in films and especially on television. This is rather like trying to combine love and hate or life and death. Sex and violence could not be further apart on the spectrum (unless we're discussing sexual violence, which I will address below), yet they are often attacked as one conglomerate evil by parent, religious, and other groups. In fact, if given a choice, many of these advocates would prefer to see sex eliminated from the land than violence!

Sex is life-affirming. Violence, by definition, destroys life. When it comes to these issues, most industrialized nations in the world are exactly opposite to the United States. They see no problem with nudity or lovemaking, but abhor the violence we embrace. We are seen, for all our "home of the free" rhetoric, as one of the most repressed and puritanical nations in the world, ranking somewhere just above those nations where women still wear veils. This sort of sexual repression, many believe, is why the United States is also one of the leading producers of pornography in the world.

The Motion Picture Association of America (MPAA), which is charged with rating films, has been accused of a "double standard" that favors violence over sexuality, wherein any detailed depiction of sex brings an almost automatic "R" rating, and explicit sex will render an "NC-17." In contrast, a film containing violence can still be given a "G" or a "PG" rating. To support this theory, researcher Joel Federman points to *Natural Born Killers*[1] and *Pulp Fiction*,[2] both graphically violent films that received R ratings, while *Showgirls*,[3] which contained graphic sexuality and nudity but no violence, received the much harsher NC-17.[4] In other words, it takes a great deal more violence, comparatively, to cross that threshold and earn that same MPAA rating.

German television broadcasters, some of the most powerful buyers of American entertainment overseas, will buy American product containing sex—even explicit sex—but will stop short of buying American violence. In fact, many European countries, as well as Latin American countries and Australia, are opposed to this violence over sex mind-set, and routinely edit violence out of U.S. entertainment, yet allow a certain amount of healthy sexuality to be shown to their young people. Says Federman, author of *Media Ratings, Design, Use and Consequences*, "[I]n Britain, American films are rarely edited for sexuality, but are often cut for violence ... For example, violent scenes were cut from *Robin Hood: Prince of Thieves*,[5] *Lethal Weapon 3*,[6] and *Teenage Mutant Ninja Turtles*,[7] [of all films!] so they could be approved for a younger audience."[8]

Making movies is all about compromise. You've got a whole group of people. But usually the pressure for a given amount of vulgarity or the wrong decision doesn't come from the people you've chosen to work with. It comes from the people who are paying the bill.
—Gordon Willis

Yet back home, the mere flash of Harvey Keitel's buttocks[9] is enough to earn a movie an "R" rating under the MPAA rating system,[10] disqualifying anyone under 18 from seeing the movie without an adult, at least in theory.

The issue is really not sex, per se, but the *cheapening* of sex and sexuality. It is certainly true that, in today's entertainment, we use sex, sex appeal, and the hint of sex absolutely everywhere. Are there ethical issues here? Does it matter, for example, that no high-powered lawyer who wanted to be taken seriously would ever show up in court in an *Ally McBeal*[11] microskirt? Does it matter if New York City Hall employees do not come to work in peek-a-boo blouses à la ABC's *Spin City*?[12] Does it matter that the character Seven of Nine's spray-painted-on uniform on *Star Trek: Voyager*,[13] although it looks great, seems perhaps not the ideal style for work on a starship? It's all just harmless fun, you say! Perhaps, but let's explore a bit deeper.

Advertising is the most obvious example of the rampant use of sexual content. Because the Madison Avenue dreammakers are experts at tapping into our most primal instincts, we now live in a world where sex is used to sell laundry soap, the latest sports utility vehicle, and even aluminum screen doors. Imagine: An enormous percentage of all advertising in the United States would disappear if advertisers were forced to simultaneously pull all ads using sex in any way to sell a product or service. Think of all that dead airtime, all those empty magazines and billboards, and all those blank pages on the Internet!

Sex is certainly overused as a media tool today. We are saturated with sexual innuendo in the media on a daily basis, yet we recoil at the thought that our children might see a woman's breast or a caring couple making love on TV or in the movies—a natural sight with which other industrialized nations have no problem. As far as media portrayals go, American society seems more comfortable with sophomoric jokes about sex on sitcoms between seductively dressed characters (often in the workplace) with no consideration of the loving relationships that might provide context for the sexual content.

The result is that we seem to take the mystery of sex and trade it for an attempt at shock value or some quick laughs. Yet, as time goes by and we sit constantly bombarded with nudity and sexual imagery, we as an audience become harder and harder to excite. Ever-increasing blatancy is required to maintain our interest, much as in the case of portrayals of violence (see "Portrayals of Violence"). This can and I believe does have the effect of cheapening and routinizing this most human, potent, and mystical instinct of our physical existence. *That* is the problem with too much sex being portrayed in the media, not the destruction of our moral fiber, whatever that may be.

Now, let it be said that it is not by any means just the right-wingers and the religious conservatives who mix sex and violence. Hollywood itself mixes them constantly onscreen, and it is that mixture, especially, that is volatile and potentially problematic.

Sexual Violence, Public Health, and Sex Among Minors

When considering portrayals of sexual content in the media, certain areas warrant very careful ethical consideration. One of these is, of course, sexual violence.

In both movies and television, female characters are regularly victimized in one way or another. The sexualizing of violence has been commonplace in film for decades. Perhaps the most egregious examples of this process are found in the so-called "slasher" films.[14] As Harvey Weinstein, cofounder of Miramax Films and now chief of Dimension Films has stated, "[i]n the '70s and '80s, the women in those types of films used to be the victims. They were there for eye candy. They would be the girl getting killed in the shower so there could be nudity."[15]

This trend has changed to some degree in the last decade or so, as Annette Insdorf discusses in her essay at the end of this section. Women have ceased to be powerless. They are now armed. As Weinstein has suggested, "[w]hat's happened in the '90s is that the females are the heroines."[16]

Of course, in one view, all we have done is moved from the sexualizing of violence through the inherent sexuality of the victim, to the sexualizing of violence through the inherent sexuality of the perpetrator heroine.

Rape and other sexual abuse should not be tolerated on a societal level. Therefore, as creators, we ought to be very careful about depicting these crimes. Rape is *never* deserved (just as murder is *never* deserved) and women never enjoy rape, in spite of what sophomoric movie fantasy might suggest. We should illustrate these crimes only when they are absolutely required by the story, and then, work to minimize graphic depiction and titillation, maximizing perceived negative consequences at the same time.

Taking the low road with excesses of sex and violence is not just a bit of creative mischief but an abuse of the freedom American filmmakers are guaranteed, because it's clearly harmful to the social fabric. When sex is debased and violence glorified, repeatedly on the screen and usually in realistic contexts, the scenes cannot be shrugged off as mere movie make-believe.
—*Les Brown*

The other area in the vast universe of sex to be taken very seriously is sex between minors, or worse, statutory rape. Again, these activities are both illegal, and perceived by many as harmful, the latter more than the former.

Now, of course, minors do have sex ... often. That is a reality that will not go away simply because many groups in our society would wish it to. A study conducted in 1997 reported that more than 48 percent of high school students nationwide have engaged in sexual intercourse.[17] This, of course, brings myriad unfortunate consequences for society and for the teens themselves, although they may enjoy themselves in the process. Teen pregnancy and teen birth rates in the United States are the highest of any industrialized nation in the world.[18] Nearly a million teenagers get pregnant each year in this country, and more than half of these pregnancies are carried to term.[19] In addition, of course, is the less tangible, yet incalculable damage caused by forcing these children to grow up much too fast and take on adult responsibilities long before they are mentally or emotionally ready to do so.

What does all this mean for us, as creators? Two illustrations: first, research with adolescents has shown that heavy television viewing can lead to negative attitudes toward remaining a virgin;[20] second, further research has found a correlation between watching a great deal of television and early initiation of sexual intercourse.[21] Although research should obviously not be the final arbiter of what we do creatively, these sorts of conclusions drawn from legitimate study data would seem to argue for some caution on our part. If what we do makes a bad problem worse, even if it doesn't cause the problem in the first place—let's face it, teens have been having sex since the dawn of our history—we should attempt to minimize these negative effects.

These subjects are not solely the province of so-called "T&A" films or teen sex comedies either. In the Academy Award winning film *American Beauty*,[22] Kevin Spacey's character treads a very fine moral line—he fantasizes about his daughter's *teenage* female friend, who by all indications seems sophisticated and sexually experienced. The film then becomes even more disturbing when he actually attempts to have sex with her and her true innocence is revealed. She is, despite outward appearances and demeanor, a young girl. Spacey's character makes the choice to respect that innocence. Certainly, though, the graphically depicted fantasy scenes throughout the film posed ethical considerations for the filmmakers, and the very graphic nature of these scenes suggests to many that perhaps more scrutiny might have been in order.

However, portrayals of consensual sex between adult partners are a different matter. It is enough that societal puritanism and conservative antisex advocates have made the United States a world laughing stock on this issue. We need not conform to these ideas and remove all sexual activity from our materials. This would be unnatural and an extreme overreaction. And yet, the ethical filmmaker will attempt to use portrayals of sexual content in a responsible manner; this includes portrayals of sexually transmitted diseases, HIV/AIDS, and other sensitive issues. In particular, AIDS should never be used as a simple dramatic prop or thematic device. Neither should cancer, for that matter. These diseases are too serious to offend people worldwide through flippant or casual manipulation.

Sex and the Working Girl: Roles for Women

Closely related to the issue of the overuse of sex in the media is that many critics believe women are depicted two-dimensionally as sexual objects in most media portrayals, which leads to the objectification and degradation of women in society as a whole.

Many a prominent actress has complained in the past several decades that there are too few good dramatic roles for women outside of their function as sex objects, girlfriends, and conquests for the male protagonists. Meg Ryan, for example, has been quoted as saying "I am irritated that the only power in movies that goes to women is sexual power."[23] Demi Moore remembers that when a studio was reviewing the script for *A Few Good Men*,[24] a nameless studio executive, in his notes to the writer, asked "Why is Jo (Moore's character) female? She doesn't take her clothes off, and there's no love scene."[25]

Now, it's true that both of these interviews were from 1993. This was dubbed the "Year of the Woman," during which roles for women and the respect they were accorded in Hollywood were slated to blossom. Perhaps the most biting satirical comment on the Year of the Woman came from none other than Michelle Pfeiffer:

> So, this is the Year of the Woman. Well, yes, this has been a very good year for women. Demi Moore was sold to Robert Redford for $1 million. Uma Thurman went for $40,000 to Mr. De Niro. While just three years ago, Richard Gere bought Julia Roberts for ... what was it? ... $3,000? I'd say that was real progress.[26]

Why the fascination with prostitutes? Kim Basinger,[27] Elisabeth Shue,[28] Mira Sorvino,[29] and Sharon Stone[30] have all played prostitutes in recent years, scoring a raft of Golden Globe Awards, Academy Award nominations, and box office dollars among them. Could it be that these accomplished and talented actresses chose these roles because there was such a dearth of alternatives?

Of course, prostitutes are not *always* included for mere excitement value. Prostitutes often have power or drive the plot in some way, unlike the girlfriend character so prevalent among women's roles.[31] Also, as screenwriter Paul Hapenny comments:

> While I write about prostitutes and I'm aware they may be perceived as strictly titillation, I use them to turn that exact perception on its head. Perhaps as a result of my lower middle class, urban upbringing, I tend to write about marginalized characters; people I used to see every day. You very rarely see, especially in American Film of the last 30 years, hookers being shown as three dimensional.[32] This very disturbing trend toward black/white characterizations tends to simplify storylines and is, ultimately, an insult to the audience. Can they not be trusted to follow along in the grey areas of a character's life, thoughts and soul, where I believe most human interaction takes place?

A Word About Teens and Sex

Let's start with something positive. The previous statements notwithstanding, the entertainment community has been increasingly sensitive in recent years about portrayals of teen testosterone, portraying the negative consequences necessary to drive home the point that becoming pregnant in high school statistically most often leads to young mothers bringing up their children alone and on welfare.[33]

In films and television programs across the networks, young people are going through the pain and emotional scars of abortion; relationships are being destroyed; pregnant girls and their boyfriends are dropping out of school; and other realistic consequences of "that one blissful night" of unprotected sex are providing a balance for young viewers. Characters now routinely speak of using condoms, an important deterrent in avoiding unwanted pregnancies as well as spreading sexually transmitted diseases, including HIV/AIDS, a phenomenon unheard of just a few decades ago.

This trend represents a collective shift in ethical consideration. In our portrayals, we're beginning to reflect the unfortunate and extremely unpleasant facts that often accompany that dreaded phrase of the teen years: "I'm pregnant," or the horror at any age of the statement "I'm HIV positive."

Although for the moment we're not discussing documentary projects, where one strives for truth, neither should we blithely portray false truths, especially to the particularly susceptible teen audience. If our portrayals show that unprotected sex is both fun *and* consequence free, we definitely send out the message: "It's OK for you too." Ethically savvy portrayals of these sorts of issues should show what the negative consequences of these actions might be. This might mean the difference between that crucial second thought and leaping blithely from the parapet. Perhaps we can help to reduce the incidence of teen pregnancy by showing some of the stark realities, making viewers somewhat more careful.[34]

Q: It's been observed that violence and sex on TV have a seesaw relationship. When violence escalates and Congress makes noise about it, the violence quotient dips and the sex quotient rises and vice versa. Are they cyclical?

It's all at a higher level. We're just a much freer society. When the Hays Office was in charge of censoring movies you couldn't have a scene where a man or a woman had both feet off the ground.

—*Bridget Potter*

In the WB show *Popular*,[35] the two sisters carefully planned their first sexual relationship with their boyfriends. The writers created a very moving and realistic portrayal of the events surrounding the "first" time for each of the sisters as well as some of the supporting characters, with the "popular" sister actually regretting the experience afterwards. Programs such as these help bring issues of a sexual nature into the living rooms of teens across the country and at the same time tell compelling stories.

The same is true of teenage prostitution and runaways. Films such as *Angel*[36] and others[37] have placed attractive heroines in the position of either running away from home or working as prostitutes, or both in combination. Somehow, they have usually managed to come out on top in the end. Even when Angel's school friends discover what she does at night out on the boulevard and she is ostracized briefly, she finds a way to prove that she can triumph.

The realities, of course, are much darker. Every year thousands of children run away from home, sometimes with good reason, often because they are unable to get along with their family or friends. Many of these runaways end up on the streets with no money and nowhere to live. At this point, they become easy prey for pimps, drug dealers, and other pond scum. A significant proportion of them, boys and girls, end up as prostitutes and/or junkies. This is a dark and depressing pattern, with very little hope that the teens involved will escape once caught in this web.

It is hard to construct any but the grittiest, darkest, nastiest film or television story from this reality. Therefore, the tendency when dealing with this subject matter is to "tart it up" as the English say. We choose a heroine of outstanding character, beauty and intelligence, place her in terrible but unavoidable circumstances not of her making (absolving her of guilt) and send her into this world. We hope that the audience will sympathize with her plight and her strength in the face of it, and will therefore care what happens to her. It is relatively clear right from the beginning that she will be one of the lucky few that makes it out alive and in one piece.

What Does All This Mean To Us?

Responsible portrayals. Of course, there's the rub, as Shakespeare would say. What does "responsible portrayal of sexual content" really mean? This is a question creators must answer for themselves on an individual basis. However, certain overall suggestions present themselves.

Creators who want to tell great stories with real characters can avoid the easy pitfalls of titillating sexual innuendo and depictions of gratuitous sexual content that are often the hallmark of weak storytelling. If your scripts call for characters to engage in sexual activity, depict these scenes with dignity and respect, and you will be starting down the ethically higher road. More specifically:

First, your ethical radar should be on full alert when depicting so-called negative sexual behaviors—sexual violence and sex with or between those who are underage.

If you're going to use this material, examine the point of it repeatedly. Use the READR method to analyze the component parts of your project to determine if graphic scenes are essential to your story and your characters. Minimize any unintended demeaning or degrading messages. Analyze how much of the negative behavior you actually want to show onscreen, as opposed to alluding to it in subtler, perhaps more creative ways. Are there more sensitive ways to relay your message? Are the consequences of negative sexual behavior depicted? Are you inadvertently glorifying potentially harmful behaviors?

Second, consider not using sex simply because it sells. Perhaps explore creative ways to play into your audience's yearning for romance rather than the graphic "in your face" side of sex, so to speak. Try not to accede to the element of the lowest common denominator of the audience. The market imperative can be satisfied in other ways, and it may not be worth the societal cost to constantly use sex as a blunt instrument. As always, you may make yourself a better filmmaker if you try to think your way around certain elements, rather than simply relying on blatant commercial precedent. This way, when you determine that a portrayal of sexual content is important to the story, your portrayal will not be something you have done to death and therefore do by rote. It becomes, in effect, a scalpel rather than a bludgeon.

Q: What draws the line between a tasteful sex scene and something that's played for gratuitous titillation?

Like everything in society these days, we're in the ultimate overkill about everything. I'm not a moralist but I do perceive taste as an important part of things. Sexuality on the screen is again about selectivity, your choice.
—Gordon Willis

Through publicity you sell literary and cultural aspirations and through advertising you sell the food and sex. Or in the case the case of The English Patient, *the romance and the exotic locations for women—and for men, the sex, spies, intrigues, and battles.*
—Mark Gill

Third, know your intended audience, and try not to surprise them in the realm of sexual content. In fact, work *very* hard not to surprise them. This sounds counterintuitive and antithetical to good storytelling and good moviemaking, but it is extremely important. A concern of many who advocate reducing or eliminating portrayals of sex is that they are uncomfortable being constantly subjected to what has been called "the squirm factor," a phenomenon mostly found among parents who have settled in to watch a movie or television program with their children that they believe is family friendly.

As an illustration, adults watching *NYPD Blue*[38] in the 10 p.m. drama programming slot or attending an "R" rated movie are, or should be, well aware of the fact that portrayals of sex may appear in this programming.

Forewarned is forearmed. If these viewers don't wish to view such portrayals or have their children view them, they can simply elect not to watch the program or pay to see the movie.

If, however, these same adults sit down with their children to watch television during what has been called the "family hour" (between 7:00 P.M. and 9:00 P.M.), or take their children to see a "G" or a "PG" movie, they expect that they will see so-called family entertainment. If suddenly, sexual content appears without warning, parents recount literally "squirming" as their child turns to ask: "Daddy, what are they doing?" There is no time to switch channels or leave the theater—which, in any case, would simply serve to shine an unwanted spotlight on the incident rather than minimize it.

It seems clear that what we have done in this scenario is to take away the parents' right to choose entertainment content for their children, not to mention to choose where and when they want to explain the facts of life to them. This we have no right whatsoever to do. Rather, it seems responsible, necessary, and only fair that in our family friendly content, we actually *be* family friendly. We should not presume to force lessons on the viewer or expose them to content, even if we believe it would be "good" for them, "loosen them up," or give their children a "good education." This is not our choice to make, nor should it be.

See, I warned you there might be a little "feeding" of opinion at various places in this book.

Exercise in Sex: Tracking Through the Process

Back to our now infamous scenario of the "rogue" cop pursuing the bad guy. We have already illustrated the use of violence, stereotypes, and substance use with this scenario. Now, we'll examine how sex can crop up and be emphasized and re-emphasized throughout the film's development and production process. How does sex end up on film and television screens? How does it get carried through the major departments of a film, being molded and shaped by each department? As a hypothetical exercise, the following section will trace a rather extreme example of exactly that process.

Let's assume we have our character-driven screenplay about our "rogue" cop hero tracking our villain in order to get him before he can murder his next victim in a serial murder spree.

1. The writer has come up with a characterization of our villain. He has not filled in a lot of detail about his character, preferring to leave that to casting and the director. For reasons described in the "Portrayals of Violence" chapter, the writer has included the stabbing of an innocent victim in Central Park; a successful escape from the hero on foot in an alleyway with several shots fired; and a final shoot-out with the hero, in which our villain is injured and arrested.

2. A producer now options this script. The producer works with the writer to hone the story and the characters. She is also thinking about casting and marketing. She decides she needs a good villain, a worthy adversary for the hero that will make the film attractive to a studio or financier. She decides that to create a really solid, three-dimensional villain, she needs to give him certain quirks or habits. He needs to be a real threat in the audience's eyes. The writer begins to expand on the villain's personality. He has limited page

space in which to accomplish this, as the producer also wants more action, violence, and of course, sex to ensure overseas sales. Therefore, the writer must shorthand this development. He decides to make the villain's weakness the fact that he is obsessed by sex. He thinks about where, when, how, and, most importantly, with whom almost constantly.

Now, the producer and the studio executives or financiers ask for a rewrite from the writer, and ask him to include a sidekick for the villain, who can both cause mayhem on her own and give the villain a dramatic foil. She, too, has to have a compelling personality. But, if the writer has little page space to expand the portrayal of the villain, he has virtually none to flesh out the role of the sidekick. Therefore, he decides to give her a killer figure and a self-awareness of it that is almost preternatural. She oozes sex. Each time she and the villain are about to engage in any illegal or difficult behavior, she teases him mercilessly to pump up both of their energy levels.

Q: What offends you?

Anything I find gratuitous or over-the-top. It can be all-out sex on the screen for a given amount of time if it offers humor or wit in it, and moves the audience in the right direction for that moment.
—Gordon Willis

The studio executives or financiers decide the film needs a villain that the audience will love to hate, but will also secretly admire. They demand that the script be changed, again. Now, among other changes, not only will the villain be obsessed with sex, he will easily be a match for the sidekick in raw sexuality.

In order to preserve some semblance of originality and pride in his work, the writer also explores the hidden past of the villain. He decides that the watershed event of the villain's past must be specified. He decides the villain was on the straight and narrow, growing up to be normal, when the twin sister he adored committed suicide as a result of being sexually abused by their stepfather. She died when he was 15 and he has never been the same. Perversely, her death has caused his obsession with sex, and taught him to use it as a weapon.

In addition, the villain's sidekick must become as beautiful as she is lethal to inject more sex and sex appeal into the project. This will also serve to heighten the hero's allure and sense of mystery. To make her more dangerous, she is given a drug habit, sniffing amyl nitrate ampoules, which causes violent fits of rage and periodically scares the crap out of everyone around her. This addiction will be the source of her power and control that amplifies her sexuality in moments of tension.

Further, the final shoot-out is changed. As the villain is making his escape, he'll stab a homeless man, reinforcing what a danger he poses to society. As he kills the man, his facial expression and body language clearly indicate an almost orgasmic rush.

The villain will be given a veritable arsenal, so there is a fierce firefight. In addition, the villain cannot be injured and captured without demystifying him. Rather, he and his sexy sidekick must be killed outright in a hale of bullets, à la *Bonnie & Clyde*. The writer adds a brief scene of them *both* using amyl nitrate and kissing hungrily behind a dumpster, just prior to courageously charging out into a hale of bullets, guns blazing.

This may be a sure sign of moral decay, but I felt that Kids *had more going for it morally than most movies only because, as* The New York Times *put it, it was a wake-up call to American parents. These were not kids who parents conventionally might expect to be wandering into trouble. And by the way, they were not kids out of the ordinary. They weren't hardened New York City kids who do not exist anywhere else. They were pretty representative of a large chunk of the teenage population. It showed what's going on. Now what about the notion of underage sexuality? We might wish it wasn't there, but the fact is that it exists in bigger and bigger ways.*

—Mark Gill

The writer chooses to have the villain be a Russian Mafia gangster, to add a specific personality. This allows him to be brutal, unprincipled, and hateful.

3. A director is hired. She, too, must have her hand in the creation of this gradually changing picture. She brings in a new writer just to "polish" the screenplay for production. She decides that the villain should be "an Arab," for reasons discussed at the end of the "Portrayals of Stereotypes" chapter. Aside from these reasons, she feels that the picture of a Russian Mafia gangster is of an older, scraggly bearded man. She is looking for a younger, swarthier, sexier type.

   The villain is still thought to be too generic, and not well-rounded enough (or diseased enough, depending upon your point of view).

However, the studio executives or financiers have come to like the sex addiction, so that is to be kept. It is felt that this will help in the marketing. The villain will also be referred to as a westernized Arab, which provides the major benefit of making casting easier, as the "whiter" and more westernized the villain is, the greater the chance of casting a "name" actor.

Once our villain is in place, the stakes of the entire picture are raised. Maniacal, cruel, and completely unpredictable as a result of sex addiction, mood swings, and drug and alcohol addictions, the villain is no longer just a serial killer. Now, he becomes an international terrorist, seeking to plant a chemical bomb that will poison much of the eastern seaboard and paralyze the government.

He is rabidly anti-U.S. Although he was raised and educated in the United States, he has developed a profound hatred for that government that stems from his observation of the disrespect Americans show for their leaders and institutions on television and in the movies. How can a government be strong, good, and virtuous, he reasons, if the very people it is intended to govern ridicule, mock, and disrespect it at every turn? This hypocrisy would never be allowed in his native country, where the traditional government rules with an iron hand. Similarly, he has come to despise the American family, where the children have no respect and are only trying to get the most for themselves, rather than listening to their elders—these lessons he again learned from the media. He finds western religion to be the greatest hypocrisy of all, with preachers seemingly existing merely to ask for money on television and from the pulpit. This is all made worse by the fact that his brother was killed in our raids on the terrorist bases in the Sudan, which he will never forgive.

Now, the hero must stop the villain to "save the world." Finally, the producer has a larger canvas for her movie.

During the first shoot-out, our villain takes a woman hostage to use as his human shield. He holds her prisoner in an old warehouse and tortures her, obviously enjoying some sort of sexual thrill from the process. The choice of victim is not to be made at random, of course. The hostage must be young, helpless, and terrified, as well as gorgeous and probably rather underdressed. When the audience sees her tied up in some provocative position following torture, they will assume her ordeal somehow involved taking a shower, as she will somehow have become drenched, with her blouse now noticeably form fitting and all but transparent.

4. The director casts a handsome, but hard-looking and swarthy man as the villain, likely without much concern for his native acting ability. He is cast as someone rather slight of build, intense, but with a confidence and authority that allow us to believe he is a real threat. He is also twitchy, which

illustrates the effects of his various addictions. The moll is cast in the Faamke Janssen mold, smart, sexy, loony, and absolutely lethal.

The executives, the producer, and the director are thrilled. They have a large-scale good versus evil picture, with very high stakes, and clearly defined good guys and bad guys. The original writer would not recognize his script, but this doesn't matter, as it's not shown to him in any case.

5. Designers are brought on board. The production designer suggests that everything connected with our villain be shown as murky, silky, and dark, with as much Middle Eastern mystery as possible. He adds a few authentic touches of Arab culture to help this illusion along. He also adds drug and alcohol paraphernalia as an element in many of the scenes, as well as sexual illustrations and pictures of the villain's beautiful conquests, like trophies, throughout his lair.

6. In addition, working with the props department, the designer determines that the threatened bombing should occur in a way not seen before. Because the writer did not provide anything interesting or unique and the director is always looking for fresh ideas, they come up with one. They determine that the enormously powerful explosive device, hidden in the Statue of Liberty as a symbolic gesture, will be detonated unknowingly by the hero himself. At the appointed time, the trigger will be set off by the frictional heat of copulation on the hero's mattress, picked up by a small sensor hidden in his bed. The delicious irony of the hero's screwing the eastern seaboard (as well as himself) to death thrills the villain and his moll, and drives them to some extracurricular activity of their own. A great sex scene is added to the movie in this way, and the director buys the designer and props people an expensive present. Very visual, very sexual. Perfect.

   In addition, the designers suggest a cigar for the sidekick, Cuban of course. Giving a cigar habit to a sexy gun moll, they feel, will add an element of sex appeal. The director agrees, and comes up with the idea that the sidekick cuts her cigars (for the uninitiated, the process of cutting the mouth-end tip off the cigar so air will flow throught the cigar) with an oversized switchblade with Arabic symbols carved on the ivory handle. This will make the whole process seductive, showy, and interesting. It will also draw attention to the sidekick's lips.

7. The director of photography now decides how to photograph the villain and sidekick to create maximum villain-ness. He decides on a primarily low angle approach, making them look as imposing and dangerous as possible. The cigar smoke will be used to cast an air of silky mystery over the characters.

   Overall, each department goes to the director with their own ideas as to how to make these characters sexier and more evil, playing on the fact that American audiences will define them as evil and despicable the moment they see them.

Finally, the film goes into production, and all departments pull together (so goes the theory) to maximize the "bang for the buck."

The picture is released to great fanfare and makes a quarter of a billion dollars overseas, about three-quarters of that in the domestic markets, and lives forever on video.

Everyone is happy, except perhaps anyone of any sort of Arab nationality, and society as a whole, as sex and sexuality have become, in this case, a trick used in the service of film commerce.

Ethical Gymnastics

1. You're writing a comedy for a prime-time TV series slated for the family hour—7 P.M. to 8 P.M.; your director urges you to "spice up the sexual tension" between your lead characters. Discuss what you think this means. Are there ethical issues at play here?

2. Create a scene where two sitcom stars fall in love. Discuss ways in which you could portray their love without having sex (just for the fun of it).

3. Name your favorite feature film, and use the READR method to break down and analyze the sex scenes, if there are any. Were any important ethical choices presumably made or ignored making the movie?

4. Discuss the film *The People vs. Larry Flynt*[39] in terms of all of the issues raised in this chapter. Analyze the film using the READR method.

5. You're writing a screenplay about a runaway teenage girl who joins a gang for protection and camaraderie on the streets. For her initiation, she must have sex with each of the top gang leaders. Discuss how you would portray this scene if your story was about this one girl's tragic choice.

6. Now you're writing this same story, only from the point of view of the gangbangers, whom you personally see as misguided but basically good-hearted youth merely trying to find meaning (and safety) on the streets. How would you rewrite the scene above?

7. You're directing your first feature film, and your female star tells you she feels very uncomfortable shooting an explicit sex scene involving her and two male characters in a ménage à trois. She is uncomfortable not only as

an actress, but because she also feels that her character would not engage in this sort of activity, particularly while her children are asleep down the hall. What do you do?

8. Write a scene between two teens that shows “responsible” sexual behavior while being believable and entertaining.

9. Use the READR method to analyze the film *American Beauty* in light of what you have read in this chapter. Discuss the sexual fantasy scenes in the film. Do you see any ethical issues here?

10. Discuss whether or not you believe it is possible to construct a weekly television series about teens that does *not* revolve around sexual issues. Are there enough other topics pertinent to the lives of your teen audience to support a full season of programming? What part would concerns about academics play? Relationships (nonsexual)? Spirituality? Athletics? Home life?

Notes

1 1994 D: Oliver Stone, Warner Bros.

2 1997 D: Quentin Tarantino, Miramax Films.

3 1995 D: Paul Verhoeven, United Artists.

4 Federman, Joel. *Media Ratings: Design, Use and Consequences* (Studio City: Mediascope, 1996), p. 33.

5 1991 D: Kevin Reynolds, Warner Bros.

6 1992 D: Richard Donner, Warner Bros.

7 1990 D: Steve Barron, New Line Cinema.

8 Federman, 1996.

9 *Piano, The,* 1993 D: Jane Campion, Miramax Films.

10 Federman, 1996.

11 1997–present, Fox Television.

12 1996–2000, DreamWorks SKG.

13 1995–present, Paramount Television.

14 Carbone, Stephanie. *Picture This: Diversity in Film and Television,* (unpublished).

15 Bernstein, J. “Growing Up in the Dark,” *Premiere: Women in Hollywood*, 1999.

16 Bernstein, 1999.

17 *CDC Surveillance Summaries*, Center for Disease Control and Prevention, August 14, 1998.

18 *Whatever Happened to Childhood? The Problem of Teen Pregnancy in the United States*, National Campaign to Prevent Teen Pregnancy, May 1997, p. 3.

19 “Boys Have a Role Too in Curbing Teen Pregnancy,” *USA Today*, January 6, 1998.

20 Brown, J. and Newcomer, S. "Television Viewing and Adolescents' Sexual Behavior," *Journal of Homosexuality* 21 (1991): 77–91.
21 Princeton Survey Research Associates. *A Review of Public Opinion About Teen Pregnancy* (Princeton, N.J.: The National Campaign to Prevent Teen Pregnancy, September 1996).
22 1999 D: Sam Mendes, DreamWorks SKG.
23 Griffin, N. "Table Talk," *Premiere*: *Special Issue*, 1993.
24 1992 D: Rob Reiner, Castle Rock Entertainment.
25 Griffin, 1993.
26 Pfeiffer, M. "Honor Society," *Premiere: Special Issue*, 1993.
27 *LA Confidential,* 1997 D: Curtis Hanson, Warner Bros.
28 *Leaving Las Vegas*, 1995 D: Mike Figgis, MGM-UA.
29 *Mighty Aphrodite,* 1995 D: Woody Allen, Miramax Films.
30 *Casino,* 1995 D: Martin Scorsese, MCA/Universal Pictures.
31 Carbone.
32 The notable exception to that is, of course, *Klute,* 1971 D: Alan J. Pakula, Warner Bros.
33 See, for example, *The Substitute*, 1996 D: Robert Mandel, LIVE Entertainment; *Say Anything,* 1989 D: Cameron Crowe, 20th Century Fox; *Teen Angel* (TV), 1989 D: Max Reid, *Teen Angel Returns* (TV), 1990.
34 See, for example, *Wish You Were Here*, 1987 D: David Leland, Zenith Productions; *Summer School*, 1987 D: Carl Reiner, Paramount Pictures.
35 1999–present, The WB Television Network.
36 1984 D: Robert Vincent O'Neill, New World Pictures.
37 See also *Boogie Nights*, 1997 D: Paul Thomas Anderson, New Line Cinema; *Dawn: Portrait of a Runaway* (TV), 1976 D: Randal Kleiser; *Where The Day Takes You*, 1992 D: Marc Rocco, Cinetel; and, *Taxi Driver*, 1976 D: Martin Scorsese, Columbia Pictures Corporation.
38 1993–present, ABC Network.
39 1996 D: Milos Forman, Columbia Pictures.

From "Boys with Toys" to "Babes with Bullets"

Annette Insdorf

Annette Insdorf, author of "From 'Boys with Toys' to 'Babes with Bullets,'" is a professor in the Graduate Film Division of Columbia University's School of the Arts, and director of Undergraduate Film Studies. She is a frequent contributor to the *The New York Times* and a national commentator on film, and has published articles in *The Los Angeles Times*, *The Washington Post*, *The San Francisco Chronicle*, and *Rolling Stone*, as well as several books on the subject of film.

> Hitchcock shoots love scenes as if they were murder scenes, and murder scenes as if they were love scenes.[1]
>
> —*Francois Truffaut*

If the violence that characterizes much of American cinema has been evolving from "boys with toys" to include "babes with bullets," have we really come a long way? Is it progress when a heroine's hand—which in an earlier decade tried to cover her exposed breast—now points a loaded gun? Are women any less objectified when their seminude bodies are juxtaposed with weapons in the ironic mode of Quentin Tarantino's *Jackie Brown*[2] or the opening title sequences of James Bond movies? These questions reflect a discomfort with how women have been—and continue to be—portrayed in a cinema that seems to value not only violent male action but the gimmick of disrobed female bodies. The only evolution during the 1990s might be from an image of women flaunting their sexuality—using it to manipulate men, like Sharon Stone in *Basic Instinct*[3]—to that of muscles replacing curves, as when Demi Moore becomes "one of the boys" in *G.I. Jane*.[4]

In the late nineteenth century, movies were originating in the penny arcades as "peep shows." What were those pre-cinematic experiences about? Kiss-kiss and bang-bang, in particular. We have advanced quite a bit since then, especially in terms of technology, but sex and violence continue to be primary attractions for the more sophisticated voyeurs today. The problem lies in the frequent equation between eroticism and assault—sex that is indeed violent, and violence that provides a thrill so visceral, a release so powerful, that it functions as a turn-on. In some films, sex functions as foreplay to orgasmic shoot-outs or explosions.

As a film professor, a woman, and a concerned citizen, I continue to be perturbed by the escalation of violence as a commodity, especially when directed against women, as occurs in mainstream movies like *Fatal Attraction*[5] and art-house cinema like *Blue Velvet*.[6]

The celebration of violence is, of course, a problem hardly limited to contemporary film. Why should we expect the American cinema to be any different from American society? After all, doesn't film reflect the world we inhabit? But the screen has a double edge: movies also condition how we see ourselves. And given that the largest percentage of the American moviegoing public consists of rather impressionable young people, one wonders about the effects of films whose appeal lies primarily in titles like *Natural Born Killers*,[7] *Young Guns*,[8] *Lethal Weapon*,[9] *Die Hard*,[10] and their sequels.

This is not exclusively a male issue, even if most of the screen heroes are men, from Clint Eastwood and Bruce Willis to Sylvester Stallone and Arnold Schwarzenegger. In *Beverly Hills Cop II*,[11] a huge commercial success of 1987, one of the comic moments is particularly discomfiting: as the voluptuous villainess played by Brigitte Nielsen is finally shot, the hero (Eddie Murphy) mutters, "Women!" Hearing the audience cheer this misogynistic moment is hardly heartening. The episode is a cheap shot akin to the end of *Fatal Attraction*,[12] another box-office hit of the same year. This contemporary drama begins with a happy New York family, but when Anne Archer is away for the weekend, husband Michael Douglas does not resist the lure of the independent career woman played by Glenn Close. After their one-night stand, however, Close obsessively follows Douglas and turns his life into a nightmare.

The original ending of *Fatal Attraction* was somewhat more sympathetic to her character, as she committed suicide. But preview audiences did not find this satisfactory, so Paramount had the director Adrian Lyne re-shoot a more confrontational climax: in the final version, Douglas smacks her, and his wife shoots Close in self-defense. As critic Dave Kehr wrote in the February 1988 issue of *Premiere* magazine,

> the cheers and laughter that greeted Douglas's assault on Close … were heard again … when in *Fatal Beauty*[13] a fuzzily asexual Whoopi Goldberg punched Jennifer Warren … knocking her through a plate glass window. As trends go, this isn't an encouraging one: when there is money to be made slugging women around, women will be slugged around.[14]

Whether male or female characters are doing the slugging, such images do not exist in a vacuum. An article in *The New York Times* of May 7, 1991, cites a study conducted at UCLA that found that "30 percent of men are sexually aroused by watching portrayals of violence against women, leading researchers to assume that they fantasize about such violence."[15] It's bad enough when a rape scene is graphically presented onscreen; but when a film depicts a female character's willing complicity in her physical degradation—as in *Blue Velvet*[16]—it's time to question romantically grotesque conceits.

Written and directed by David Lynch, *Blue Velvet* is a stylish, compelling, and perverse mystery. At the beginning, we see a brightly colored, harmonious suburban world. But after a man gardening is almost strangled by a mysterious string, we seem to be in the science-fiction realm. When Jeffrey (Kyle MacLachlan) enters the film, it becomes his story: Like the audience, he is sucked into the mystery, an innocent who becomes tainted by what he sees and feels. Jeffrey sneaks into the apartment of a singer named Dorothy (Isabella Rossellini). After she finds him hiding in her closet, she makes him undress. Then Frank (Dennis Hopper) arrives, so she puts Jeffrey back in the closet, and he observes the degrading sex: Frank inhales from a green mask, and then stuffs blue velvet material into Dorothy's mouth as well as his own. Frank hits her, and doesn't let Dorothy look at him (although Jeffrey—and we—are looking). When Frank leaves, she still comes on to Jeffrey. Dorothy asks him to hit her, which he can't bring himself to do … this time. When he returns and she asks again, he does hit her during lovemaking. With slow motion romanticizing the scene, Lynch would have us believe that Jeffrey is enacting a female fantasy of eroticism. But *Blue Velvet* offers merely a male projection of what are perhaps the director's own fears and desires.

Whether mainstream or independent, American films have had a hard time dealing with female sexuality. As far back as the silent era, women were either vamps or victims: the former were sexual aggressors who, like the vampires from which the term originates, drained the spirit from men; the latter, when seduced, lost their reason if not their life. Some 60 years later, Hollywood had not matured in terms of presenting women's eroticism with courage, respect, or tenderness. Both Paul Schrader's *Cat People*[17] in 1982 and Tony Scott's *The Hunger*[18] in 1983 exemplify male nightmares about female sexuality unleashed. Nastassja Kinski in the former and Catherine Deneuve in the latter are beautiful even as they incarnate bestial violence: the moments of erotic climax in both films are shown in terms of bloody murder. In these horror movies accompanied by fashionable punk-rock soundtracks, sex literally turns the "heroines" into destructive animals. Femme fatale may be a French term, but it captures a problematic concept inherent in many American movies: gorgeous women are lethal—whether to themselves or others. Sexually defined female characters have led men to their deaths (as in film noir); more often, they have been objects of violent behavior.

The 1980s had no monopoly on violence, pornography, or cynicism. In every era of filmmaking, women onscreen have been subject to excesses and distortions, or at least pernicious clichés. Already in the justly celebrated work of Alfred Hitchcock, one finds many of these problems. He is arguably the greatest director of suspense or thriller material in the history of the cinema, a popular entertainer with a genuine vision of human corruption or corruptibility. But *Psycho*[19] is a prime example of how Hitchcock manipulates audience sympathy so that we identify with someone who turns out to be a Peeping Tom and murderer (Anthony Perkins), while subliminally blaming the sexy woman (Janet Leigh) in a black brassiere. As Leo Braudy suggests in his perceptive essay, "Truffaut, Hitchcock, and the Irresponsible Audience,"

> We follow Norman into the next room and watch as he moves aside a picture to reveal a peephole into Marion's cabin. He watches her undress and, in some important way, we feel the temptress is more guilty than the Peeping Tom ... Whether we realize it or not, we have had a Norman-like perspective from the beginning of the movie ... this time, like the first time, we know we won't be caught. We tend to blame Marion and not Norman because we are fellow-voyeurs with him, and we do not want to blame ourselves.[20]

We might ask, what is the sexual morality in such films? Beyond the fact, as Francois Truffaut put it, that Hitchcock shoots love scenes as if they were murder scenes and murder scenes as if they were love scenes, it appears that a woman—usually blonde—can be killed because she is promiscuous. That a nude female body invites a knife must be demystified and revealed as a facile conceit, whether the audience is rooting—as at the end of *Fatal Attraction*—for the murder of the sexually predatory blonde, or gasping at the audacity of Brian De Palma's *Body Double*.[21] Here, for example, the response to the semi-clad woman (Melanie Griffith) is not a knife but an electric saw! De Palma has emulated the master's work, and gone even further than Hitchcock in offering cheap thrills. At least Hitchcock invited the audience into a discomfiting moral realm: to the degree that we identified with his troubled protagonists—as in *Rear Window*[22]—we had to question our own responses and darker desires. But films like De Palma's early work are made in a moral vacuum, indulging our voyeuristic tendencies without making us aware of the price that must be paid for peeping.

It is too easy to attribute these limitations to the fact that most filmmakers are men, because female directors are not exempt from objectifying their heroines. The opening credit sequence of Kathryn Bigelow's *Blue Steel*,[23] for example, shows Megan (Jamie Lee Curtis) preparing for graduation from the police academy. This includes loving close-ups of shiny bullets being placed into a gun, juxtaposed with the buttoning of Megan's blue shirt. The metaphoric counterpoint of breasts and ammunition being tucked away suggests the closing off of sexuality. Not only the heroine but also the filmmaker seems to be proving her new status as one of the boys, able to deal with violence just as graphically as her male counterparts. When Caryn James compared *Blue Steel* with Sondra Locke's *Impulse*[24] in *The New York Times* of April 15, 1990, she called attention to these filmmakers' ability "to out-tough and out-macho any man at his own game," but lamented how "both of their policewomen show symptoms of insidious, inescapable female stereotypes. And while there is something exhilarating about women's ability to make whatever kind of movie they want, these directors are caught in sexist clichés you'd think they would have been shrewd enough to avoid."[25]

If David Lynch suggested in *Blue Velvet* that a woman wants to be hit during lovemaking, the directorial debut of his daughter, Jennifer Chambers Lynch, with *Boxing Helena*,[26] fuels another pernicious myth born of male fear: a beautiful woman is likely to mistreat and humiliate the man who loves her, and deserves to be punished. This film—an excuse for soft-core pornography as well as indulgence in a voyeurism that would be reviled if the director were a man—invites identification with Nick from the very beginning: he is first seen as a little boy whose beautiful, rich mother seems to hate him (and before whom she flaunts her lovers); later, Nick (Julian Sands) is a successful surgeon obsessed with Helena (Sherilyn Fenn). Like Norman in *Psycho*, he is the audience surrogate for voyeurism, as when he climbs a tree across from Helena's window (open, of course) to watch her make love with Ray (Bill Paxton).

> *It's happened a couple of times that I've gone in for a meeting and just knew that the ideas I was going to have were not what they wanted to hear. They would want to stay with what is traditional. That begs the question of just how long it takes to make a tradition!*
>
> —*Pat Golden*

Helena is cruel to Ray, dismissing him after she says he bores her. At a party thrown by Nick, Helena disrobes to frolic in the fountain, picks up his young colleague, and accidentally leaves her pocketbook behind. This leads to her return to Nick's mansion ... and to being hit by a car. In the next scene, Nick is caring for the suddenly legless Helena, who continues to berate him. He shuts himself off from work and friends, devoting himself to the paralyzed Helena—who taunts Nick about never having had an orgasm with him. In the next scene, she has no arms as well! (Has Nick's sophisticated scalpel punished her?) He brings home a prostitute and has sex with her while Helena watches, her eyes expressing arousal. Helena seems to desire Nick, but Ray comes in and attacks the good doctor. *Boxing Helena* ends with a twist: in the hospital, Helena has all her limbs. If what preceded was a dream, was it Nick's or Helena's? Is the film a fantasy of male revenge or of female masochism? And is one version any less reprehensible than the other?

Fortunately, other images of women (as well as men) proved more popular in the 1990s. Even if the stereotype of the whore-with-a-heart-of-gold has not disappeared from movies—as with Julia Roberts in *Pretty Woman*[27] or

Melanie Griffith in *Milk Money*[28]—fresh characterizations emerged in the 1990s. From Tom Hanks's childlike incarnations in *Big*[29] or *Forrest Gump*[30] to the female "heroes" of *Silence of the Lambs*[31] or *Thelma and Louise*,[32] gender roles on film were being reassessed. Earlier in the decade the centrality of the ammunition-toting hero was already in question: in *Terminator 2*,[33] for instance, Linda Hamilton made a speech about a cyborg perhaps being a superior father because he is never too busy to nurture! Films like *Regarding Henry*[34] and *The Doctor*[35] presented Harrison Ford and William Hurt as professionals who needed to reevaluate their priorities. Other movies—as diverse as *Hook*,[36] *Father of the Bride*,[37] and *The Prince of Tides*[38]—implied the centrality of the family. The value seemed to lie in being a good father, a sensitive listener, and a nurturer.

Q: Have you encountered pressures to cast younger women?

Always.

—Pat Golden

I think you're starting the stereotyping by asking for advice for gay and lesbian producers. The main thing is to make great films.

—Christine Vachon

The year 1991 began with the release of *Silence of the Lambs*, starring Jodie Foster as an FBI agent who gets her man—not in the traditional sense of romance, but the professional meaning of capturing a killer. As she remarked upon accepting the Best Actress Award from the New York Film Critics Circle, it was a "hero" role to which women had not had access before. In the same year, three studio releases—*V.I. Warshawski*[39] (with Kathleen Turner), *Thelma and Louise*, and *Terminator 2*—suggested that women were moving from vulnerable object to weapon-wielding subject.

Directed by Ridley Scott from Callie Khouri's Academy Award-winning screenplay, *Thelma and Louise* is an engaging feminist road movie that touches a raw nerve in audiences: it acknowledges that women might have both sexual urges and the potential for violent action. When Louise (Susan Sarandon) shoots a man who has attempted to rape Thelma (Geena Davis), the waitress and the housewife become outlaws. Although some viewers are made nervous by what the women do, many more are disturbed by what the men in the film do not do. The male characters range from the ineffectual to the fatally sleazy. If a single one had been able to "save the day" by saving the heroines, fewer viewers would have been offended. But *Thelma and Louise* rejects the traditional notion of the male: the characters played by

Michael Madsen, Christopher McDonald, and Harvey Keitel do not succeed in protecting either the women or their territory. None is able to tame the narrative as they do in conventional American movies.

But is it a step forward for women to pack pistols, or a step backward because violence is still cathartic? *La Femme Nikita*[40] is a compelling French thriller by Luc Besson, but its heroine Nikita (Anne Parillaud) exists as a function of violence. Her transformation is merely from the anarchic destructiveness she displays at the beginning, to the focused and sanctioned killing she performs by the end. Nikita is hardly sympathetic in an early scene when she rams a pencil through a police inspector's hand, but she is rendered a heroine when she commits the murders assigned by her mentor Bob (Tcheky Karyo). The fact that Besson's film led not only to a Hollywood remake but an American television series suggests that the title character resonates with the public. (John Badham's *Nikita*[41] is a faithful imitation that merely has Bridget Fonda walk through the steps of her French predecessor.) But why does Nikita translate so well? Because the "hit man" is an attractive young woman?

An affirmative answer to this question is provided by *G.I. Jane*[42] when a feisty female senator (Anne Bancroft)—who is pushing to integrate women into the military—looks over applicant dossiers. After passing over a few unattractive women, she lights upon the file of the shapely Lt. Jordan O'Neill (Demi Moore): "This is really top-drawer—with silk stockings," she says approvingly. Jordan, who has been denied operational experience that was afforded her boyfriend—also a lieutenant—is thus the first woman accepted into the elite Navy SEALS training program. From a script by David Twohy and Danielle Alexandra, Ridley Scott directs the controversial *G.I. Jane* in a return to the tense women-in-male territory that he explored in *Thelma and Louise*. Violence is the norm: as the senator replies when a female reporter asks if certain jobs are not for women, "How strong do you have to be to pull a trigger?" Because the drop-out rate for the grueling SEALS program is 60 percent, politicians expect the little lady to disappear from the male enterprise. But the indomitable Jordan won't give up.

Goaded by the surly chief (Viggo Mortenson) as well as her fellow male trainees, Jordan hangs in there by discarding femininity. The trademark Demi Moore locks fall to the ground as she shaves her own head. She works out, growing increasingly muscular, and even loses her menstrual period (the doctor says this is normal because she is shedding body fat). Jordan is finally accepted by the guys because of her transformation into an essentially male SEAL: she fights back physically when abused, curses, drinks shots with them, and hurls the vulgar (subsequently oft-repeated) epithet, "Suck my dick." Seeing she won't quit, politicians try to smear her as a lesbian because they have taken secret photos of her at a party with other women.

When it turns out that the smear campaign has been orchestrated by the female senator, *G.I. Jane* takes on an insidious aspect: it is women who keep women from succeeding. Whereas the men are direct in their condescension to Jordan, Bancroft's character is duplicitous, willing to sacrifice her prodigy for political advancement. She has presumably risen to her position by indeed becoming "one of the boys"—playing political games through ruthless manipulation. The central climax in the film is not the famous scene of the chief assaulting Jordan in front of her peers—testing their ability to withhold military secrets while witnessing an attempted rape—but Jordan's confrontation with the senator: realizing that this politician is her real enemy, Jordan fights back ... and is reinstated. By the end, she manifests courage as well as physical strength, rescuing the chief in a Libyan attack and getting her men out of danger.

From the numerous shots of Moore exercising to become a lean weapon-wielder, one is reminded of her previous film, *Striptease*,[43] in which her character bared her curves. Much like Sharon Stone moving from sexual icon in *Basic Instinct* to gun-toting broad in *Gloria*,[44] Moore represents a possible cinematic transition from woman-to-be-ogled: instead, we have woman-to-be-reckoned-with ... because she's armed.

The association between babe and bullets informs *Jackie Brown*,[45] Quentin Tarantino's first feature after the wildly influential *Pulp Fiction*.[46] Adapted from Elmore Leonard's *Rum Punch*,[47] the heist film with well-drawn characters centers on a clever and mature stewardess (Pam Grier). But before we get into her story, an opening scene simultaneously engages us in and distances us from women with guns. Weapons dealer Ordell (Samuel L. Jackson) proudly shows his buddy Eddie (Robert De Niro) TV ads for his product. Bikini-clad chicks smile seductively as they hold massive weapons, as Ordell explains that every guy wants the gun he sees on a screen. Ordell articulates what Tarantino is attacked for: seeing violence onscreen creates a desire to imitate it! The seminude females are simply repeating what they do in traditional advertising—showing their bodies to sell a product.

What is literalized in *Jackie Brown* is figuratively presented in the opening title sequence of *Tomorrow Never Dies*.[48] As in previous James Bond movies, gorgeous, almost-naked young women hold guns and other paraphernalia, creating a visual association between females and phallic worship. These beautiful creatures are simultaneously voyeuristic objects and a tool for selling weapons. While one can focus on the self-conscious—and thus ironic—aspect of this depiction, the objectification is doubly troublesome: read literally, the women in both films want their undraped bodies to be ogled, and they want to fondle instruments of assault.

> *I wish we were ready to deal with the subtleties of body type. Everyone is body-beautiful, no matter what they had to do to get themselves that way. They know it's not acceptable to be fat or out of shape, unless they're playing a character role.*
>
> —*Pat Golden*

Fortunately, the narratives of *Jackie Brown* and *Tomorrow Never Dies* transcend the opening imagery. Jackie turns out to be vulnerable but tough, a black woman who is able to outsmart criminals and feds of every color and age. And Pierce Brosnan's 007 seems less the hero than Michelle Yeoh, playing a super-competent martial arts expert working for the Chinese. When compared with their 1970s counterparts, these heroines are a blast of fresh air. As the star of "blaxploitation" films like *Cleopatra Jones*[49] and *Foxy Brown*,[50] Pam Grier played the first sexy black heroine to brandish weapons. Two decades later, the same actress defined by Foxy is "Jackie," allowed to show smarts rather than flesh, and maturity rather than ammunition. Similarly, "Bond Girls" used to be primarily what the term suggests—babes to be bedded and easily sacrificed by the plot. Without Yeoh's warrior, on the other hand, Bond might not survive for a sequel.

Women holding weapons may seem liberating, but the image is potentially facile and harmful. *The New York Post* of January 5, 1998 recounts that

> Four women looking for 'kicks' kidnapped a man at gunpoint, took him on a terrifying three-hour ride and robbed him of $500 after watching a flick about female bank robbers, police sources said.... The suspects' inspiration was *Set It Off*,[51] a 1996 movie, starring Queen Latifah, Jada Pinkett, Vivica Fox and Kimberly Elise, about four Los Angeles women who rob banks, the detective said. It was described by one critic as *Thelma and Louise* times two.[52]

(If this sounds like the young male criminals who said their crimes were inspired by *Rambo*[53] or *Money Train*,[54] it's hardly coincidental.) Although we would like to think that the screen violence of the late 1990s uses irony—that it doesn't take itself as seriously as earlier films did—viewers are less likely to come away with cultural critique than desensitization.

Speaking at a Columbia University film class in 1993, Philip Kaufman lamented that whereas movies can show a female breast being shot, they still can't show a breast being caressed. The director of such stunningly provocative films as *The Unbearable Lightness of Being*[55] and *Henry and June*[56] should know: the latter was the first American movie to receive the NC-17 rating—a classy X. Violence is a commercially viable commodity in motion pictures, whether enacted by men or women. Erotic tenderness is not.

What can be done? Certain senators and their supporters would have us believe that art is subject to the morality of the most vocal legislators—a position that leads, regrettably, to censorship. Imagine banning *Romeo & Juliet*[57] on the grounds that Shakespeare could inspire teen suicide! It is dangerous to impose on the filmmaker the obligation to be "moral," especially because the word needs constant redefinition. But it's also dangerous to absorb movies without reflecting on their potentially harmful effects.

As the Women in Film International Coordinating Council stated in 1993,

> We are committed to raising awareness of the destructive repercussions of excessive screen violence particularly on young audiences. The disproportionate number of women brutalized on screen, and of ethnic minorities cast as violent characters, perpetuate negative stereotypes. Great drama is created through the development of characters and the relationships between them, not through bullies, bullets and bombs. This is not a call for censorship. It is a call for sensitivity, responsibility and accountability.[58]

Critics must continue to seek out and make known great films—to celebrate the skill—but also to question the clichés. Filmmakers are responsible for what is on the screen, and so are enlightened viewers.

Notes

1 Insdorf, Annette. *Francois Truffaut* (Cambridge, N.Y.: Cambridge University Press, 1994).
2 1997 D: Quentin Tarantino, Miramax Films.
3 1992 D: Paul Verhoeven, TriStar Pictures.
4 1997 D: Ridley Scott, Buena Vista Pictures.
5 1987 D: Adrian Lyne, Paramount Pictures.
6 1986 D: David Lynch, DeLaurentis Entertainment Group.
7 1994 D: Oliver Stone, Warner Bros.
8 1988 D: Christopher Cain, 20th Century Fox.
9 1987 D: Richard Donner, Warner Bros.
10 1988 D: John McTiernan, 20th Century Fox.
11 1987 D: Tony Scott, Paramount Pictures.
12 1987 D: Adrian Lyne, Paramount Pictures.
13 1987 D: Tom Holland, MGM-UA.
14 Kehr, Dave, *Premiere*, February 1988.
15 Goleman, Daniel. "New View of Fantasy: Much is Found Perverse," *The New York Times*, May 7, 1991.
16 1986 D: David Lynch, DeLaurentis Entertainment Group.
17 1982 D: Paul Schrader, Universal Pictures.
18 1983 D: Tony Scott, MGM-UA.
19 1960 D: Alfred Hitchcock, Paramount Pictures.
20 Braudy, Leo. "Truffaut, Hitchcock, and the Irresponsible Audience," *The World in a Frame: What We See in Films* (Chicago: University of Chicago Press, July 1984).
21 1984 Brian DePalma, Columbia Pictures.
22 1954 D: Alfred Hitchcock, Paramount Pictures.
23 1990 D: Kathryn Bigelow, MGM-UA.
24 1990 D: Sondra Locke, Warner Bros.

25 "Women Cops Can Be A Cliché in Blue," *The New York Times*, April 15, 1990, Section 2, p. 17.
26 1993 D: Jennifer Chambers Lynch, Main Line Pictures.
27 1990 D: Garry Marshall, Buena Vista Pictures.
28 1994 D: Richard Benjamin, Paramount Pictures.
29 1988 D. Penny Marshall, 20th Century Fox.
30 1994 D: Rober Zemeckis, Paramount Pictures.
31 1991 D: Jonathan Demme, Orion Pictures.
32 1991 D: Ridley Scott, MGM-UA.
33 1991 D: James Cameron, Carolco Pictures.
34 1991 D: Mike Nichols, Paramount Pictures.
35 1991 D: Randa Haines, Touchstone Pictures.
36 1991 D: Steven Spielberg, Amblin Entertainment.
37 1991 D: Charles Shyer, Touchstone Pictures.
38 1991 D: Barbra Streisand, Columbia Pictures.
39 1991 D: Jeff Kanew, Warner Bros.
40 1990 D: Luc Besson, Gaumont.
41 *Point of No Return*, a.k.a. *Nikita* 1993 D: John Badham, Warner Bros.
42 1997 D: Ridley Scott, Buena Vista Pictures.
43 1996 D: Andrew Bergman, Columbia Pictures.
44 1999 D: Sidney Lumet, Columbia Pictures.
45 1994 D: Quentin Tarantino, Miramax Films.
46 1997 D: Quentin Tarantino, Miramax Films.
47 Leonard, Elmore. *Rum Punch* (New York: Doubleday, 1998).
48 1997 D: Roger Spottiswoode, MGM-UA.
49 1973 D: Jack Sarrett, Warner Bros.
50 1974 D: Jack Hill, American International Pictures.
51 1996 D: F. Gary Gray, New Line Cinema.
52 Messing, Philip. "Woman Abduct Man In 3 Hour Terror Ordeal," *The New York Post*, January 5, 1998, p. 6.
53 *First Blood*, 1982 D: Ted Kotcheff, Orion Pictures Group.
54 1995 D: Joseph Ruben, Columbia Pictures.
55 1988 D: Philip Kaufman, The Saul Zaentz Company.
56 1990 D: Philip Kaufman, Walrus & Associates.
57 William Shakespeare. *Romeo and Juliet*, *Encyclopedia Britannica Online*: www.eb.com.
58 Women in Film International Coordinating Council Statement, 1993.

Documentary and Reality-Based Programming

Hollywood Recasts History?

"Ain't Nothing Like the Real Thing"

What happens when Hollywood meets journalism? Let's imagine that you're a reporter for *NBC News*. If you appear on a television news program with an editorial categorically stating that President William Jefferson Clinton impregnated a young girl while he was the governor of Arkansas, and have no hard evidence to back up this statement, you most likely will be sued. NBC will certainly censure you in some way.

However, if you protect your statement under the veil of fiction, as Joe Klein did in his book *Primary Colors*,[1] you can make the very same statement, whatever that statement may be, without fear of direct retribution. In this book, Klein created a fictional presidential candidate that was so closely drawn to Bill Clinton that most readers immediately made the identification. The book was then made into a film by the same name,[2] starring John Travolta and Emma Thompson. When questioned about the parallels, director Mike Nichols protested that *Primary Colors* was "only a movie," and hence, not intended to be taken literally. However, as Les Brown comments:

> The parallels between the fictive Stantons and real-life Clintons were the main source of the book's notoriety and undoubtedly the reason the movie was made in the first place. It is a stretch to give Nichols the benefit of the doubt here, but perhaps in his own mind the screen adaptation of any book renders it pure make-believe, a mere movie, one of those confections destined to be left in the theatre when the patrons go home. His protestation to the contrary, it's probable that millions of people in the U.S. and abroad formed some lasting impressions—fair or not—of the President and the First Lady from this film.[3]

As if the book itself was not a strong enough influence, the power of seeing such stars as Travolta and Thompson playing the fictional first family on-screen without a doubt affected people's perceptions of the Clintons, whether positively or negatively.

Q: Is there an advocacy role that you should have played more strongly?

That's a moral issue that we go back and forth on. On many different levels and in many different categories of philosophical debate, we ride a line. We're constantly examining which side of the line we're on.
—Joe Berlinger

But, what are the responsibilities of the filmmaker in situations that are either reality based, or wherein reality is so closely mimicked as to have substantially the same effect on the audience?

As a preliminary point, what are some of the legal ramifications of dealing in reality-based programming? The First Amendment gives you the right to say most anything these days, verbally, in writing, or in film, but it does not protect you from being sued by those private citizens whom you may wrong with your speech, as we discussed in previous sections.

Most importantly, you're not permitted by law to engage in the oral (crime of slander) or written (crime of libel) defamation of a person, which includes damaging the social esteem in which he or she is held (say by printing a false story about their being arrested), damaging through ridicule, damaging by falsely implying that the subject has a disease or mental illness, or damaging the subject in his or her occupation (by falsely impugning his or her business reputation). You are also liable if you libel a corporation by making statements damaging to the company's ability to do business (such as stating that the company cannot pay its bills).

In the area of libel, the law in its several forms is confused at best. For example, sometimes truth is a defense. In other words, if you can prove that what you have said in whatever form is true, you are not liable. However, sometimes this defense does not hold. Similarly, sometimes lack of malice in intent is a defense, but not always. Sometimes freedom of speech is a defense, but again, not always. Suffice it to say that past legal precedent is not a foolproof guide to the results of a legal action in this area.

Now, when you create fiction, you, as the creator, have almost unlimited license to express yourself in whatever way you see fit. You can cast historical facts in the best light to serve your purposes and to make for the best entertainment possible.

Let it be said that history has been recast for effect throughout history, but several things have changed in recent times: first, our ability, through film and television, to reach a mass audience; and, second, our ability to integrate actual historical footage into our work and manipulate it outrageously, as, for example, in

Q: Is a documentarian first and foremost a journalist or an entertainer?

I think it's a blending of the two. I think our films are entertaining in the sense that—although they're not musicals—they entertain the mind. A lot of documentaries are unfortunately illustrated lectures. Ours are very experiential. People watch the films and come up with many different feelings. When Joe and I first started making Brothers Keeper *and* Paradise Lost *we had one feeling. A month into the journey we felt differently. Two weeks later we felt exactly as we did a month before.*

—Bruce Sinofsky

Forrest Gump.[4] In cases like *Gump*, this type of manipulation is done purely for the entertainment value and to make for a more enjoyable movie.

Filmmakers also rewrite historical events to create more dramatically compelling stories. As special effects expert Rob Legato has suggested about his work on *Titanic*:[5]

> We're hopefully telling things in a way that's a tad more exciting than they really were, but we're not forcing someone to believe something that wasn't there. What we contributed to the retelling of the Titanic legend was depicting it in such a real way that audiences comprehend how horrible that night must have been...[6]

In this case, the manipulation of history to whatever degree seems to present little in the way of ethical dilemmas. Survivors' accounts differ, and, having lived through a terrible tragedy, they might not wish to have their stories distorted in any way. However, the insertion of the story of the fictional lovers was a simple and clever dramatic invention that allowed the audience into the drama, gave the tragedy a human face, and, not coincidentally, earned enormous, record-breaking box office in the process.

But what if these manipulations are used to change facts or context in an attempt to reconstruct history in a certain, somewhat slanted way? Does this present different issues? Legato says:

> If you went back and recreated Hiroshima or the Zeppelin disaster, and did it so expertly that you altered the impression of it, or took something historical and distorted it, that would be one thing. I don't think we made it look like real footage and distorted it. We were faithfully retelling the story and upping it a bit dramatically just to make it fun to watch, but not changing it. It starts to get a little funny in a film like *Contact*[7] when you have the current President of the United States with a real actor. It looks so realistic that

> you believe that the President took time out from his day to do it. At least it was tastefully done and they didn't alter the footage to make him look silly. But it could have ramifications.[8]

Ramifications? Indeed. The classic contemporary example of a filmmaker's attempt to recast history according to his own viewpoint is Oliver Stone's *JFK*.[9] From the fictional black and white footage used throughout, to the constant replaying of the actual historical Abraham Zapruder home movie of President John F. Kennedy's assassination, to the hand-held camera style and quick edits, this movie looks like a realistic peek behind long-closed historical doors.

It is possible that young viewers who did not live through the actual events and who have engaged in little or no serious study of the subject accept this film as history, or in other words, reality. To them it feels like an accurate expose of a

> *At the beginning of our film you buy into what the local people bought into: terrible murders. You see the body footage, grieving parents of the murdered kids. That's all anyone ever saw. We show the other side of the coin. What we do is show the human side of the three defendants and their families. We let you add up the evidence, including what the defendants' families were like. We felt that the audiences were intelligent and sophisticated enough to make up their own minds about innocence or guilt, about politics, about the justice system and so many more issues.*
>
> *—Bruce Sinofsky*

historical event. Now, does the film present some intellectually fascinating fodder for trying to unravel what is essentially a modern mystery? Absolutely. However, the need for *JFK* to be compelling entertainment first and an accurate rendition of history second becomes clear in certain of Stone's choices.

One of those choices that received the most criticism, and made the material presented less believable for many, was most assuredly made for dramatic purposes as opposed to historical accuracy. The choice of New Orleans District Attorney Jim Garrison as a noble hero and of Kevin Costner as Garrison was clearly made to give the audience an accessible hero to follow through the story, and through which Stone's message and the movie's reality could unfold. This choice works exceedingly well, right down to Garrison's stirring "Do not forget your dying King" closing argument at the end of the film. Hollywood at its best. However, these choices were made to make the film compelling as entertainment, not for the sake of historical accuracy.

Those who were adults at the time of the Kennedy assassination, and therefore, presumably at least, were aware of what was happening, often express a very different view of District Attorney Garrison. To many, he was not a hero, but one of the "bad guys," a little man whose primary motive was self-aggrandizement. We need not debate the truth or lack thereof in these pages. Perhaps Mr. Stone's version of reality is correct. Clearly, it is thought-provoking. However, whatever the truth (which we may never know for certain), it is enough for our purposes to suggest that Garrison was used for the entertainment side of the equation, and built up to attract an actor of Costner's stature, not to adhere to any literal truth.

There is nothing wrong with this per se. It was obviously a good dramatic and casting choice on Stone's part, helping to make for a powerful, thought-provoking, and successful film that posed some interesting theories. There is nothing wrong with Stone's choice from an ethical point of view either, *except* that much of the audience was not equipped to question his rendition of the facts or his interpretational liberties.

Q: Were those the issues that originally attracted you to the story?

We're attracted to sensational stories because we like to blow the myth the media presents, that stories are black and white. When you go beneath the big headlines the story is always more gray. Paradise Lost *is not about three devil-worshipping teens who killed three eight-year-olds.* Brothers Keeper *is not about rural fratricide with subhuman farm brothers in the valleys. It goes much deeper than that.*

—Joe Berlinger

The same is true for Stone's later political foray, *Nixon*.[10] Even though "dramatic license" and fictionalizing of the truth for maximum entertainment impact or to fill in gaps in the public record were used constantly, many accept the film as the literal truth. In fact, several of the people who were part of Nixon's inner circle in the final days of his presidency came forward after the film's release to claim that the truth was different from that presented in the film. However, it is the film that had the greater impact, and the version of history it presented as entertainment is what much of the public has now filed away as the literal truth. Herein lies the ethical issue.

That issue revolves around people's perception of the facts and meaning of history. Film and television have incredible power, not only to inform, but also to persuade and influence. If the material being depicted is presented as historical fact, but is a somewhat altered or "jazzed-up" version of historical fact, we are, in effect, changing people's perceptions of history. One might ask if this matters. Because history offers the only accurate barometer of how we got to where we are as a society, the answer seems emphatically to be yes. Our perceptions of the past will influence our building of the future; that is our nature. If our historical foundation is a "house of cards," that might, in the long run, pose a real problem.

Are we journalists or entertainers? We're storytellers who are also journalists. But storytelling is the most important aspect to us. That doesn't mean we have a license to not be truthful.
—*Joe Berlinger*

It's factual storytelling. It's not an intrusion because of the way we handle ourselves. We never force the camera on them. With the Ward brothers we visited them four or five weekends before we began filming. Some of the people in Paradise Lost *we didn't even film interviews with until six months had passed. Unfortunately a lot of documentarians question our ethics in forming these relationships with people on the grounds that we're taking advantage of them and using them.*
—*Bruce Sinofsky*

By amalgamating matters of fact and considerations of entertainment, it's easy to give the false impression that what is seen onscreen is literally true. Filmmakers, of course, all have a point of view in their work, but once a filmmaker working with historical fact begins to alter that fact to serve his or her point of view, it would seem that an ethical line is crossed.

If really abused, the end result is not the depiction of history, but propaganda. The most dazzling case of reality-based filmmaking morphing into outright propaganda is Leni Riefenstahl's *Triumph of the Will*,[11] allegedly a documentary film record of Hitler's 1934 Nuremberg Nazi Rally, that crossed the line to become, arguably, the most powerful, brilliant, and disturbing propaganda film ever made. With almost unmatched visceral power, this film seduces the viewer into the politics of its subject, quite against his or her will.

Although this is obviously an extreme example, sometimes we can only check our own direction on the downhill by seeing the end of the slope.

Television Journalism

At the same time, television journalism is also under constant pressure to become more entertaining in order to grab viewers and sell advertising. For this reason, it's becoming more and more Hollywood in its approach to delivering the news.

In January 2000, a most extreme example of this came to light. In support of American journalists, this example came from Russia, not the United States, but it is a bizarre foreshadowing nonetheless. Since its inception in October 1999, the highest rated show on the Russian M–1 Channel has a news show where the beautiful female anchor strips on the air while reading the news. In one broadcast, the now-naked newscaster chewed suggestively on a banana while giving the sports news! This represents perhaps the ultimate ratings grab at the expense of the dignity of journalism. The justification, when the newscaster was questioned, of course, was that people were listening more closely to the news than ever before![12] However, this does seem to neglect the fact that the newscaster could have been reading insurance policies or reciting bad Haiku and people still would have watched! The news of the day seems largely irrelevant at this point.

In the United States, we have already reached the stage where many news broadcasts are so anxious to entertain that the "on-air personalities" (who used to be referred to simply as anchors) are increasingly becoming the show, rather than being conduits for the news they report. Their humor (or most often lack thereof) and perky personalities are woven into the delivery of the news, taking up precious airtime and diluting what is reported. In addition, given the fact that television is a medium driven by pictures, producers need "good video" to accompany a story, and this plays an enormous part in determining which stories get aired. Stories that have the desired footage will often get aired rather than their drearier counterparts, regardless of the relative importance of the news content of each. This is one reason, for example, that so many local newscasts nationwide will lead off with stories of dramatic fires. Even if the fire is not of primary concern for its news value, the elemental drama of fire on video works wonders to grab the audience. The techniques of entertainment have taken serious reality-based programming and news and begun to turn them into something of a circus.

Even the sophisticated network newscasts, which pride themselves on being pillars of journalistic integrity, are not immune to this type of temptation. In January 2000, *The New York Times* reported that *CBS Evening News* had digitally erased a billboard outside a window onto Times Square on New Year's Eve and replaced it with an advertisement for its own programming.[13]

So what, you ask? Who cares? The point is that a line was crossed with this small and seemingly innocuous move of self-promotion. The trust between *CBS Evening News* and its viewers that the news being reported as live was *really happening* was impugned. What could be digitally changed next? Is the president really in Beirut, or does he just appear to be? Was his background digitally enhanced as well?[14] As Allen Kuczynski wrote for the *Times*:

> Inserting digital images has become an increasingly common in sports and entertainment programming—usually to insert advertising and corporate logos ... but has generally been considered out of line on news shows, a type of programming in which the assumption of reality is considered sacrosanct and not informing viewers is considered a breach of journalistic guidelines.[15]

The point is that as technology advances along with the ability to manipulate what we see onscreen, producers and writers of media shoulder an increased burden to use this technology responsibly.

Furthermore, as forcefully illuminated by Martin Koughan in "Reality-Based Filmmaking Versus Reality," the essay at the end of this section, the lines have become blurred between news and the "docu-drama" or fictional drama, between reporting the truth and enhancing it to make it more compelling, and even sometimes between straight journalism and entertainment. This has happened in several ways.

Lines of technique have blurred. Slick production values and elements borrowed from the entertainment industry have replaced the straight news delivery format of the past. It is no longer enough to have Edward R. Murrow or Walter Cronkite sitting in what looked like, and undoubtedly was, an actual newsroom presenting the news. Gone are the days when the look and feel of a piece could tell you instantly whether you were watching entertainment or reality-based content or news. As creators, we now use both the tone of reality-based programming and a variety of journalistic techniques to add credibility, verisimilitude, and impact to our entertainment programming.

On the other side, journalists, documentarians, and creators of reality-based programming are presenting an ever-increasing number of entertainment stories on news programs. People are interested in these stories, and they sell. In fact, as Koughan points out, a survey of the period from 1990–1993 showed that almost as many entertainment stories were aired on network newscasts as stories about the environment and education combined! These stories sell newspapers, magazines, and advertising for news programming.

There has been a proliferation of pseudo-news programming in recent years, aptly dubbed the "news magazine." These shows make a pretense at providing the viewer with responsible reporting. It may even be that they follow the ethical strictures of journalism. However, their raison d'être, in general, is to report sensationalized news and gossip as news content that appeals to the audience's more prurient impulses, generating ratings.

The net result of these programs' combined assault on the audience is to confuse where serious news ends and entertainment begins. Because the shows' content is presented as news, and quite convincingly so much of the time, viewers often take it as such on faith.

It is interesting to note that traditional journalists are asked to adhere to a formal code of professional ethics, and are taught this code as part of the core curriculum of most every journalism course they take. In stark contrast, film and television creators working outside the traditional news arena but still engaged in reality-based programming very often come from an entertainment background. With rare exceptions, creators with a background in entertainment are not even exposed to the formalized concept of ethics in

But we believe that any time you make a film this personal, entering into people's lives, you do cross the line a little bit. Not in the sense that you're manipulating them. But you form relationships and bonds and those trusts that allow us to film the intimate scenes that you see in our films. We don't prejudge. But it raises a series of interesting ethical dilemmas for us. You enter into people's lives. You establish a relationship; yes, I would even use the word friendship, which raises the hair on the necks of many documentarians.
—*Bruce Sinofsky*

(One of the families) felt we had violated a trust and a friendship by putting graphic footage in the film. There was an expectation on their part that we would totally tell their side of the story and not do anything disturbing to them. That was never a promise.
—*Joe Berlinger*

their work, let alone asked to adhere to a code of behavior. We could theoretically go out tomorrow and create a story about a Martian landing, present it as news, using all the techniques of news presentation, and not once be confronted with the ethical considerations of what we had done, at least not until after the fact.

In what is still one of the most remarkable instances of this phenomenon of duping through verisimilitude, Orson Welles, with his legendary broadcast of H.G. Wells's *The War of the Worlds*[16] on October 30, 1938, had many viewers convinced there had been an actual alien landing in Grovers Mill, New Jersey. Because he presented the story realistically as news, thousands of listeners actually abandoned their homes and sought shelter as a result of this broadcast.

We wrestled mightily about using that footage or not. We felt that if you made a film about Auschwitz and never showed victims, then how is anybody ever going to believe that this happened?
—Bruce Sinofsky

The knife was given to our cameraman as a Christmas gift. We opened it up in our hotel room and there was blood on it. Mark (Buyers, a possible suspect in a murder case) had said he had never used it before because he didn't like it. We went back to HBO and decided that the civically responsible thing to do was to turn this knife over.
—Bruce Sinofsky

By far the best contemporary example of this phenomenon to date is the low-budget film *The Blair Witch Project.*[17] This film caused quite a stir, as it created a new Internet marketing paradigm in the independent film industry, or at least showed conclusively that such a paradigm could succeed. For our purposes here, *Blair Witch* also added some new wrinkles to the reality-based versus fiction debate.

The story conceit of *Blair Witch* is that three filmmakers went off alone into the woods to make a documentary about the Blair Witch, an actual figure in Maryland supernatural folklore. They were never seen again. The rough footage that was released as *The Blair Witch Project* was left in the woods by these filmmakers and found one year after their disappearance. It provides a (to some) terrifying record of their trek through the woods to certain doom.

So, right from the start, the film was marketed as a documentary, which of course it was *not*. Although the Blair Witch is a real legend, that's where reality ends. The entire idea of three filmmakers lost and ultimately dying in the woods and leaving this film behind as their testament was the brilliant brainchild of two young Florida filmmakers, and was entirely a fictional device.

Blair Witch was marketed solely on the Internet prior to its attracting a U.S. distributor (Artisan Entertainment). The filmmakers created a Website that provided basic information about the film. Once Artisan stepped in, paying $1 million for a film that cost just $100,000 to make, the distributor took over the Website.

At this point, the idea that *Blair Witch* was based upon a true story really began to take hold. Artisan posted the colorful legend of the Blair Witch on the Website. The company also posted a fabricated journal of one of the doomed filmmakers, fake police reports about the disappearance, and so on. A video cassette claiming to provide further evidence and details of the disappearance appeared on video store shelves soon after the original release. The debate about whether the disappearance of the filmmakers was real or a hoax generated much interest on the Internet. Again, entertainment blurring into reality or at least steeped with verisimilitude was the key to creating the buzz around this film.

By the time Artisan released the film, a complete *Blair Witch* mythology had been created, spawning a ready market for the film, which made back its costs on its opening weekend. The film went on to make a staggering $140.5 million domestically. Both a sequel (*Blair Witch Two*), and a prequel (*Blair Witch 3*) are due to be released in the next two years. Of the sequel, Artisan President Amir Malin has said, "We'll keep that sense of reality and add a little more meat to the bone ... you try to create a sense of realism. That's what [the Director] is going to bring to the table."[18]

The selfish, manipulative filmmaking thing to do would have been to not give the knife over. When we gave it over, we thought it was going to destroy the film.
—Joe Berlinger

I'm 35. When I was in high school almost no one was sexually active until his or her last year of high school. Now if you're not, you're laughed at. So for me Kids *was partly about mirroring reality and waking people up to it. I don't think the movie did anything to glorify it. If anything, by the end of it you had a knot in your stomach.*
—Mark Gill

Interestingly, the director Malin is talking about for the sequel is Joe Berlinger, an interviewee for this book, and ironically, an award-winning *documentarian.*

The ultimate, brazen presentation of fiction as reality that was *The Blair Witch Project* worked for the filmmakers better than anyone could have dreamt. However, for our purposes here, this example shows that it's no longer easy or even possible to tell with certainty what is true and what is just made to seem true. This is a powerful realization, open to much manipulation and abuse by creators of fiction. However, since creation of fiction does not abide by the same strictures, legal or ethical, as either legitimate journalism or serious documentary filmmaking, it will prove very difficult, if not impossible, to rein in this trend now that the genie has escaped from the bottle.

Was the selling of *The Blair Witch Project* more than simply a brilliant marketing plan? Were there ethical issues that were not considered that should have been? The answer would seem to be no, in this specific case. This was simply a great idea and the filmmakers deserve all the credit (and profit) in the world. However, the deeper question is, what about the trend this will spawn, or at least accelerate, given the profit potential involved?

The READR method should provide a good "reality check" here, no pun intended. When you use this method to examine a project, ask yourself in Step 1 ("Review") whether the project is pure fiction, to be presented as such, or whether its impact will depend, in some part, on it appearing factual.

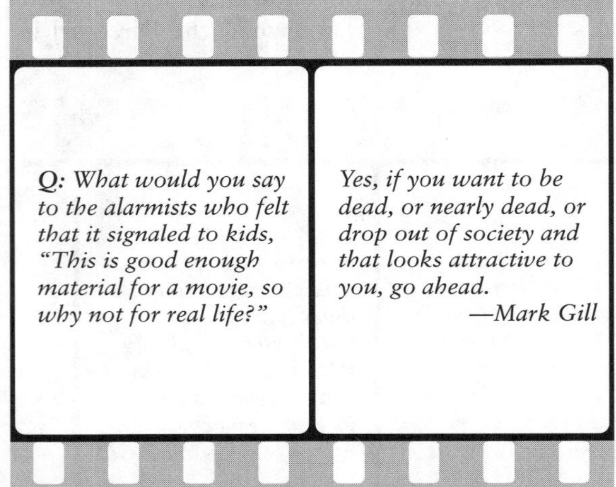

If the piece is purely fictional, when you engage in Steps 2 ("Enumerate") and 3 ("Analyze"), see what sorts of reality your components are depending upon in their presentation. In Step 4 ("Determine"), make sure that you are ethically comfortable in the fact that you're not using reality factors to mislead or trick the audience in any way, unless you are creating the next *Blair Witch* and that's the point of the exercise. Finally, in Step 5 ("Reintegrate"), make sure that your judgment of reality versus fiction is still the same as when you started the process.

If you are creating reality-based programming, that's another matter. Then, in Step 1, you must ascertain what story you are telling and to what degree you will stick with the truth of the reality. Then, in Steps 2 and 3, make sure that each component maintains a roughly consistent reality level, or at least make yourself aware of where you're simply exaggerating or filling in gaps in knowledge and where you're making things up out of whole cloth. Remember that amalgamation of real historical characters or events to make a point or tell a story can rise to the level of manipulating history, which may pose ethical concerns.

In Steven Spielberg's compelling *Amistad*,[19] for example, Anthony Hopkins' character's stirring speech before the court is an amalgamation of antislavery sentiment, actually built up over many decades throughout our history. It is quite simply a fiction as regards the individual character who delivers it. As storytellers by profession, we're entitled to a certain amount of "dramatic license" in order to create compelling tales. However, a problem arises when we cross the line from entertaining to educating. For example, study guides for classrooms were developed from *Amistad* with the purpose of educating youth about the evils of slavery. However, at least some of what was presented in these study guides was taken from the movie, not from history, and enhanced to increase the dramatic impact. This is pure invention, noble in cause, but dangerous to the entire concept of historical study.

In Step 4, make sure that you are comfortable with the message and the reality that you are portraying through each character, milieu, backdrop, line of dialogue, and so on. Finally, in Step 5, after breaking down the project in this manner, make certain that you're comfortable with the entire picture you are presenting, taking all its component parts into account.

On another topic, consider for a moment all of the "disease of the week," trauma, crime, or sex scandal Movies of the Week and miniseries that are based on real people and real events. Are these news? Are they documentaries, docu-dramas, or mixtures of all three? Where does fact end and entertainment begin?

Greatly adding to the blurring trend is the fact that most news and reality-based programming outlets and the programming itself are now owned by entertainment conglomerates. It has become clear that those individuals or entities that own the means of distribution of electronic product ultimately call the shots. This does not mean that legitimate news is no longer legitimate news. However, it does in large part account for the fact that more and more entertainment stories are finding their way into legitimate news broadcasts. It helps explain the increasing cross-pollination between units of these conglomerates, including the news arms.

Documentaries have suffered from the entertain-at-all-costs phenomenon as well. Documentaries, although not in the studio feature film realm, are not inexpensive to produce, at least not if they are produced for television. In many cases, in order to receive funding the documentarian must sell the funder on the idea that the documentary will be entertaining to a significant enough portion of the audience to make it a good risk. Koughan explains in vivid detail what this means for serious documentarians, who were once primarily driven by the subjects they were exploring and are now increasingly enslaved by monetary concerns and the need to entertain. Reality programming, in many ways, has become the hostage of entertaining and entertainment.

When we make entertainment feel like news or news feel like entertainment, when we blur the distinction between reality and fictionalized reality, let alone fiction, we create large potential ethical landmines.

Ethical Gymnastics

1. Based upon your reading, what do you believe are the differences between documentary and reality-based filmmaking and propaganda? Be as specific as possible.

2. You're producing a documentary about the assassination of President John F. Kennedy. You have found definitive proof that the phone company was responsible. You've also found a small, unconfirmed bit of information that leads you to suspect that your "definitive proof" might not be so definitive after all. What are your ethical concerns at this point? Should the unconfirmed bit of information be ignored? Should it be mentioned, but not emphasized in your documentary, or should it be featured? What are your responsibilities, if any, to confirm the information? What if you found out that the man who actually shot Kennedy was still working at the phone company today? Would this alter your ethical concerns?

3. Watch the film *All The President's Men*.[20] Use the READR method to break down and analyze the movie. Discuss examples of Woodward's and Bernstein's ethical or unethical "verification of the facts."

4. As a documentarian, should your main purpose be to objectively present all the facts and issues, or to influence the audience using those facts and issues? Do you think most documentarians working today follow the ethical choice you're suggesting in your answer? Choose a current documentary and discuss.

5. Discuss the range of ethical choices you're likely to face as you write and produce your documentary entitled *The Historical Significance of the Ku Klux Klan*. How will you present an accurate picture? Will your own feelings intrude? You know this will be uncomfortable for the African American segment of your audience. What, if any, ethical choices do you have that might minimize this discomfort (assuming you believe you should try)?

6. You're producing a segment for a TV news magazine entitled *Green Day and Green Balls of Death*, about incendiary household decorations. You're appalled that you haven't come further in your career! However, a number of sources have confirmed that playing Green Day songs on a radio in close proximity to growing Chia pets will sometimes cause them to explode. In 13 separate attempts, you've been absolutely unable to cause such an explosion. Discuss the ethical issues involved in creating an explosion using conventional means, simply to illustrate what your sources assure you is happening in the real world on an almost daily basis. If you decide to

proceed, what are your ethical concerns? Would you plaster "Dramatization" across the screen while showing the explosion? Would you modulate the explosion to keep it in proportion to the size of the reported explosions happening to real Chia owners? Discuss and be specific.

7. You've been asked to write, produce, and direct a massive, extremely expensive, hour-long documentary about the social, religious, and economic impact of Satan throughout history. When word gets out, you're besieged with information, opinions, and propaganda from groups and organizations as wide ranging as the religious right and organized satanists. You've been handed a subject on which it's very difficult to know the truth. Discuss how you would go about completing your assignment.

8. You're assigned to produce a TV news magazine segment about a recent G-8 economic summit that took place behind closed doors in Kansas. Although the delegates may have been perplexed at the choice of location, you are extremely concerned because you have no video available for the summit itself, as cameras were prohibited. The matter being discussed is extremely technical, having to do with agricultural credits versus International Monetary Fund (IMF) obligations. You don't even have footage of the arrival of the delegates, as your piece is a last minute fill-in for a story about a dying elephant (the animal got better) and those delegates are already in Kansas. Discuss ways in which you can still make your piece of interest to a television audience.

9. Choose three movies that, in your opinion, handled historical subject matter ethically, then choose three that did not, and discuss why you've made these choices.

10. Do you believe it matters if an accurate picture of history is presented in a film that allegedly deals with historical subject matter? In other words, is it somehow essential that viewers of a movie see truth, or is it enough that the movie is entertaining and may lead the viewer to want to learn more about the subject? Discuss.

11. Map out a strategy for creating your own *Blair Witch Project*. Be specific about the story, so that you're able to discuss ways of blurring the reality/fiction line to ensure the success of your picture.

12. Now, use the READR method to determine if creating your own *Blair Witch Project* is a good idea from an ethical decisionmaking point of view. How might you vary the new paradigm created by this project to present the material in the least problematic manner?

Notes

1 Klein, Joe. *Primary Colors: A Novel of Politics by Anonymous* (New York: Warner Books, November 1996).
2 *Primary Colors*, 1998 D: Mike Nichols, Universal Pictures.
3 Brown, Les. *The Artist as Citizen* (unpublished).
4 1994 D: Robert Zemeckis, Paramount Pictures.
5 1997 D: James Cameron, 20th Century Fox and Paramount Pictures.
6 Interview with Laura Blum, Summer 1998.
7 1997 Rober Zemeckis, Warner Bros.
8 Interview with Laura Blum, Summer 1998.
9 1991 D: Oliver Stone, Warner Bros.
10 1995 D: Oliver Stone, Buena Vista Pictures.
11 *Triumph des Willens*. 1934 D: Leni Riefenstahl, Connoisseur Video.
12 Broadcast, *Fox News at Ten*, January 22, 2000.
13 Kuczynski, Allen. "On CBS News, Some of What You See Isn't There," *The New York Times*, January 12, 2000, p. 1.
14 See, for example, *Wag the Dog*, 1997 D: Barry Levinson, New Line Cinema.
15 Kuczynski, p. 1.
16 Wells, H.G., Broadcast by Orson Welles, October 30, 1938. A film version (*The War of the Worlds,* 1953 D: Byron Haskin, Paramount Pictures) was made without Mr. Welles' participation.
17 1999 D: Daniel Myrick and Eduardo Sanchez II, Artisan Entertainment.
18 Malin, Amir. *Daily Variety*, January 4, 2000.
19 1997 D: Steven Spielberg, DreamWorks SKG.
20 1976 D: Alan J. Pakula, Warner Bros.

Reality-Based Filmmaking Versus Reality

Martin Koughan

Martin Koughan, author of *Wrestling with Ethics in Documentaries*, produced a documentary on the gambling industry in association with *Frontline*, and has served as a multiple Emmy-winning producer, director, and writer with *CNN* and *CBS News*.

It was an image that literally burned itself into memory. You're careening down a country road at 50 miles per hour heading directly at a pickup truck stalled in front of you. Your car slams into it broadside, triggering an instant explosion. A ball of flames comes roaring right at you. Right over you.

If seeing is believing, that breathtaking sequence would have been all viewers needed to know about the safety problems of GM pickups with side-mounted fuel tanks. These vehicles clearly were the "firebombs" that their critics were charging.

General Motors believes that the emotional impact of that *Dateline NBC*[1] story—seen by 11 million viewers—was reflected in the size of the company's next courtroom judgment. A few months after the broadcast, a Georgia jury awarded the family of 17-year-old Shannon Mosely, who died in a GM pickup fire, an astonishing $105 million dollars in damages.

But truth is no longer necessarily what you see with your own eyes. Electronic image manipulation is now so advanced that truth lies solely within the control of the television journalist and the filmmaker. In the case of the GM truck story, the facts that viewers saw could not have been more conclusive, more convincing, or more wrong.

The story that aired on *Dateline NBC* on November 17, 1992—prophetically titled "Waiting to Explode?"—was a textbook case of truth falling victim to the seductive power of the image and competitive pressures to maximize the emotional impact of a story.

Numerous newspaper articles concerning the problems with the sidesaddle fuel tanks on GM pickup trucks detailed how these crash fires had caused more than 300 deaths—more than 10 times the number that died in fires involving the infamous Ford Pinto. Those facts alone were sobering and terrifying, but that kind of statistical data is too slow, too static on TV. Nor would a dry legal story dispassionately laying out both sides attract and hold viewers. Balance is neither dramatic nor does it move the story forward. Increasingly, viewers—and network producers—see the prime time news magazine as just another TV drama.

To grab that *Dateline NBC* audience, the rules of TV drama demanded that the story match the emotional tone of a murder trial, not a driver education class. It became not just useful for a GM pickup to burst into flames on camera. To the producers, it was absolutely essential.

What the audience saw lasted a terrifying 57 seconds. Three cameras recorded the crash and resulting blaze. Slow motion was used to chilling effect. Viewers were told that the crash punctured the gas tank and that the fire was ignited by the filament in the crash car's headlights. In fact, there was no puncture in the truck's gas tank, nor was the headlamp filament necessary to start a fire. The *Dateline NBC* team had rigged the trucks with gunpowder-packed charges that were remotely triggered at the moment of impact.

How could there have been such a dramatic fire if there was no breach of the gas tank? The producers had overfilled the tank, which caused a spray of gasoline to shoot out on impact. In real life, the fire lasted only 15 seconds. The rest was the invention of multiple camera angles and slow motion. In fact, the truck itself never caught fire at all.

How is it possible that journalists could concoct such an elaborate deception? Simply, the NBC team had convinced itself that because these trucks were indeed prone to fires—the pivotal dramatic element of the story—creating one for the cameras merely fulfilled the requirements of the script. But unlike prime time dramas, news and documentary production is not supposed to start with a script. Journalism is a process of discovery in which information is gathered, premises tested, and conclusions drawn from the facts.

Producing journalistic documentaries for television, however, is an enterprise riddled with ethical and moral dilemmas. First, there are the enormous costs associated with film and TV production. If you need $400,000 to produce a documentary, you're not likely to earn the confidence of funders by telling them you'll let them know what their money is buying once you finish your process of discovery. As a rule, you sell a fully formed idea, a story absent only the final script. The challenge is to then maintain the intellectual honesty to allow the story to evolve as the facts dictate—and inevitably the courage to defend the truth from interference by the very people who paid for it.

Then there's the problem of both management and audience expectations of storytelling techniques. If documentaries are regarded as just a variant of TV drama, then the temptation to distort the story for the purposes of excitement or pacing is unavoidable. Truth is often seriously at odds with the competitive demands of the marketplace. It takes enormous integrity to reexamine a very effective sequence and conclude, "it works, but it's just not honest."

I still cringe when I recall one moment from my early work in documentaries. I had been reporting on how political insiders were funding junkets to Europe and other exotic places by drawing large amounts of cash from the estates of people who died without relatives. The guiltiest parties managed to successfully avoid my cameras; only one lowly operative from the court, who was along for the ride, was not nimble enough to stay out of camera range.

Worse, the long tracking shot of him walking down the sidewalk was terrific; he looked thoroughly unnerved and furtive (not unreasonable considering he stepped out of his front door in the morning only to find a TV crew laying in wait). Worst of all, the scene just screamed "guilty."

I used every inch of it along with a voice-over that carefully noted all the responsible parties. It was not until the night of air, when I watched on my home TV, that I realized the narration had been completely overwhelmed by the image. In the viewers' minds, this one man bore the entire responsibility for the crime.

The problem here is that, although the visual image has impact and endures, it only incidentally carries a rational message. The message of TV and film reaches the brain only after passing through the gut and the heart.

Viewers of my surrogate's court story understood on a visceral level that this angry, nervous man scurrying away from my camera crew was guilty as hell. My attempt to create a context with just words had completely failed. The newspaper story, in contrast, must first be processed by the rational mind in order to decode the language message. The television image can carry countless messages that connect instantly—and often unpredictably—with the audience.

Consider that mainstay of the news, the burning building. Even if the fire itself does not have much news value, the visual image does. Fire is pure emotion—wild and dangerous. And emotion is perhaps television's most important product.

Emotional messages make a deep and lasting impression. Did you ever stop to wonder why you often have trouble remembering what you had for lunch, but when a 30-year-old song comes on the radio you can not only sing along but you probably know the performer's every vocal inflection? You're not drawing from some rational memory but rather a vast reservoir of stored emotional experience associated with the music itself.

You almost certainly never saw the lyrics on paper, and yet the words emerge effortlessly. Absent the musical cues, however, the words would be as impossible to recall as that lunch menu. (You've undoubtedly caught yourself humming a tune just to retrieve those lyrics from memory.)

Your mind has absorbed an emotional experience and preserved it perfectly in some remote part of the unconscious. All that's required to summon the experience back is a few bars of music. It is this reservoir of the audience's collective emotional experience that the filmmaker can influence with virtually every creative decision.

It is precisely because of the potential for emotional manipulation that when I began at *CBS News* the use of music in news reports was strictly forbidden, even as the theme motif for the evening broadcast. Music can be so powerful that it infuses the image with cues on how to feel about the information being presented.

Every network journalist I know has learned the hard way just how powerful—and volatile—vivid imagery can be. I once produced a feature for the *CBS Evening News*[2] about an upcoming congressional hearing on pesticide reform, a thoroughly nonvisual story. To emphasize the importance of the issue, I seized upon one agricultural chemical commonly used on apples that, when heated, produced a highly toxic breakdown product with the same chemical properties as rocket fuel.

To underscore the importance of the issue—or so I rationalized—I began my story with a playground full of preschoolers at snack time, eating applesauce and drinking apple juice. Over a smiling, angelic face smeared with applesauce, I introduced the thought that Mom might be interested to know what else besides vitamins is in the applesauce she feeds junior. The messy face takes a quizzical turn, then there is a startling roar and a hard cut to the launch of a Titan missile. It turned out I had made a bigger point than I intended.

Within seconds, the switchboard at *CBS News*, New York, was overwhelmed with calls from frantic mothers horrified to learn that with the best of intentions they had been poisoning their babies. And it was not just in New York. Affiliates from across the country experienced a similar panicked response—and unfortunately, local station personnel did not have the slightest idea what these callers were referring to. The affiliates' displeasure—not to mention the needless panic I had triggered among young mothers—was later forcefully called to my attention.

Not incidentally, the real message of the piece—the problems facing the congressional committee rewriting the pesticide law—had been obliterated. By trying to add a little dramatic spark to the story, I managed to burn down the house.

It was that kind of desire for high impact drama that combined with economic imperatives to completely undermine the integrity of the GM truck story. Increasingly, economics can shape a story's message in ways that are invisible to the audience. NBC's reporters in the field had been hamstrung by austerity measures at the network. The old days of "whatever it takes to get a story right" were long gone at all three networks in the 1990s. Automakers normally spend $250,000 to perform a crash test. *Dateline's* budget allocated only $3,500.

Imagine the pressure the producer felt on location. A section of country road in Indiana had been closed off and a local fire department was in attendance along with state and local law enforcement. Despite a very tight budget, *Dateline's* team numbered more than a dozen, including two video crews, support personnel, the editorial team, and their experts—and only two target trucks to capture the fire scene. With the meter running on an image considered critical by the series' executives, incendiary charges to ensure a burst of flame on the first try must have seemed perfectly reasonable.

Almost certainly, no one on location thought much about the fact that what they were doing violated the strict ethical guidelines established at *NBC News* in a time when network news people were encouraged to ignore ratings. The late Richard Salant, one of the most respected presidents of *CBS News*, used to remind the staff: "Our job is to give the people what they need to know, not what they want to see."[3] In the early days of network television, news producers were forbidden to film any scene that was not actually happening in real life—an approach that was high-minded but very, very expensive.

Today, network news is no longer "pure." Prime time magazines must compete for audience on the same terms as TV dramas and sitcoms. For all practical purposes, network news has become an arm of show business—with a growing emphasis on the business.

"The most important question in most television newsrooms today," observes Dan Rather, "is not, 'Do you know this for a certain fact?' but 'Do we have the video for that?' That's why you get pictures of trees falling on houses instead of analysis of the Asian economic crisis."

The danger of television news, which has operating ethical guidelines, falling under the sway of the entertainment industry, which has no such guidelines, is obvious. But increasingly the lines between the two are not only blurring but merging.

It's not uncommon to find real-life newscasters appearing as themselves in feature films (often made by the same conglomerate that owns both the film company and the news operation). This raises the question of whether their appearance increases the verisimilitude of the movie or undermines the credibility of the broadcast journalist—a main reason they are not allowed to do commercials.

In *Independence Day*[4] familiar faces soberly report the arrival of an armada of alien spaceships, an image preserved in that collective reservoir of emotional memory. Is it possible they may take subsequent real-world pronouncements from these journalists less seriously? It's a legitimate question but one that is enormously difficult to answer.

The unseemly marriage can work in the other direction. *60 Minutes*,[5] widely accepted as the most credible of network news magazines, aired a story in September 1997 about the threat of nuclear terror resulting from the lax security protecting the nuclear arsenal of the former Soviet Union. What the audience did not know is that the freelance producer of the piece was also coproducer of the DreamWorks SKG feature, *The Peacemaker*,[6] on the same subject.

Was this sound reporting or Hollywood hype? The producer—also the author of a nonfiction book released at the same time—heatedly denied that the movie skewed the treatment of the *60 Minutes* report. It was solid journalism that inspired the movie, all involved insist, but critics claim that the piece significantly oversold the threat.

"When you examine the level of hype in the piece and compare it with available data, it is hard to believe," observed MIT security policy expert Ted Postol. In the book, the central character is the real female scientist and former National Security Council staffer who was leading the campaign to expose the danger. Yet the book jacket carries a photo of Nicole Kidman, her fictional counterpart in the movie. It's easy to see how difficult it is for the audience to draw the line between reality and invention.

TV journalists and filmmakers now have the tools to not only reflect reality but to substantially alter it. With such influential industry players as George Lucas' Industrial Light and Magic and cutting-edge computer technology from companies like Silicon Graphics, viewers no longer have any idea what is real and what is invention.

Electronic sleight of hand is now a widely accepted tool of broadcast journalism, as well. For example, the set of *Discovery News*[7] on the Discovery Channel features Art Deco columns, a cluster of monitors, and a world map. But none of it is real. Every design element is virtual, the creation of computer generated images and advanced ultramat technology.

Virtual sets are now common in mainstream news operations. *ABC News*' 1996 election coverage was broadcast from a virtual set. Local news operations have begun to discover that using computer-generated illusion gives them more flexibility at a lower cost. But where does manipulation of the package stop and the presentation of the content begin? The risks of art shaping reality are obvious, and the opportunities presented by technology grow every day.

To most observers, the excesses of *Dateline NBC's* GM truck story are simple and obvious, but what of the filmmaker who deals with reality-based material? What sort of obligation is there to literal truth? If entertainment aims more directly for the emotional, what effect could that have on our intellectual understanding of the real world around us?

The answers to these questions are becoming more and more critical as real life increasingly becomes the subject of Hollywood filmmaking. When news embraces the techniques and tricks of docu-drama, and filmmakers employ the conventions of newsmen, there is a significant risk that the audience will lose confidence in their truthfulness. In short, both risk betraying the public trust.

The work of Oliver Stone represents to many critics perhaps the most troubling example of the dangerously thin line between truth and invention. Real life has been the source of most of Stone's films. His earliest work, such as *Platoon*[8] and *Born on the Fourth of July*,[9] share a gritty authenticity largely because of Stone's personal experiences with the Vietnam War.

But as the filmmaker has matured, his confident interpretations of history have left many critics cold. *The Doors*,[10] his version of the life of rock star Jim Morrison, contains precisely detailed scenes of wretched excess; even if they happened as Stone imagines, it is unlikely that the drug-addled Morrison would remember. Even the scene of Morrison's death, so carefully wrought and serene, is in reality the subject of significant controversy.

Even more disturbing to critics are Stone's forays into national politics, such as *Nixon*.[11] Much of President Nixon's most baffling behavior is explained by the dialogue and context in which Stone places the character. But from the moment of release, *Nixon* was bitterly criticized by individuals who were privy to those final days and insist that the words and situations Stone assigns to the late president are not only wrong but contradictory and misleading.

But even those fact-based movies, which are widely accepted as responsibly reported history, almost always diverge from the facts in order to accommodate the storytelling requirements of film.

What sort of Pandora's box is opened? Exactly who decides which facts are relevant, which evidence is confusing, which fictional characters or situations can be added to help make the story's message more "correct"? After all, it is precisely this subtle manipulation of reality to achieve specific ends that defines propaganda. One might endorse Spielberg's choices in the film *Amistad*, for example, but how does the audience determine whether or not the motives of the filmmaker are insidious?

If it is a slippery slope, it's one that filmmakers and documentarians have been perched upon for quite some time. Taking liberties with the facts has rapidly become the rule rather than the exception in fact-based filmmaking. Reality is little more than a first rough draft of history to Hollywood, a useful guide but one that in the minds of many practitioners definitely needs some "punching up."

Worse, real history is now frequently used as a marketing tool to promote feature films. That movies inspire curiosity about history is indisputable. For example, interest in the story of the Titanic among teens was minimal before James Cameron's blockbuster was released; now teachers report their students cannot get enough of it. But some of these classroom learning aids are transparently pure promotion—like those for the movie *The Jetsons*[12] or the big screen version of the campy sci-fi TV series, *Lost in Space*.[13]

Study guides often create the same fuzzy boundaries between reality and invention. For example, the character of Theodore Joadson in *Amistad*, played by Morgan Freeman, is referred to frequently in the study guide released with the film. It even includes conversations between Joadson and John Quincy Adams—only Joadson never existed. He is a dramatic device created by the filmmaker to represent the attitudes of black abolitionists in the nineteenth century.

Film critic Michael Medved called the marketing of *Amistad* a "new low ... (I)n the study guide they made no distinction between fictional or real characters or between actual and invented dialogue."[14]

Again, it is perhaps easy to rationalize the use of such a composite character to help students understand period attitudes toward slavery, but who makes such decisions and on what basis? And then there's the matter of how that affects the audience's understanding of the reality on which such inventions are based. If fictional characters are powerfully drawn, they will remain submerged in that reservoir of emotional memory and emerge along with truth when recalled. Can we really expect the audience to keep this tangle of real and imagined details straight?

If the hateful propaganda of Nazi Germany was clearly evil, and the liberties taken by Spielberg to explain attitudes toward slavery are socially acceptable, exactly where does one draw the line between these extremes? This weighty responsibility, with its ethical implications, is the filmmaker's alone.

Why should we expect the film industry to adopt the ethical standards of journalism at a time when broadcast journalists are embracing the more liberal standards of Hollywood? Because when dealing with actuality, the risks of sensationalizing truth to play to the viscera of the audience is fraught with dangers—for both practitioners. A fact-based movie may not be journalism, but, to coin a phrase, it plays like one on TV.

The competition for real human drama is now so intense that we are treated to such spectacles as a major network airing a TV movie on alleged murder by military academy lovers from Texas before their case even came to trial! Amy Fisher, the Long Island high school girl convicted of shooting her lover's wife, earned no fewer than three TV movies. All three presumed to show intimate moments that shed light on the crime, moments designed to motivate the action. In essence, the filmmakers were intuiting the characters' motives in the absence of any direct evidence.

So what is the viewer to think when, as in the case of the Fisher troika, those moments differ significantly? Hollywood cannot be expected to literally embrace journalistic ethics, but given their influence, filmmakers assume an enormous responsibility when dealing with actuality. More and more, history will be learned on the screen and not in the classroom, yet there is little evidence that Hollywood ever reflects on the broader significance of routinely giving form to the unknowable.

Meanwhile, the push to produce news and documentaries as compelling and dramatic as Hollywood movies has spawned a terrifying trend of manipulation and outright falsehood.

Take the case of *The Connection*,[15] an hour produced by the British network Carlton TV, which takes the viewer on an astonishing journey deep into the underground world of heroin smuggling. The producer, Marc de Beaufort, claimed he spent a year winning the trust of the Cali cartel in order to document a shipment of pure heroin from its source in Columbia to the streets of London.

The audience accompanies the producer while, "blindfolded ... and risking his life," he is taken to meet the number three man in the Cali cartel at "an unknown location"; they witness the drug courier, known as a mule, swallowing a kilo of heroin in the form of latex-wrapped pellets; they travel with the mule as he flies to England and, we are told, slips through Customs to make his delivery.

In short, it is unique, even breathtaking journalism—so much so that the film won eight international awards and was praised worldwide for "risk-taking investigative reporting."

Only one problem. Not a word of it was true. The "unknown location" the blindfolded producer visited was actually his own five-star hotel room; the high-ranking cartel members were hired to play their roles, as were most of the story's criminal characters. The mule was not swallowing heroin—in fact, there never was any heroin. The courier did fly to London, but not on cartel business. He was using a ticket paid for by the producer. In fact, the mule never even got through British customs; he was immediately deported because of a prior criminal record.

Even more disturbing than these deliberate deceptions is what happened after the program aired. Because the material was so compelling, such a riveting drama, it was quickly sold to 14 countries including the United States, where versions of it aired on both Cinemax and *60 Minutes*. All purchasers were operating on the reasonable but increasingly risky assumption that this award-winning documentary produced by a major British network was honest and accurate.

It appears to be messier than a simple producer deceiving his superiors at Carlton TV. According to the expose in *The Guardian* (May 6–7, 1998), the 28-year old associate producer of the film, a Colombian woman named Adriana Quintana, presented the head of documentaries for Carlton (Roger James) and the head of compliance for the network (Don Christopher) with a nine-page statement that outlined many of the deceptions *a week before the original broadcast*.[16]

James and Christopher recall the meeting with Quintana was all about money she claimed she was owed (Christopher denies even reading her memo). Even so, there is no indication James or Christopher confronted de Beaufort with the allegations. In fact there is no indication that anyone expressed anything but delight over this sexy, highly marketable documentary.

There has been much hand-wringing within the TV news community about the perils of the convergence of journalism and filmmaking, but there are no simple answers. "We have more tools at our disposal, and we are more skillful at applying them than any previous generation of journalists," laments Ted Koppel of *ABC News*, "But we're afraid of the competition, afraid of earning less, afraid of losing our audience."[17]

Journalists trying to resist the temptations of filmmaking, and filmmakers grappling with the responsibilities of journalism, are now a permanent part of the media landscape. All would do well to heed the advice of a speaker at a New York University symposium:

"The truth is very tricky in this life, very elusive, especially when it comes to contemporary issues. People have a stake in it, and it's fought over like a civil war. So be careful."[18]

The speaker? Oliver Stone.

Notes

1 1992–present D: Guy Pepper, NBC Television.

2 Personal recollection of Martin Koughan.

3 Buzenberg, Susan and Bill, Eds. *Salant, CBS and the Battle for the Soul of Broadcast Journalism: The Memoirs of Richard S. Salant* (Boulder: Westview Press, 1999).

4 1996 D: Roland Emmerich, 20th Century Fox.

5 1969–present, CBS Television.

6 1997 D: Mimi Leder, DreamWorks SKG.

7 Nicholson, Leslie. "Computer Generated Television Sets Help Producers Save Money," *The Philadelphia Inquirer*, January 8, 1998.

8 1986 D: Oliver Stone, Hemdale Film Corporation.

9 1989 D: Oliver Stone, Universal Pictures.

10 1991 D: Oliver Stone, Imagine Entertainment.

11 1995 D: Oliver Stone, Buena Vista Pictures.

12 1990 D: Joseph Barbera and William Hanna, Hanna-Barbera.

13 1998 D: Stephen Hopkins, New Line Cinema.

14 Medved, Michael. "Spielberg Film Warps History, Deceives Students," *USA Today*, December 9, 1997, p. 15A.

15 1998 D: Marc de Beaufort, Carlton TV.

16 "The Fake Connection: How Carlton's Filmmakers Deceived 3.7 Million ITV Viewers," *The Guardian*, May 6, 1998, p. 4.

17 Remarks made at the Committee to Protect Journalists' International Press Freedom Awards.

18 McKinley, Jesse. "An Irreverent Director Advises Reverent Fans," *The New York Times*, October 13, 1997.

Children's Programming

Children: A Higher Standard

Kids Are People Too

Clearly, media has become an important learning tool for children, as well as a primary means of socialization for many. Children look to the media, particularly television, for role models. They also learn styles of dress, ways to act, and certain attitudes from the characters in the programs they watch. If you consider that, in the United States, children spend an average of 28 hours per week watching television—more than they spend in school on an average week[1]—you begin to understand the hold the media has on the young minds of America. And this hold is ever-tightening.

If you thought there were ethical issues to consider and choices to be made in creating material for an adult audience, you "ain't seen nothin' yet." Creating and producing for children is both exceedingly simple and inordinately complex at the same time.

The process is simple because there are fewer moral "gray areas" with which to struggle. All of our arguments in favor of simply putting all our material out there and allowing viewers' powers of discrimination to filter out problematic, violent, or undesirable content go right out the window when producing for children. The "caveat emptor" approach ("let the buyer," or in this case, the viewer, "beware") is completely inappropriate.

Creators must make very definite choices when generating material for this audience. We should check, recheck, then check again to make sure we are not intentionally or inadvertently sending out any potentially harmful messages. In other words, we have a responsibility to be the front line ethical arbiters of the messages children receive from our work. The READR method should prove helpful here, as it will guide you through a complete breakdown of all elements of your project, and bring to light the messages, both intended and unintended, implied in each.

The entertainment industry has rallied, to an extent, and has created guidelines for writers who are interested in learning more about content issues involved with creating quality programs for children.[2] Also, many production companies now routinely hire educators and child psychologists as "technical assistants" to help develop their children's programming. If we, as creators, are interested in programming for children, professional advice and an understanding of child development can be extremely helpful in creating compelling, entertaining, and responsible stories.

This may all sound uncomfortably like censorship to you, or some kind of restriction of creativity, no matter how voluntarily it is exercised. It is not. It is merely an acknowledgment that children are considered a protected class in our society, one for whom speech should be regulated, both for the good of the children and for the future of society. The reason for this protection, of course, is that children are uniquely vulnerable to media and other influences, and have not yet developed the capacity or analytical processes to filter out negative or harmful messages. *That* is a responsibility that we, as creators, bear. *That* is the "easy part," believe it or not.

> Q: *Are any of the issues* OZ *deals with pushing it too far?*
>
> *If it's smart and it's there for a reason, no. The purpose of the project was to shed light on a human condition. I have no problem showing* OZ *to my children.*
>
> *—Bridget Potter*

The more difficult aspect of all of this is determining who fits in the protected class of minor children in what way, and what content may be harmful at what stage. By definition, all children are minors, of course. Beyond this, however, common sense tells us that not all children are alike and that, at the very least, age group lines must be drawn in order to accurately analyze content in terms of its appropriateness. Obviously, parents have the strongest role in determining what their child should watch, but a filmmaker rooted in ethical decisionmaking will certainly consider carefully the program content he or she knows will be attractive to a young audience.

Also of concern is the enormous issue of programming that is not designed specifically for children, but is often viewed by them—for example, *Friends*,[3] *South Park*,[4] and almost any "R" rated film shown on television during hours when children watch. However, we will deal here with programming intended for children, for the most part.

As children grow, their attention span, the amount of mental energy invested in watching programming and the very way in which their brains process information changes drastically.

For purposes of discussion, we will examine one generally accepted framework for understanding key stages of child development and for determining what elements children are actually absorbing as they watch television—and by extension films and other media. The research was developed by Canadian child psychologist Wendy Josephson, who has broken down the ages and stages of a child's understanding in the following way:[5]

Birth to 18 Months

From a child's birth until the age of approximately 18 months, the child can only pay attention to a television screen for extremely short periods of time. He or she is easily distracted by toys, sounds, people, and other activities. At this age, the primary experience of television programming, and by extension movies, is of color, light, and sound. These children are unable to grasp the content of the programming, although one theory posits that it is possible they can recognize various characters even at this stage.

Eighteen Months to Three Years Old

From 18 months to approximately three years of age, most children have become full-fledged television viewers. This seems to happen around the age of two-and-a-half. Once they reach three years, many actually have a "favorite program." Their attention span increases and they are able to concentrate more on the programming and comprehend and extract meaning from some of what they view.

Now for creators, here's the most difficult part. Children of this age are likely to begin to imitate behaviors they see and hear on television and in the movies. Yes, it starts that young. They seem to prefer educational programming designed for them, but also appear to like comedies, game shows, and cartoons with a great deal of action.[6] This makes sense if you assume that, at least to some degree, they're still watching programming more for its spectacle value—lights, sound, motion, and color—than for its dramatic content. The comedies and game shows provide lightness and humor, as embodied in the laugh track, and they are usually bright and colorful by design. The visual and audio riot of most action-oriented children's cartoons functions as the world's most engagingly insane over-the-crib mobile.

Ages Three to Five

Between three and five years of age, children are beginning to discover meaning in the content of the programming they watch. They are already able to discern so-called "good guys" from "bad guys," although for them, the definition of bad guys seems to be premised upon those characters being scary as opposed to what adults might define as "bad."

At this age, children are especially drawn to cartoon violence because it is extremely active and accompanied by loud music and sound effects. All this visual and audio commotion stimulates children's senses and keeps them engaged in the program.

Also, it appears from research[7] that this age group cannot always differentiate between fantasy and reality. In other words, they can identify with puppet or cartoon characters as easily as if they were human characters. This means that, in these cases, the elaborate creations of our fancy, whether good guys or bad guys, read as real to children. What messages, then, are we sending through the creation of characters, perhaps without realizing that our audience's "filters" are not yet developed sufficiently to allow them to accept the characters as mere entertainment (if indeed any viewers, children or adult, can ever truly accomplish this)?

Perhaps the reason for greatest pause in all this is that some research also shows that after watching cartoon violence, children in this age group play more aggressively than after watching other programming.[8]

Six to Eight Years Old

Children from six to eight years of age actually begin to watch less television than they did just a year or two earlier. The reason, of course, is the dreaded start of school. Although they may have been involved in preschool programs or prekindergarten programs, school takes up significantly more of their time, on average, when they hit this age group.

When they do watch, children at this age are more interested in situation comedies, cartoons, and programming with a great deal of action than they are in any kind of so-called educational programming.[9] They appear to watch for relaxation and fun, probably feeling that education is now something to be relegated to school hours. This makes them relatively passive about content. They are not highly critical, nor do they engage in a great deal of content analysis. They can generally understand television and movie plotlines, and can generally interpret those plotlines in relation to the character motivations and emotions they are shown.

Research has shown that, in the absence of sufficient character information being provided to them, children at this age will use stereotypes to fill in the blanks in deciding if a character they see is good or bad.[10] This further illustrates that the use of stereotypes, in one form or another, is an innate tool that the human mind uses to help it interpret the vast amount of information that bombards us constantly.

The issue of media violence rears its ugly head again here. At approximately the age of eight, the development of aggression in children becomes critical. Children at this age, particularly boys, appear to identify with aggressive, violent, and often unrealistic media heroes.[11] The attraction of these heroes seems to be more the power they display than the violence they use to achieve their goals or any form of sex role identification through stereotyping. This would explain why boys at this age are fascinated by superheroes and others who have the power to

The most violent things in the world, if you're counting acts of violence, are Saturday morning cartoons. But if you count violence as pure acts of violence, you're counting crazy stuff. You're counting people falling on a pie. Is it an act of violence or is it a joke? You can't make any of these judgments outside of the context of the piece of drama that you're doing.
—*Bridget Potter*

shape reality and affect their surroundings.

Common sense would suggest that this leaning toward the powerful is in direct response to the fact that children at this age feel powerless. They have just recently been plunged, usually against their will, into a school situation in which an entire cadre of unfamiliar adults begins directing virtually every move they make. This is in addition to their parents waiting at home, whom they have probably already learned to manipulate, but who try to direct their behavior out of school nevertheless. The children long for more control over their lives, a feeling that will continue to grow for at least a decade or more—if not for the rest of their lives! If they could only be their favorite superhero, no one would dare tell them it was time for bed!

Nine to 12 Years Old

By the time children reach the nine- to 12-year-old age group, they will very likely have come to believe that what they watch on television is a reflection of real life. By age 10, "real" has generally come to mean "possible in real life."[12] The interesting thing is that, when asked who they wanted to be like in one study, children aged eight to 10 named unrealistic characters from television programming far more often than they named those that were more realistic, more possible in real life. The traits boys seem to strongly favor in their heroes are bravery, power, and strength, all classic aggressive tendencies.[13]

There is a growing recognition, supported by the research, that girls are less aggressive in general, which may well account for their comparative lack of interest in viewing violence in the media and statistically lower likelihood of using aggression in real-life situations.[14] However, studies do show that girls who do watch a significant amount of violent content are often more aggressive in real life than those who do not watch such programming.[15] Hence, a question arises: Are boys and girls subject to the same influences of violence in the media? This is a classic nature versus nurture question, sadly beyond the scope of our discussion here.

Teenagers

Finally, we come to the age group of 12- to 17-year-olds, so-called adolescents. These young adults actually tend to watch less television than their younger counterparts. The reason for decreased viewing is that generally, teens have many more activities competing for their leisure time than do younger children.

In addition to the amount of viewing, adolescents' tastes differ markedly from those of younger children. They begin to favor dramas, including soap operas, as well as sports and music videos. They continue to watch comedies, but tend to watch fewer cartoons. Adolescents tend to doubt the reality of television, and are less likely to identify with television characters. Those who continue to identify with characters, especially those of the aggressive heroic school, tend to be more aggressive than those who do not. About 80 percent of adolescents deliberately watch movies that frighten them.[16]

There is a much greater body of research on the effects of media on children than presented here, and some of it is contradictory in nature. For example, one study shows that children who watch television with their parents are more likely to recognize that what they are watching is fantasy.[17] A different study concludes that it makes relatively little difference whether a child watches television alone or in the company of adults.[18] However, the basic point of all of this research for our purposes is that children, taken as a whole, process programming differently than adults. The "how" and "how much" of the difference depends largely upon the age of the child.

What this research implies is that we as creators should be exceedingly aware that children do not filter information in the same way as adult audiences, nor in the same way as we do ourselves, and that their "filters" change often as they age. The message we *think* we are sending may not at all be the message the child is receiving. It is not merely the overall content of our programming (i.e., does this seem like a good story for children?), but also *everything* related to the presentation of that story that is important. The characters through whom the story is told are the most vital element, but so too is the music, the action level, the sound effects, and many other elements. We should probe for hidden messages at each step along the road of developing programming for this audience, and constantly double-check ourselves to confirm that we are communicating what we think we are communicating. Again, allow the READR method to be a tool in this process.

> *As a parent I'm responsible for what my children watch on TV. I don't think it's a bad idea to give parents the simple ability to block out things they don't want their kids to look at. All parents should have that responsibility and that ability about everything.*
> —*Bridget Potter*

The children's entertainment industry has become more sensitive to these issues in recent years. Key members of the creative community have endorsed voluntary guidelines for developing programming[19] that encourage heightened consideration when illustrating character and values, conflict and violence, and diversity and stereotypes in media for children. At the same time, the federal government is pushing the industry to be more responsible to their younger viewers, passing such legislation as the Children's Television Act of 1996, which requires three hours of educational programming for children per week on each FCC-licensed station.

Creators considering entering the realm of children's programming should realize that this is an area where ethical considerations are an everyday fact of life, and are, in certain cases, codified by law.

Ethical Gymnastics

1. Discuss appropriate and inappropriate subject matter for preschool age programming.

2. Young boys enjoy action-oriented programming. Write a treatment for an action program for television, to be marketed to eight- to 12-year-old boys, that would send positive messages and avoid violent and aggressive reactions in light of what you have read in this chapter. Discuss the ethical choices you have made.

3. Write a treatment for a drama or comedy to be marketed to teenage girls. Discuss the issues you might explore for this audience. Also, discuss how your program might differ were it marketed primarily to teenage boys.

4. Discuss appropriate and inappropriate subject matter for programming aimed at six to eight year olds. Discuss different categories of subject matter and attempt to determine what age you think an audience member should be before they should view this subject matter in light of what you have read in this chapter.

5. Many parents are concerned about the way in which their child learns about sex. What are the ethical choices involved in presenting material that deals with human reproduction or sexuality to a preteen audience? If you determine by ethical choice that it is not appropriate to present such material, what about the issue of presenting such material concerning mammals? Flowers? Because any information of this kind can lead normally to a child's questioning of human sexuality, where would you "draw the line?"

6. You must write, produce, and direct (lucky you) an in-depth after school special for grade school children entitled *The Stranger*, in which a young girl gets into trouble of some kind by talking to a stranger. What are the

ethical choices you must make in accurately portraying this material? For example, should you show a child fending off an attacker to drive the point home? Will you be glorifying the violence? Will you terrorize your audience? Should you? Should you make the stranger sleazy and dangerous looking to make him or her less attractive to the viewers? Discuss the construction of the ideal special in light of what you have read in this book.

7. Discuss the themes you feel are most relevant and entertaining for a teenage audience, and how these might conflict with ethical considerations, if any. How you would propose dealing with those issues in a television format?

8. Choose three current television programs marketed to young children and discuss the apparent ethical choices made by the creators. Use the READR method to break down and analyze each program. What would you have chosen to do differently in light of what you have read in this book?

9. Discuss a program or film that you believe presents compelling entertainment in an ethical framework designed for a teenage audience. How are the issues presented to keep them interested? What ethical choices would you wish to urge other creators to make in producing programming for this audience?

10. You are the show-runner producer for a hot new program slated for 18- to 34-year-old males. The Nielsen ratings come back, revealing that your steamy adult characters have become the heartthrobs of the week for eight- to 12-year-old girls across the nation. Should you be concerned? What are the ethical considerations involved here?

Notes

1 *Facts About Media Violence*," American Medical Association, 1996.

2 See Trotta, Laurie A. "Special Considerations for Creators of Children's Media," in *Building Blocks: A Guide for Creating Children's Educational Programming* (Studio City: Mediascope Press, 1998).

3 1994–present. Bright/Kauffman/Crane Prods. and Warner Bros. Television.

4 1997–present. Comedy Partners and Comedy Central.

5 Josephson, Wendy L., Ph.D. *Television Violence: A Review of the Effects on Children of Different Ages*, 1995.

6 Josephson, p. 15.

7 Skeen, Patsy, Brown, Mac. H., and Osborn, D. Keith. "Young Children's Perception of "Real" and "Pretend" on Television," *Perceptual and Motor Skills,* 54 (1982): 883–887.

8 Josephson, p. 17.
9 Josephson, p. 17.
10 Josephson, p. 28.
11 Josephson, p. 29.
12 Josephson, p. 29.
13 Josephson, p. 29.
14 Josephson, p. 30.
15 Josephson, p. 30.
16 *The National Television Violence Study,* Universities of: California, Santa Barbara; Wisconsin, Madison; North Carolina, Chapel Hill; Texas, Austin (Studio City: Mediascope, 1996).
17 Messaris, P. and Kerr, D. "Mothers' Comments about TV: Relation to Family Communication Patterns," *Communication Research*, 10, (1983): 175–194.
18 Nikken, Peter, and Peeters, Allerd L. "Children's Perceptions of Television Reality," *Journal of Broadcasting & Electronic Media*, Volume 32, Number 4, (Fall 1988): 441–452.
19 The "Children's Entertainment Media Summit" took place at Dic Entertainment in Burbank, California, in September 1999. Sponsored by Dic and Mediascope, the summit included all networks and major production companies as well as representatives from the children's interactive community. The result is a set of voluntary guidelines, *Special Considerations for Creators of Children's Media.*

The Virulence of Violence

Neil Hickey

Veteran journalist Neil Hickey has written about the television industry for more than 30 years and is currently the editor-at-large of *The Columbia Journalism Review*. He was *TV Guide's* New York bureau chief for 25 years, and senior editor for five years. He is an adjunct assistant professor in the graduate divisions of New York University and Fordham University. In his essay entitled "The Virulence of Violence," Hickey briefly traces the history of both government and academic concern about this issue.

For almost half a century, since the dawning of commercial television just after World War II, the matter of violent television programming and its effects has been examined and debated like few other issues. The debate has gained intensity as television gained audience.

As it became clear to parents, legislators, academics, and child experts in the early 1950s that this astonishing new conduit for entertainment, information, and sports had an awesome capacity to enthrall, apprehension about its social impact began to be felt. Congress invited broadcasters (there were as yet no cable casters) to defend themselves against the rising concern that some of their more violent programs might cumulatively have harmful effects, especially on children. All the early hearings and symposia ended inconclusively, as broadcasters rightly argued that nobody had yet produced reliable empirical evidence that televised mayhem had any serious, long-term effects on children or adults.

Into that vacuum stepped the academic community and governmental agencies, often in tandem. Scores, then hundreds, then a thousand studies appeared in the ensuing decades. Violence research became a thriving new industry among government agencies, universities, and broadcasters themselves.[1] Many of those studies found a connection between televised violence and aggressive behavior.

Q: A distributor can serve as a pre-editor if you are involved at the early stage, the pre-buy. Can it be said that a distributor plays a moral role?

You have the opportunity to do that. The decisions can and should be—but aren't always—ethical.
—Mark Gill

One of the most ambitious studies, conducted by Dr. Leonard D. Eron and others, concluded that the more frequently eight-year-olds watched television, the more serious the crimes they were convicted of by age 30; the more aggressive their behavior when drinking; and the harsher the punishment they inflicted on their own children. The study's bottom line:

> There can no longer be any doubt that heavy exposure to televised violence is one of the causes of aggressive behavior, crime, and violence in society. The evidence comes from both the laboratory and real-life studies. Television violence affects youngsters of all ages, of both genders, at all socioeconomic levels and all levels of intelligence.[2]

Gradually, the conviction was hardening that indeed a direct, demonstrable link existed between violence on television and violence in society, and that other unwanted effects were apparent in children and adults who were heavy TV users.

Responsible scientists were at pains to point out that not all societal violence could be laid at the door of television. Clearly, most of it derived from lamentable social circumstances—such as poverty, poor schools, urban blight, broken homes, and racial inequality. Dr. Eron estimated that perhaps 10 percent of real violence resulted from observed violence on television.[3] But that's plenty, if one happens to be a victim or a perpetrator within that 10 percent.

Nonetheless, through the 1970s, the broadcasters and a handful of contrarian scholars continued to resist the notion of linkage. Their first line of defense was the First Amendment, which they invoked with great success for the freedom to broadcast violent programs if they chose. Normally the First Amendment would preclude any government interference with program content, but TV licenses are granted by the government with a requirement to serve the public interest, and where the well-being of children is involved, it is clear where the public interest lies.

During the 12 years of the Reagan and Bush administrations (1980–1992), deregulatory fervor in Washington was at a new high, and TV people relaxed in the knowledge that government would keep its hands off the broadcasters' business. "Let the market decide," was the mantra, and that meant no meddling in what programmers were beaming out on the public airwaves. One Federal Communications Commission chairman of the period, Mark Fowler, even likened the television set to a toaster, just one more appliance in the home, implying that it deserved the same level of government attention.[4]

Q: How have you ever re-angled, changed, or decided not go for a film because of your hesitations at that early stage of pre-buy?

In Scream *we felt that the most extreme violence in the early cuts was a little gratuitous. But so did the director.*
—Mark Gill

Then, in the early 1990s, a groundswell of public dismay about the clear increase of violent programming on television schedules brought a response from legislators in Washington, who saw it as an issue that was bound to play well in their home districts. A few, like Senator Paul Simon, a Democrat from Illinois (and a former school teacher), appeared genuinely concerned about the potential damage to the society's fabric from the torrent of violent images invading American homes. As he became involved in the issue, said Simon, he found a "remarkable consensus" on "the harm excessive TV violence does to children and adults." And he also found confirmation that television in the United States "is more violent than ever before and may be the most violent of any industrialized society."[5]

As to why TV and movie companies were creating so much violent entertainment, a few answers were clear. Violent scenes are simple to write and place no subtle demands on actors' skills. For many viewers, violence—as rendered onscreen—is a kind of mind candy: easy to absorb, visually engrossing, involving a very low level of mental strain and concentration. Also, violence travels well abroad, being instantly comprehensible and needing little translation.

Some advertisers choose not to associate their products with programs that feature violence, but most are more often interested in ratings than in content. When *NYPD Blue*[6] first came on the air, for example, many potential advertisers righteously declared their aversion to the series because its content was objectionable, but when it became a runaway hit that concern quickly vanished.

In 1992, as a senior editor of *TV Guide*, I produced a special issue of the magazine devoted to televised violence, for which I commissioned the Center for Media and Public Affairs in Washington to conduct a content analysis of broadcast and cable programming. The center monitored 10 channels over 18 hours on a typical day, and in those 180 hours these were the findings:

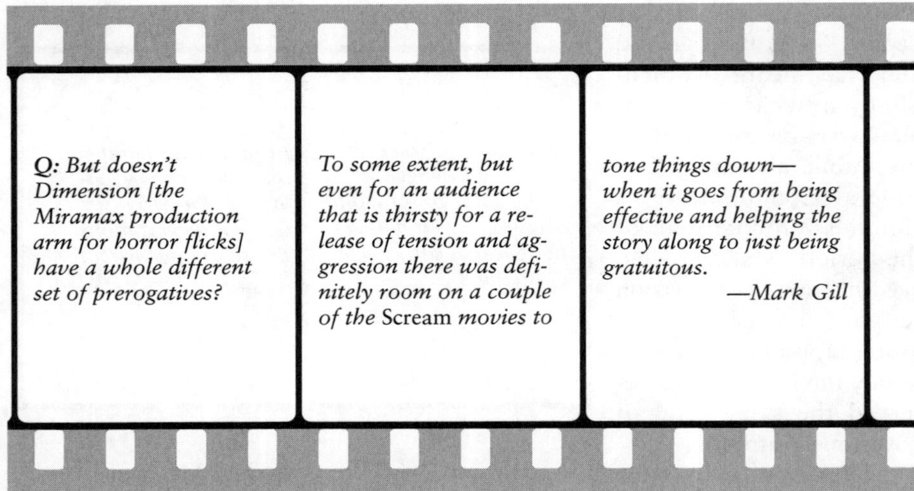

Q: So you don't see that movies play a role in societal violence?

We have a worldwide control experiment that says it is not so. It may well be that there's some influence there somewhere, but to draw a direct link is clearly not accurate. Just see how the rest of the world responds, and they are all seeing American movies.

—Mark Gill

- 1,846 individual acts of violence—purposeful, overt, deliberate behavior involving physical force against other individuals,
- 175 scenes in which violence resulted in one or more fatalities,
- 389 scenes depicting serious assaults,
- 362 scenes involving gunplay,
- 673 depictions of punching, pushing, slapping, dragging, and other physically hostile acts,
- 226 scenes of menacing threats with a weapon.

The program genre with the highest incidence of violence was children's cartoons. Then, in descending order of violent content: promotional announcements for television programs; theatrical and made-for-TV movies; toy commercials; music videos; commercials for theatrical movies; TV drama series;

news; reality shows like *Cops*[7] and *Hard Copy*;[8] situation comedies; and soap operas. Unmeasured in the survey were the many hundreds of hours of VCR-watching that went on that day—much of it devoted to theatrical films with violent content. The survey concluded: "Violence remains a pervasive, major feature of contemporary television programming; and it's coming from more sources and in greater volume than ever before."[9]

In VIG, *the violence was disturbing because it was carried out by people who look like each other. Yes, there were some differences between Irish and Italian, male and female, young and old, but they were all white. And because we could so readily identify with both sides of the conflict, the violence was heightened to what I call "psychic violence." The enemy is our husband/wife/neighbor/friend. The enemy is us. And knowing that, understanding that duality exists in all of us makes the story much more real, thus much more powerful.*

—Paul Hapenny

An important phrase in that statement is "more sources." Up until the early 1970s the three major broadcast networks—ABC, CBS, and NBC—had a virtual monopoly on TV viewing, usually attracting more than 90 percent of the audience in prime time. Then the cable industry began its spread across the country, eventually penetrating more than two-thirds of television homes, and bringing with it an array of new networks that scarcely could have been imagined in the 1960s—CNN, ESPN, Lifetime, USA, MTV, A&E, Nickelodeon, and scores of others. It also brought "premium" (pay) channels like HBO, Showtime, The Movie Channel, and Cinemax that aired commercial-free, largely unedited theatrical movies. In 1986 a fourth broadcast network, Fox, sprang from the brow of Rupert Murdoch, later to be followed by a pair of part-time, studio-owned terrestrial networks, WB and UPN.

One of the most phenomenal media stories of the 1980s was the explosive proliferation of the VCR, which spurred the establishment of tens of thousands of video rental shops across the land.[10] With that came video games and, later, computer games, which collectively have annual revenues in the United States alone of more than $10 billion,[11] exceeding the amount Americans spend on tickets to the movies.[12] From the start, the games involved forms of violence, but in later generations the violence became graphic, and because the user participates in the violence (unlike the passive experience of watching television), a new set of questions is raised about their effects on the devotees, who mainly are children.

Studies conducted so far have suggested that the predominant emotional responses to video games are aggression, anger, and hostility.[13] A game called "Postal" was described in a video magazine review:

> Armed with shotguns, flamethrowers and napalm, you mow down entertainingly innocent bystanders, ranging from church congregations to high school marching bands. Your maimed and dying victims beg for mercy or run around on fire, screaming for help ...[14]

With these new media the definition of television expands. Whatever arrives in the home via the television set is now thought of as television. Many of the basic cable networks at first depended on old reruns from ABC, CBS, and NBC, and those included action-adventure series, cop dramas, and Westerns, with a heavy freight of gunplay, fistfights, murders, explosions, car crashes, stabbings, and bludgeonings. They also drew heavily from the Hollywood vaults of B-movies from the 1930s through the 1950s, many of them crime and war stories. The premium cable channels, meanwhile, were delivering more recent, uncut theatrical films into the home, a good many of which were (and are) disturbingly violent.

In Jaws, *Mr. (Daryl) Zanuck, Mr. (Steven) Spielberg, Mr. (Peter) Benchley, and I tapped into one of the great fears of humankind, which is that water is not the kind of natural element that air is. I don't know (why it is such a) powerful symbol. I think it's because one person's death—I'm looking at our ad for* Jaws, *where the swimmer is at the surface of the water and the shark is lurking below with his jaws agape—somehow one death is more personal, obviously, and more frightening than a thousand, because one can relate only to the individual suffering.*

—*David Brown*

To that mix add the VCR, which allows children unaccompanied by parents to graze in the video stores and bring home the most recent products of the American movie industry. In latter years, these have included some of the most extravagantly violent films ever, often with spectacularly gory special effects, which have hugely increased the quotient of media violence in the nation's living rooms.

In her excellent book, *Deadly Consequences*,[15] Deborah Prothrow-Stith, M.D., of the Harvard School of Public Health, posited that in the United States, "our movies, our broadcast talk, our television drama, our children's TV, our toys, our sports, our music for adolescents, our print and broadcast news are awash in violent words and violent pictures. In the media world, brutality is portrayed as ordinary and amusing."[16] And usually, we don't even notice it, she says; we're inured to it, we take it for granted. Americans used to reject the notion that the end justifies the means, she writes, but no more. "At least not in the movies. In the movies, violence is limitless, and it is fun. The violent hero cannot wait for the opportunity to, in the words of President Bush, 'kick ass.'"[17] The mass media quite blatantly misrepresent the emotional and physical consequences of brutality, Prothrow-Stith maintains.

Early in 1996, the U.S. government took action on the television violence matter. First, on February 6, President Clinton signed into law a new Telecommunications Act, which was designed to update the outmoded Communications Act of 1934, eliminating the barriers that had kept media industries artificially compartmentalized, and paving the way for more choice and presumably lower prices for consumers. Tucked into the new law was a provision requiring television set manufacturers to equip new receivers with the so-called 'V'-chip, a device that would let parents screen out objectionable programming.

> *Maybe it was John Huston who said that putting in a garden can be art or making a movie can be art: it's all in the way you do it. So there is that fine line between how you perceive things. Though it sounds a little crude, I think there has to be a certain amount of style and romance. Films like* The Godfather *have violence for a reason. They are all hung on it. I think that's important.*
>
> —*Gordon Willis*

The television industry planned to fight the ratings system necessary to the operation of the 'V'-chip in court until the *National Television Violence Study*[18] was released. Within days, the industry agreed to design and abide by one.

Later that month, 30 of the most powerful executives in the movie and television industries convened at the White House at the invitation of President Clinton and pledged to create a voluntary system that would rate television programs for their violence content. Implicit at the meeting was the threat that if the entertainment industry didn't voluntarily create a rating system, the government would find a way to *impose* one on them. The handwriting was on the wall.

Nearly a year later, the industry unveiled its "TV Parental Guidelines," which were closely modeled on Motion Picture Association of America President Jack Valenti's system for motion pictures with its age-based classifications. The TV version was: Y, material suitable for children of all ages; Y–7, material suitable for children seven and older; G, material suitable for all audiences; PG, parental guidance suggested; 14, material inappropriate for children under 14; and M, for mature audiences only.

Reaction to the plan was instant and harsh. Children's advocacy groups such as the PTA, the American Psychiatric Association, and the Children's

Defense Fund, along with legislators, media researchers, and TV critics, declared almost unanimously that an age-based system was too vague and too ambiguous to be of much help to parents, and besides, left crucial distinctions about what's okay for the several age groupings in the hands of program producers, the folks with a vested interest in attracting large audiences for their shows.

Valenti and his colleagues reluctantly returned to the drawing board, and on July 10, 1997, produced an amended rating scheme that would simply add content advice to its already-proffered age guidelines—V for violence, FV for fantasy violence, S for sex, L for language, and D for dialogue.[19] Said Valenti: "This is not something we celebrate as a great victory. This is something we did because we had to do it."[20] But NBC promptly broke ranks and pronounced the new plan a further intrusion on its First Amendment rights: "NBC is disappointed that the industry capitulated to political and special-interest pressure and did not look more seriously at the implications of the flawed process in which they engaged. Therefore, NBC will not be a part of the new agreement."[21]

Meanwhile, a clock was ticking. All television sets sold from 1998 forward were obliged by the Telecommunications Act to contain a 'V'-chip, even as disagreement raged on over how, and if, it would ever be fully operable and efficient.

On a personal note, as a graduate of the emergency room, I know better than most that in real life the sight of mashed and mangled bodies is terrible. And so is the emotional pain violence causes. The remorse of those who resort to violence, even justifiably; the unremitting anger and humiliation of victims; the life-altering, dispiriting impact of permanent injury; the endless grief of family members; the scarred psyches of children who see a parent die in a violent act—these are crucial elements of the story usually left untold on television and in the movies.

Film violence occurs in a moment: a gun is fired, a person dies, and on to the next scene. But in real life, the impact of the moment of violence reverberates through time. This sense of action without consequences that popular films convey reinforces the dangerous "magical" way many children think. Did the school-aged kids who shot and killed classmates and teachers in several small southern cities in the late 1990s really understand that death is permanent, unalterable? Television and movies certainly never told them so. Several years before, in a National Public Radio documentary on pre-teen inner city kids who own guns, an 11-year-old told of a shoot-out in which he was wounded. "I didn't know it was supposed to hurt."[22]

Notes

1 A few of the more exhaustive studies: the National Commission on the Causes and Prevention of Violence (1968), the Surgeon General's Report (1972), the National Institute of Mental Health report (1982), and the U.S. Attorney General's Task

Force on Family Violence (1984). The findings were endorsed by the American Medical Association, the American Pediatric Association, the American Academy of Child Psychiatry, and the American Psychological Association.

2 Eron, Leonard D. and Huesmann, L. Rowell. *Television and the Aggressive Child: A Cross National Comparison* (Hillsdale, N.J.: Lawrence Erlbaum Associates, Inc. Publishers, 1986), pp. 45–80.

3 Eron and Huesman, pp. 256–257.

4 "[The TV] is just another appliance—it's a toaster with pictures." Tucker, Elizabeth. "FCC Weighs Role of Hostile Bids for TV Networks," *The Washington Post*, July 21, 1985, p. H1.

5 Simon, Paul. "Reducing TV Violence," *The Courier-Journal* (Louisville, Kentucky), August 31, 1989, p. 15A.

6 1993–present, ABC Television.

7 1989–present, 20th Century Fox Television.

8 1989–1999, syndicated.

9 Research files of Neil Hickey.

10 Doan, Michael. "As The Video Craze Captures U.S. Families," *US News & World Report*, January 28, 1985, p. 58.

11 "Video Games and Their Effects," *Issue Brief Series* (Studio City: Mediascope Press, 1997).

12 "Video Games and Their Effects."

13 "Video Games and Their Effects."

14 Research files of Neil Hickey.

15 Prothrow-Stith, Deborah. *Deadly Consequences* (New York: Harper Collins, 1991).

16 Prothrow-Stith, pp. 29–30.

17 Prothrow-Stith, pp. 30–31.

18 *The National Television Violence Study,* Universities of: California, Santa Barbara; Wisconsin, Madison; North Carolina, Chapel Hill; Texas, Austin. (Studio City: Mediascope, 1996).

19 Motion Picture Association of America's Website: www.mpaa.org/tv.

20 Motion Picture Association of America's Website.

21 Pietrucha, Bill. "TV Ratings Compromise Halts Legislative Action," *Newsbytes*, July 10, 1997.

22 "Boys and Guns: What Does It Really Mean?" Siegel, Robert, host, National Public Radio, December 25, 1992.

Bibliography
Filmography

Appendix A
Bibliography

Foreword

Berton, Lee and Harris, Roy. "Reel-World Accounting," *CFO: The Magazine for Senior Financial Executives*, Volume 13, Number 3, March 1999, pp. 34–46.

Diamond, Jared. *Guns, Germs, and Steel: The Fates of Human Societies* (New York: W.W. Norton & Company Inc., 1997).

Dupre, A.R., Hampton, H.L., Morrison, H., and Meeks, G.R. "Sexual Assault," *Obstetrical and Gynecological Survey* 48 (1993): 640–648.

Graves, Robert, *The White Goddess: A Historical Grammar of Poetic Myth,* (New York: Noonday Press, 1997).

Hollywood Production Code, 1934–1966.

Internet Movie Database: www.imdb.com.

Pearsall, Judy, Ed. *Concise Oxford English Dictionary*, (Oxford: Oxford University Press, 1999).

Awash in Media Culture

"Cable Television Advertising Bureau Research Update," *Cable Avails*, April 1999, Volume 9, Number 3, p. 17.

Maeder, Libby. "How to Live Happily Ever After," *The Buffalo News*, January 9, 2000, p. 14M.

Mann, Jennifer. "For Cinema Chains, Record Sales Not Balancing Costs of Overbuilding," *The Kansas City Star*, November 9, 1999.

Schroder. "Home Video Will Remain Studio Breadwinner," *Video Week*, January 10, 2000, Section: This Week's News.

Smith, Samantha Thompson. "Despite Rise in Ticket Sales, Cinema Owners Count Losses," *News & Observer*, December 24, 1999.

"Statistical Abstracts of the United States 1993." *Country Reports,* Walden Publishing, January 30, 1995.

Stern, Christopher. "U.S. Ideas Top Export Biz," *Variety*, May 11–17, 1998, p. 50.

"VCR Households," *PRC News*, December 20, 1999, Volume 1, Number 12, p. 3.

World Almanac & Book of Facts 1999, (Primedia Reference Inc., March 1999).

Entertainment in Our Extended World

Brown, Lester L., *The Business Behind The Box*, (New York: Harcourt Brace Jovanovich, Inc., 1971).

Entertainment Monitor, December 1995.

Grauer, Neil A. "Gone With The Wind: The Movie Houses That Once Dominated Washington Were Elegant, Palatial and, Ultimately, Doomed," *The Washington Post*, July 4, 1999.

Howe, Peter J. "Massive Media: Viacom CBS Merger Plan Raises Questions over Trend of a Few Giant Conglomerates Controlling What We Hear, Read and See," *The Boston Globe*, September 12, 1999.

Klein, Jonathan D., M.D., MPH; Brown, Jane D., Ph.D.; Walsh Childers, Kim, Ph.D.; Oliveri, Janice, M.D.; Porter, Carol; and Dykers, Carol. "Adolescents' Risky Behavior and Mass Media Use," *Pediatrics* 92 (July 1993): 24–31.

Morgenstern, Joe. "Film: Cosmic Crashes, Comic Cons," *Wall Street Journal*, July 1, 1998, Section A, p. 16.

Natale, Richard. "Company Town: I Know What You Did Last Weekend" *Los Angeles Times*, June 23, 1998, Section D, p. 1.

Passy, Charles. "How Big Are Those Profits From The Tickets And Popcorn?" *Palm Beach Post*, May 18, 1997, p. 4J.

Peltz, James. "Media Mega Merger; It's No Act—Case Is An Ordinary Guy," *Los Angeles Times*, January 11, 2000.

Motion Picture Almanac QP 1999, Stevens, Tracy, ed. (New York: Quigley Publishing Company, 1999).

"Television Code of the National Association of Broadcasters," 1st Edition, 1952; 22nd Edition, 1981. *Encyclopedia Britannica Online*: www.eb.com.

USA vs. National Association of Broadcasters, Civil Action #79–1549, November 23, 1982.

How the World Sees Us: An American in Paris

Bremner, Charles. "French Isolated in Move to Build Culture Barriers," *The Times (London)*, February 15, 1995.

DePalma, Anthony. "Arts Abroad: It Isn't So Simple To Be Canadian," *The New York Times*, July 14, 1999, Section E, p. 1.

"Electric Planet," *Hollywood Reporter*, November 25, 1996, p. 14.

Ellis, Rachel. "Rising Use of Tobacco Among Young," *Press Association Newsfile*, September 23, 1997.

Klady, Leonard, Compiler. *Variety*, January 25–31, 1999, p. 36.

Maslin, Janet. "Film View: G, PG, R and X: Make the Letter Reflect the Spirit," *The New York Times*, April 29, 1990, Section 2, p. 19.

Stern, Christopher "U.S. Ideas Top Export Biz," *Variety*, May 11–17, 1998, p. 50.

Tucker, Emma and Rausthorn, Alice. "EU Loan Scheme for Filming Unveiled," *The Financial Times (London)*, October 7, 1998, p. 3.

But It's Only a Movie ... Or Is It?

Brown, Les. *The Artist as Citizen*, unpublished.

Ernst, Morris L. and Schwartz, Alan U. *Censorship: The Search For The Obscene.* (New York: The Macmillan Company, 1964).

Levy, Leonard W. *Origins of the Bill of Rights,* (New Haven, Conn.: Yale University Press, 1999).

Minow, Newton. "A Vast Wasteland," *Speech*, 1961.

Free Expression in Hollywood: First Amendment & Censorship

Black, Gregory D. *Hollywood Censored: Morality Codes, Catholics, and the Movies* (New York: Cambridge University Press, 1994).

Commonweal, May 18, 1934.

Crafts, Wilbur F. *National Perils and Hopes: A Study Based on Current Statistics and the Observations of a Cheerful Reformer* (Cleveland: O.F.M. Barton, 1910).

Currie, Barton W. "The Nickel Madness," *Harper's Weekly*, August 24, 1907.

Dubow, Josh. "CBS Back in NFL Business," Associated Press Wire, January 13, 1998.

Ernst, Morris L. and Schwartz, Alan U. *Censorship: The Search For The Obscene* (New York: The Macmillan Company, 1964).

Fell, John. *Film Before Griffith* (Berkeley: University of California Press, 1983).

Guthmann, Edward. "Black History Month: Hollywood Racism a Mirror on Society," *The New York Times*, January 31, 1999, p. 30.

"Janet Reno and TV Violence: The Government is Watching," *The Phoenix Gazette*, October 23, 1993, p. B4.

Jowett, Garth. *Film: The Democratic Art* (Boston: Little, Brown, 1976).

Lord, Daniel A. *S.J. Played By Ear* (Chicago: Loyola University Press, 1955).

"Media Use in America," *Issue Brief Series* (Studio City: Mediascope Press, 1999).

Milton, John. *Areopagitica*, 1645.

Simon, Paul. "Reducing TV Violence," *The Courier-Journal (Louisville, KY),* August 31, 1989, p. 15A.

"*Titanic*'s Box Office Passes 1 Billion Mark," Associated Press, *Toronto Star*, April 27, 1998, p. E8.

Valenti, Jack: www.mpaa.org.

White, E.B. *Removal, One Man's Meat* (New York: Harper & Row, 1938).

Dead White Greeks and Why They Matter

Bentham, Jeremy. *An Introduction to the Principles of Morals and Legislation: An Authoritative Edition.* Burns, J.H. and Hart, H., Eds. (New York: Oxford University Press, 1996).

Flatman, Richard E. and Johnson, David, Eds. *Leviathan: Authoritative Text, Background, Interpreted* (New York: W.W. Norton & Company, 1997).

His Holiness the Dalai Lama. *Ethics for the New Millennium* (New York: Riverhead Books, 1999).

Hume, David. *A Treatise of Human Nature* (Buffalo: Prometheus Books, 1992).

Kant, Immanuel. *Foundations of the Metaphysics of Morals.* Trans. Beck, Lewis White, (Indianapolis: Bobbs-Merrill, 1969).

Machiavelli, Niccolo. *Il Principe (The Prince)*, 1513.

Masters, Roger D. and Kelly, Christopher, Eds. *Discourse on the Arts and Sciences* (Hanover: University Press of New England for Dartmouth College, 1992).

Mill, John Stuart. *Mill On Liberty: Critical Essay.* Dworkin, Gerald, Ed. (Lanham, Md.: Rowman & Littlefield Publishers, 1997).

Mill, John Stuart. *Utilitarianism* (Oxford, N.Y.: Oxford University Press, 1998).

Online Bible Study: www.biblestudytools.net.

Patterson, Sylvia W. *Rousseau's Emile and Early Children's Literature* (Metuchen, N.J.: Scarecrow Press, 1971).

Rice, Daryl H. *A Guide to Plato's Republic* (New York: Oxford University Press, 1998).

Tzu, Sun. *Ping-Fa* (*The Art of War*), written/compiled sometime between 770–476 B.C.

Welldon, J.E.C., Trans., *The Nicomachean Ethics by Aristotle* (Buffalo: Prometheus Books, 1987).

The Gun: Portrayals of Violence— Do Unto Others Before They Can Do Unto You

Champlin, Charles. *Los Angeles Times*, March 19, 1972.

Federal Bureau of Investigations, U.S. Department of Justice, Louis J. Freeh, Director. *Uniform Crime Report: 1997 Preliminary Annual Release,* May 17, 1998.

Federal Bureau of Investigations, U.S. Department of Justice, Louis J. Freeh, Director. *Uniform Crime Report,* June 1999.

Feshbach, S. "The Role of Fantasy in the Response to Television," *Journal of Social Issues*, 1976, Volume 32, pp. 71–85.

Hollywood Production Code, 1934–1966.

Hornaday, Ann. "Guns on Film: A Loaded Issue," *The Baltimore Sun*; January 17, 1999, pp. 10F–11F.

Leigh, Janet with Nickens, Christopher. *Psycho: Behind the Scenes of the Classic Thriller* (New York: Harmony Books, 1995).

Naremore, James. *Filmguide to Psycho,* (London: Indiana University Press, 1973).

Rebello, Stephen. *Alfred Hitchcock and The Making of Psycho* (New York: Dembner Books, 1990).

The National Television Violence Study, Universities of: California, Santa Barbara; Wisconsin, Madison; North Carolina, Chapel Hill; Texas, Austin. Studio City: Mediascope, 1996.

The Cast: Portrayals of Stereotypes

Carbone, Stephanie. *Picture This, Diversity in Film and Television* (unpublished), Mediascope interview, July 9, 1997.

Gerbner, G. and Ozyegin, N. *Proportional Representation of Diversity Index*, Cultural Indicators Project, Spring 1997.

Graves, S.B. "Television, the Portrayal of African Americans, and the Development of Children's Attitudes," in Berry and Asamen, *Children & Television: Images In a Changing Sociocultural World* (Newbury Park, Calif.: Sage Publications, 1993).

Lippmann, Walter. *Public Opinion* (New York: Macmillan, 1922).

Lorenz, Larry. "NAACP Vigilant to Minorities," *Extra Extra, the NATPE 2000 Newsletter*, January 27, 2000.

Screen Actors Guild Press Release, May 3, 1999: www.sag.org/pressreleases/pr-la990503.html.

Wade, Carole and Tavris, Carol. *Psychology* (New York: Harper Collins College Publishers, 1993), pp. 244–247.

The Props: Portrayals of Substance Use— We're Not in Kansas Anymore

"Cigarette Smoking—Attributable Mortality and Years of Potential Life Lost—United States, 1990," Centers for Disease Control and Prevention. *MMWR* 1993; 42(33): 645–649.

Dutka, E. "Force of Habit," *Los Angeles Times*, September 5, 1996.

Growing Up Tobacco Free: Preventing Nicotine Addiction in Children and Youths, Institute of Medicine, 1994.

Hartman, Rome, producer. "Smoking Onscreen," *CBS Sixty Minutes*. November 24, 1996.

Hilts, P. "Company Spent $1 Million to Put Cigarettes in Movies, Memos Show," *The New York Times*, May 20, 1994.

Labaton, Stephen, "Gov't Seeks An Ad Ban and Label Warning For Cigars," *The New York Times,* July 22, 1999, p. 14.

Lackey, W. "Can Lois Lane Smoke Marlboros?: An Example of the Constitutionality of Regulating Product Placement in Movies." *The University of Chicago Legal Forum* (Annual 1993): 275–292.

The National Center on Addiction and Substance Abuse at Columbia University 1995 Annual Report, CASA, 1996.

The National Drug Control Strategy, 1997 (Washington, D.C.: Office of National Drug Control Policy, 1997).

Shapiro, E. "B&W Tobacco Paid to Get Brands In Films, Notes Say," *Wall Street Journal*, May 16, 1994.

Snyder, S. "Movies and Product Placement; Is Hollywood Turning Films Into Commercial Speech?" *University of Illinois Law Review* (Winter 1992): 301–337.

Somerson, Mark. "Growing Evidence Favors Moderate Use Of Alcohol," *The Columbus Dispatch*, November 28, 1999, p. 7B.

Substance Use in Popular Movies and Music, Mediascope, December 1998.

Substance Use in Popular Prime Time Television, Mediascope, January 2000.

The Girl: Portrayals of Sex— Now, We're Definitely Not in Kansas Anymore

Bernstein, J. "Growing Up in the Dark," *Premiere: Women in Hollywood*, 1999.

"Boys Have a Role Too in Curbing Teen Pregnancy," *USA Today*, January 6, 1998.

Brown, J. and Newcomer, S. "Television Viewing and Adolescents' Sexual Behavior," *Journal of Homosexuality* 21 (1991): 77–91.

Carbone, Stephanie. *Picture This: Diversity in Film and Television,* unpublished.

CDC Surveillance Summaries, Center for Disease Control and Prevention, August 14, 1998.

Federman, Joel. *Media Ratings: Design, Use and Consequences* (Studio City: Mediascope, 1996), p. 33.

Griffin, N. "Table Talk," *Premiere: Special Issue,* 1993.

Pfeiffer, M. "Honor Society," *Premiere: Special Issue*, 1993.

Princeton Survey Research Associates. *A Review of Public Opinion About Teen Pregnancy* (Princeton, N.J.: The National Campaign to Prevent Teen Pregnancy, September 1996).

Whatever Happened to Childhood? The Problem of Teen Pregnancy in the United States, National Campaign to Prevent Teen Pregnancy, May 1997, p. 3.

From "Boys with Toys" to "Babes with Bullets"

Basinger, Jeannine. *American Cinema.*

Braudy, Leo. "Truffaut, Hitchcock, and the Irresponsible Audience," *The World in a Frame: What We See in Films* (Chicago: University of Chicago Press, July 1984).

Haskell, Molly. *From Reverence to Rape.*

Haskell, Molly. *Holding My Own in No-Man's Land.*

Insdorf, Annette. *Francois Truffaut* (Cambridge, N.Y.: Cambridge University Press, 1994).

Messing, Philip. "Woman Abduct Man In 3 Hour Terror Ordeal," *New York Post*, January 5, 1998, p. 6.

"Women Cops Can Be A Cliché in Blue," *The New York Times*, April 15, 1990, Section 2, p. 17.

Wood, Michael. *America in the Movies.*

Hollywood Recasts History? "Ain't Nothing Like the Real Thing"

Brown, Les. *The Artist as Citizen*, unpublished.

Klein, Joe. *Primary Colors: A Novel of Politics by Anonymous* (New York: Warner Books, November 1996).

Kuczynski, Allen. "On CBS News, Some of What You See Isn't There," *The New York Times*, January 12, 2000, p. 1.

Malin, Amir. *Daily Variety*, January 4, 2000.

Reality-Based Filmmaking Versus Reality

Benjamin, Burton. *Fair Play: CBS, General Westmoreland, and How a Television Documentary Went Wrong*. 1988.

Boyer, Peter J. *Who Killed CBS? The Undoing of America's Number One News Network*, 1988.

Buzenberg, Susan and Bill, Eds. *Salant, CBS and the Battle for the Soul of Broadcast Journalism: The Memoirs of Richard S. Salant* (Boulder: Westview Press, 1999).

Frank, Reuven. *Out of Thin Air: The Brief and Wonderful Life of Network News*. 1991.

McKinley, Jesse. "An Irreverent Director Advises Reverent Fans," *The New York Times*, October 13, 1997.

McLuhan, Marshall. *The Medium is the Message: An Inventory of Effects*. 1967.

Medved, Michael. "Spielberg Film Warps History, Deceives Students," *USA Today*, December 9, 1997, p. 15A.

Meyrowitz, Joshua. *No Sense of Place: The Impact of Electronic Media on Social Behavior*. 1985.

Nicholson, Leslie. "Computer Generated Television Sets Help Producers Save Money," *The Philadelphia Inquirer*, January 8, 1998.

Postman, Neil. *Amusing Ourselves to Death: Public Discourse in the Age of Show Business*, 1985.

Rose, Tom. *Freeing the Whales: How the Media Created the World's Greatest Non-Event*. 1989.

Schwartz, Tony. *Media: The Second God*. 1981.

Sperber, A.M. *Murrow: His Life and Times*. 1986.

"The Fake Connection: How Carlton's Filmmakers Deceived 3.7 Million ITV Viewers," *The Guardian*, May 6, 1998, p. 4.

Westin, Av. *Newswatch: How TV Decides the News*. 1982.

Children: A Higher Standard—Kids Are People Too

Facts About Media Violence," American Medical Association, 1996.

Josephson, Wendy L., Ph.D. *Television Violence: A Review of the Effects on Children of Different Ages*, 1995.

Messaris, P. and Kerr, D. "Mothers' Comments about TV: Relation to Family Communication Patterns," *Communication Research*, 10, (1983): 175–194.

Nikken, Peter, and Peeters, Allerd L. "Children's Perceptions of Television Reality," *Journal of Broadcasting & Electronic Media*, Volume 32, Number 4, (Fall 1988): 441–452.

Skeen, Patsy, Brown, Mac H., and Osborn, D. Keith. "Young Children's Perception of "Real" and "Pretend" on Television," *Perceptual and Motor Skills*, 54 (1982): 883–887.

The National Television Violence Study, Universities of: California, Santa Barbara; Wisconsin, Madison; North Carolina, Chapel Hill; Texas, Austin (Studio City: Mediascope, 1996).

Trotta, Laurie A. "Special Considerations for Creators of Children's Media," in *Building Blocks: A Guide for Creating Children's Educational Programming* (Studio City: Mediascope Press, 1998).

The Virulence of Violence

"Boys and Guns: What Does It Really Mean?" Siegel, Robert, host, National Public Radio, December 25, 1992.

Doan, Michael. "As The Video Craze Captures U.S. Families," *US News & World Report*, January 28, 1985, p. 58.

Eron, Leonard D. and Huesmann, L. Rowell. *Television and the Aggressive Child: A Cross National Comparison* (Hillsdale, N.J.: Lawrence Erlbaum Associates, Inc. Publishers, 1986), pp. 45–80.

Pietrucha, Bill. "TV Ratings Compromise Halts Legislative Action," *Newsbytes*, July 10, 1997.

Prothrow-Stith, Deborah. *Deadly Consequences* (New York: Harper Collins, 1991).

Simon, Paul. "Reducing TV Violence," *The Courier-Journal* (Louisville, Kentucky), August 31, 1989, p. 15A.

The National Television Violence Study, Universities of: California, Santa Barbara; Wisconsin, Madison; North Carolina, Chapel Hill; Texas, Austin. (Studio City: Mediascope, 1996).

Tucker, Elizabeth. "FCC Weighs Role of Hostile Bids for TV Networks," *The Washington Post*, July 21, 1985, p. H1.

"Video Games and Their Effects," *Issue Brief Series* (Studio City: Mediascope Press, 1997).

Appendix B
Filmography

Foreword

Accused, The, 1988 D: Jonathan Kaplan, Paramount Pictures.
Big Sleep, The, 1946 D: Howard Hawks, Warner Bros.
Bonnie & Clyde, 1967 D: Arthur Penn, Warner Bros.
Cleopatra, 1961 D: Joseph L. Mankiewicz, 20th Century Fox.
Convention City, 1933 D: Archie Mayo, Warner Bros.
Easy Rider, 1969 D: Dennis Hopper, Columbia Pictures.
High Sierra, 1941 D: Raoul Walsh, Warner Bros.
Last Picture Show, The, 1971 D: Peter Bogdanovich, Columbia Pictures.
Little Caesar, 1931 D: Mervyn LeRoy, Warner Bros.
Miracle of Morgan's Creek, The, 1944 D: Preston Sturges, Paramount Pictures.
Natural Born Killers, 1994 D: Oliver Stone, Warner Bros.
Penny Serenade, 1941 D: George Stevens, Columbia Pictures.
Public Enemy, The, 1931 D: William Wellman, Warner Bros.
Rebel Without a Cause, 1955 D: Nicholas Ray, Warner Bros.
Saint Jack, 1979 D: Peter Bogdanovich, New World Pictures.
Targets, 1968, D: Peter Bogdanovich, Paramount Pictures.
To Have and Have Not, 1944 D: Howard Hawks, Warner Bros.
Tragedy of Othello: The Moor of Venice, 1952 D: Orson Wells.
Wild Angels, The, 1966 D: Roger Corman, American International Pictures.
Wild Bunch, The, 1969 D: Sam Peckinpah, Warner Bros.
Winchester 73, 1950 D: Anthony Mann, Universal International Pictures.

Introduction

African Queen, The, 1951 D: John Huston, United Artists.
Jerry Maguire, 1996 D: Cameron Crowe, TriStar Pictures.
Vig a.k.a *Money Kings, The*, 1998 D: Graham Theakston, Lions Gate Films.
Saving Private Ryan, 1998 D: Steven Spielberg, DreamWorks SKG.

Awash in Media Culture

Baywatch, 1989–Present, The Baywatch Company, Syndicated.
ER, 1994–present, NBC TV.
Friends, 1994–present, NBC TV.
Gilligan's Island, 1964–1967, CBS TV.
Seinfeld, 1990–1998, NBC TV.
Touched by an Angel, 1994–present, CBS TV.

Entertainment in Our Extended World

All in the Family, 1971–1979, CBS TV.
Armageddon, 1998 D: Michael Bay, Buena Vista Pictures.
Cheers, 1982–1993, NBC TV.
Dallas, 1978–1991, Lorimar TV.
Deer Hunter, The, 1978 D: Michael Cimino, Universal Pictures.
Dynasty, 1981–1989, ABC TV.
Graduate, The, 1967 D: Mike Nichols, Embassy Pictures Corp.
Independence Day, 1996 D: Roland Emmerich, 20th Century Fox.
Love Story, 1970 D: Arthur Hiller, Paramount Pictures.
Magnum Force, 1973 D: Ted Post, Warner Bros.
Married, with Children, 1987–1997, Fox Television Network.
*M*A*S*H,* 1972–1983, CBS TV.
Men in Black, 1997 D: Barry Sonnenfeld, Columbia Pictures Corp.
Natural Born Killers, 1994 D: Oliver Stone, Warner Bros.
NYPD Blue, 1993–present, ABC TV.
RoboCop, 1987 D: Paul Verhoeven, Orion Pictures Corporation.
RoboCop II, 1990 D: Irvin Kershner, Orion Pictures Corporation.
Sanford and Son, 1972–1977, NBC TV.
Saturday Night at the Movies (TV), 1966.
Seinfeld, 1990–1998, NBC TV.
Taxi Driver, 1976 D: Martin Scorsese, Columbia Pictures Corporation.
That's Entertainment, 1974 D: Jack Haley Jr., MGM Entertainment.
Titanic, 1997 D: James Cameron, Paramount Pictures.

How the World Sees Us

Air Force One, 1997 D: Wolfgang Peterson, Columbia Pictures.
Con Air, 1997 D: Simon West, Touchstone Pictures.
Dallas, 1978–1991, Lorimar TV.
Dynasty, 1981–1989, ABC TV.
First Blood, 1982 D: Ted Kotcheff, Orion Pictures Corp.
Full Monty, The, 1997 D: Peter Cattaneo, 20th Century Fox.
I Love Lucy, 1951–1957, Paramount TV.
Independence Day, 1996 D: Roland Emmerich, 20th Century Fox.
Now Voyager, 1942 D: Irving Rapper, Warner Bros.

But It's Only a Movie ... Or Is It?

Basketball Diaries, 1995 D: Scott Kalvert, New Line Cinema.
Birth of a Nation, The, 1915 D: D.W. Griffith, David W. Griffith Corporation.
Happy Days, 1974–1984, Paramount TV.
Prince of Egypt, The, 1998 D: Brenda Chapman/Steve Hickner, DreamWorks SKG.
Risky Business, 1983 D: Paul Brickman, Geffen Pictures.
Scream. 1996 D: Wes Craven, Dimension Films/Miramax Films.
Scream 2. 1997 D: Wes Craven, Dimension Films/Miramax Films.
Scream 3. D: Wes Craven, Dimension Films/Miramax Films.

Free Expression in Hollywood

Birth of a Nation, The, 1915 D: D.W. Griffith, D.W. Griffith Corporation.
Father Knows Best, 1954–1963, Screen Gems TV.
Flintstones, The, 1960–1966, Hanna-Barbera Productions.
Gone with the Wind, 1939 D: Victor Fleming, Selznick International Pictures.
Hollywood Wars, The, A&E Network, 1994.
I'm No Angel, 1933 D: Wesley Ruggles, Paramount Pictures.
Jetsons, The, 1962–1983, Hanna-Barbera Productions.
Jurassic Park, 1993 D: Steven Spielberg, Universal Pictures.
LA Confidential, 1997 D: Curtis Hanson, Warner Bros.
Leave It to Beaver, 1957–1963, MCA-TV.
Outlaw, The, 1943 D: Howard Hughes, United Artists.
Pulp Fiction, 1994 D: Quentin Tarantino, Miramax Films.
Reefer Madness, 1936 D: Louis J. Gasnier, G&H Corporation.
Seinfeld, 1990–1998, NBC TV.
She Done Him Wrong, 1933 D: Lowell Sherman, Paramount Pictures.
Smurfs, The, 1981–1989, Hanna-Barbera Productions.
Who's Afraid of Virginia Woolf, 1966 D: Mike Nichols, Warner Bros.

Dead White Greeks and Why They Matter

Wall Street, 1987 D: Oliver Stone, 20th Century Fox.

The Gun: Portrayals of Violence

Alien, 1979 D: Ridley Scott, 20th Century Fox.

Aliens, 1986 D: James Cameron, 20th Century Fox.

Alien 3, 1992 D: David Fincher, 20th Century Fox.

Alien Resurrection, 1997 D: Jean-Pierre Jeunet, 20th Century Fox.

A-Team, The, 1983–1987. Universal Pictures TV.

Better Off Dead, 1985 D: Savage Steve Holland, CBS Entertainment Productions

Bonnie & Clyde, 1967 D: Arthur Penn, Warner Bros.

Buffy the Vampire Slayer, WB Network/Warner Bros. TV.

Casablanca, 1942 D: Michael Curtiz, Warner Bros.

Casino, 1995 D: Martin Scorsese, Universal Pictures.

Colors, 1988 D: Dennis Hopper, Orion Pictures Corp.

Dead Poets Society, 1989 D: Peter Weir, Touchstone Pictures.

Dirty Harry, 1971 D: Don Siegel, Warner Bros.

Dr. No, 1962 D: Terence Young, United Artists.

Fargo, 1996 D: Joel Coen, Gramercy Pictures.

Fight Club, 1999 D: David Fincher, 20th Century Fox.

First Blood, 1982 D: Ted Kotcheff, Carolco Pictures.

Friday the 13th, 1980 D: Sean Cunningham, Paramount Pictures (also sequels and spinoffs).

General's Daughter, The, 1999 D: Simon West, Paramount Pictures.

Godfather, The, 1972 D: Francis Ford Coppola, Paramount Pictures.

Goodfellas, 1990 D: Martin Scorsese, Warner Bros.

Gunsmoke, 1955–1975, CBS.

Home Alone, 1990 D: Chris Columbus, 20th Century Fox.

Home Alone 2: Lost in New York, 1992 D: Chris Columbus, 20th Century Fox.

Home Alone 3, 1997 D: Raja Gosnell, 20th Century Fox.

Jaws, 1975 D: Steven Spielberg, MCA/Universal Pictures.

Lethal Weapon, 1987 D: Richard Donner, Warner Bros.

Lethal Weapon 2, 1989 D: Richard Donner, Warner Bros.

Lethal Weapon 3, 1992 D: Richard Donner, Warner Bros.

Lethal Weapon 4, 1998 D: Richard Donner, Warner Bros.

MacGyver, 1985–1992, Paramount Pictures TV.

Maltese Falcon, The, 1941 D: John Huston, Warner Bros.

Mary Poppins, 1964 D: Robert Stevenson, Walt Disney Productions, original music by Richard M. Sherman/Robert B. Sherman.

Men in Black, 1997 D: Barry Sonnenfeld, Columbia Pictures Corporation, Sony Pictures Entertainment.

Natural Born Killers, 1994 D: Oliver Stone, Warner Bros.
Nightmare on Elm Street, A, 1984 D: Wes Craven, New Line Cinema (also sequels and spinoffs).
OZ, 1997–present, Rysher Entertainment.
Public Enemy, The, 1931 D: William A. Wellman, Warner Bros.
Psycho, 1960 D: Alfred Hitchcock, Paramount Pictures.
Rambo: First Blood, Part II, 1985 D: George P. Cosmatos, TriStar Pictures.
Rambo III, 1988 D: Peter MacDonald, Carolco Pictures.
RoboCop, 1987 D: Paul Verhoeven, Orion Pictures Corp.
Robocop II, 1990 D: Irvin Kershner, Orion Pictures Corp.
Robocop III, 1994 D: Fred Dekker, Orion Pictures Corp.
Robocop: The Series, 1994 Rysher TV.
William Shakespeare's Romeo & Juliet, 1996 D: Baz Luhrmann, 20th Century Fox.
Saturday Night Fever, 1977 D: John Badham, Paramount Pictures
Saving Private Ryan, 1998 D: Steven Spielberg, DreamWorks Distribution, LLC, with Paramount Pictures.
Spin City, 1996–2000, DreamWorks SKG.
Star Trek: The Wrath of Khan, 1982 D: Nicholas Meyer, Paramount Pictures.
Star Wars, 1977 D: George Lucas, 20th Century Fox.
Terminator 2: Judgment Day, 1991 D: James Cameron, TriStar Pictures.
Taxi Driver, 1976 D: Martin Scorsese, Columbia Pictures Corporation.
Teenage Mutant Ninja Turtles, 1990 D: Steve Barron, New Line Cinema.
Teenage Mutant Ninja Turtles II: The Secret of the Ooze, 1991 D: Michael Pressman, New Line Cinema.
Teenage Mutant Ninja Turtles III, 1993 D: Stuart Gillard, Golden Harvest Films.
Teenage Mutant Ninja Turtles: The Series (Animated) 1988–1997, Fox TV.
Teenage Mutant Ninja Turtles: The Series (Live Action) 1997–1998, Fox TV.
Titanic, 1997 D: James Cameron, Paramount Pictures.
West Side Story, 1961 D: Jerome Robbins and Robert Wise, United Artists
West Wing, 1999–present, Warner Bros. TV.

The Cast: Portrayals of Stereotypes

Bonnie & Clyde, 1967 D: Arthur Penn, Warner Bros.
Do the Right Thing, 1989, D: Spike Lee, 40 Acres & A Mule Filmworks.
Executive Decision, 1996 D: Stuart Baird, Warner Bros.
G.I. Jane, 1997 D: Ridley Scott, Buena Vista Pictures.
Jungle Fever, 1991 D: Spike Lee, Universal Pictures.
Operation Condor, 1997, D: Frankie and Jackie Chan, Dimension (Miramax).
Revenge of the Nerds, 1984 D: Jeff Kanew, 20th Century Fox.
Revenge of the Nerds II: Nerds in Paradise, 1987 D: Roland Mesa, 20th Century Fox.
Revenge of the Nerds III: The Next Generation, 1992 D: Joe Roth, 20th Century Fox TV.

Revenge of the Nerds IV!: Nerds in Love, 1994 D: Steve Zacharias, 20th Century Fox TV.
Siege, The, 1998 D: Edward Zwick, 20th Century Fox.
Simpsons, The, 1989–present, 20th Century Fox TV.

The Props: Portrayals of Substance Use

Animal House, 1978 D: John Landis, MCA/Universal.
Clueless, 1995 D: Amy Heckerling, Paramount Pictures.
ER, Warner Bros. Television, 1994–present.
ET: The Extra Terrestrial, 1987 D: Steven Spielberg, Universal Pictures.
First Wives Club, The, 1996 D: Hugh Wilson, Paramount Pictures.
Gia, 1998 D: Michael Cristofer, Citadel Entertainment.
Girl, Interrupted, 1999 D: James Mangold, Sony Pictures Entertainment.
Independence Day, 1996 D: Roland Emmerich, 20th Century Fox.
Kids, 1995 D: Larry Clark, Miramax Films.
Licence to Kill, 1989 D: John Glen, United Artists.
Money Kings, The, a.k.a. *Vig*, 1998 D: Graham Theakston, Lions Gate Films, Inc.
My Best Friend's Wedding, 1997 D: P.J. Hogan, Sony Pictures Entertainment.
New Jack City, 1991 D: Mario Van Peebles, Warner Bros.
People vs. Larry Flynt, The, 1996 D: Milos Forman, Columbia Pictures.
Porky's, 1981 D: Bob Clark, 20th Century Fox.
Porky's II: The Next Day, 1983 D: Bob Clark, 20th Century Fox.
Pulp Fiction, 1994 D: Quentin Tarantino, Miramax Films.
Romancing the Stone, 1984 D: Robert Zemeckis, 20th Century Fox.
Superman, 1978 D: Richard Donner, Warner Bros.
Superman II, 1980 D: Richard Lester, Warner Bros.
Trainspotting, 1996 D: Danny Boyle, Miramax Films.
What's Love Got to Do with It, 1993 D: Brian Gibson, Buena Vista.
When a Man Loves a Woman, 1994 D: Luis Mandoki, Buena Vista.

The Girl: Portrayals of Sex

A Few Good Men, 1992 D: Rob Reiner, Castle Rock Entertainment.
Ally McBeal, 1997–present, 20th Century Fox Television.
American Beauty, 1999 D: Sam Mendes, DreamWorks SKG.
Angel, 1984 D: Robert Vincent O'Neill, New World Pictures.
Boogie Nights, 1997 D: Paul Thomas Anderson, New Line Cinema.
Casino, 1995 D: Martin Scorsese, MCA/Universal Pictures.
Dawn: Portrait of a Runaway (TV), 1976 D: Randal Kleiser.
Klute, 1971 D: Alan J. Pakula, Warner Bros.
LA Confidential, 1997 D: Curtis Hanson, Warner Bros.

Leaving Las Vegas, 1995 D: Mike Figgis, MGM-UA.
Lethal Weapon 3, 1992 D: Richard Donner, Warner Bros.
Mighty Aphrodite, 1995 D: Woody Allen, Miramax Films.
Natural Born Killers, 1994 D: Oliver Stone, Warner Bros.
NYPD Blue, 1993–present, ABC TV.
People vs. Larry Flynt, The, 1996 D: Milos Forman, Columbia Pictures.
Piano, The, 1993 D: Jane Campion, Miramax Films.
Popular, 1999–present, the WB Television Network.
Pulp Fiction, 1997 D: Quentin Tarantino, Miramax Films.
Robin Hood: Prince of Thieves, 1991 D: Kevin Reynolds, Warner Bros.
Say Anything ... 1989 D: Cameron Crowe, 20th Century Fox.
Showgirls, 1995 D: Paul Verhoeven, United Artists.
Spin City, 1996–2000, DreamWorks SKG.
Star Trek: Voyager, 1995–present, Paramount TV.
Substitute, The, 1996 D: Robert Mandel, LIVE Entertainment.
Summer School, 1987 D: Carl Reiner, Paramount Pictures.
Taxi Driver, 1976 D: Martin Scorsese, Columbia Pictures Corporation.
Teenage Mutant Ninja Turtles, 1990 D: Steve Barron, New Line Cinema.
Teen Angel (TV) 1989 D: Max Reid.
Where the Day Takes You, 1992 D: Marc Rocco, Cinetel.
Wish You Were Here, 1987 D: David Leland, Zenith Productions.

From "Boys with Toys" to "Babes with Bullets"

Basic Instinct, 1992 D: Paul Verhoeven, TriStar Pictures.
Beverly Hills Cop II, 1987 D: Tony Scott, Paramount Pictures.
Big, 1988 D: Penny Marshall, 20th Century Fox.
Blue Steel, 1990 D: Kathryn Bigelow, MGM-UA.
Blue Velvet, 1986 D: David Lynch, DeLaurentis Entertainment Group.
Body Double, 1984 D: Brian DePalma, Columbia Pictures.
Boxing Helena, 1993 D: Jennifer Chambers Lynch, Main Line Pictures.
Cat People, 1982 D: Paul Schrader, Universal Pictures.
Cleopatra Jones, 1973 D: Jack Starrett, Warner Bros.
Die Hard, 1988 D: John McTierman, 20th Century Fox.
Doctor, The, 1991 D: Randa Haines, Touchstone Pictures.
Fatal Attraction, 1987 D: Adrian Lyne, Paramount Pictures.
Fatal Beauty, 1987 D: Tom Holland, MGM-UA.
Father of the Bride, 1991 D: Charles Shyer, Touchstone Pictures.
Forrest Gump, 1994 D: Robert Zemeckis, Paramount Pictures.
Foxy Brown, 1974 D: Jack Hill, American International Pictures (AIP)
G.I. Jane, 1997 D: Ridley Scott, Buena Vista Pictures.

Gloria, 1999, D: Sidney Lumet, Columbia Pictures Corporation.
Henry & June, 1990 D: Philip Kaufman, Walrus & Associates.
Hook, 1991 D: Steven Spielberg, Amblin Entertainment.
Hunger, The, 1983 D: Tony Scott, MGM-UA.
Impulse, 1990 D: Sondra Locke, Warner Bros.
Jackie Brown, 1997 D: Quentin Tarantino, Miramax Films.
La Femme Nikita, 1990 D: Luc Besson, Gaumont.
Lethal Weapon, 1987 D: Richard Donner, Warner Bros.
Milk Money, 1994 D: Richard Benjamin, Paramount Pictures.
Money Train, 1995 D: Joseph Ruben, Columbia Pictures Corporation
Natural Born Killers, 1994 D: Oliver Stone, Warner Bros.
Point of No Return, aka: *Nikita* 1993 D: John Badham, Warner Bros.
Pretty Woman, 1990 D: Garry Marshall, Buena Vista Pictures.
Prince of Tides, The, 1991 D: Barbara Streisand, Columbia Pictures.
Psycho, 1960 D: Alfred Hitchcock, Paramount Pictures.
Pulp Fiction, 1994 D: Quentin Tarantino, Miramax Films.
First Blood, a.k.a. *Rambo: First Blood*, 1982 D: Ted Kotcheff, Orion Pictures Corp.
Rear Window, 1954 D: Alfred Hitchcock, Paramount Pictures.
Regarding Henry, 1991 D: Mike Nichols, Paramount Pictures.
William Shakespeare's Romeo & Juliet, 1996 D: Baz Luhrmann, 20th Century Fox.
Silence of the Lambs, 1991 D: Jonathan Demme, Orion Pictures.
Striptease, 1996 D: Andrew Bergman, Castle Rock Entertainment.
Terminator 2: Judgment Day, 1991 D: James Cameron, Carolco Pictures.
Thelma and Louise, 1991 D: Ridley Scott, MGM-UA.
Tomorrow Never Dies, 1997 D: Roger Spottiswoode, MGM-UA.
Unbearable Lightness of Being, The, 1988 D: Philip Kaufman, The Saul Zaentz Company.
V.I. Warshawski, 1991 D: Jeff Kanew, Warner Bros.
Young Guns, 1988 D: Christopher Cain, 20th Century Fox.

Hollywood Recasts History?

All the President's Men, 1976 D: Alan J. Pakula, Warner Bros.
Amistad, 1997 D: Steven Spielberg, DreamWorks SKG.
Blair Witch Project, The, 1999 D: Daniel Myrick and Eduardo Sanchez II, Artisan Entertainment.
Contact, 1997 D: Robert Zemeckis, Warner Bros.
Forrest Gump, 1994 D: Robert Zemeckis, Paramount Pictures.
JFK, 1991 D: Oliver Stone, Warner Bros.
Nixon, 1995 D: Oliver Stone, Buena Vista Pictures.
Primary Colors 1998 D: Mike Nichols, Universal Pictures.
Titanic, 1997 D: James Cameron, 20th Century Fox and Paramount Pictures.
Triumph des Willens. 1934 D: Leni Riefenstahl, Connoisseur Video.

Wag the Dog, 1997 D: Barry Levinson, New Line Cinema.
War of the Worlds, The, 1953 D: Byron Haskin, Paramount Pictures.

Reality-Based Filmmaking Versus Reality

60 Minutes, 1968–present, CBS TV.
Amistad, 1997 D: Steven Spielberg, DreamWorks SKG.
Born on the Fourth of July, 1989 D: Oliver Stone, Universal Pictures.
Connection, The, 1998 D: Marc de Beaufort, Carlton TV.
Dateline NBC, 1992–present, D: Guy Pepper, NBC TV.
Doors, The, 1991 D: Oliver Stone, Imagine Entertainment.
Independence Day, 1996 D: Roland Emmerich, 20th Century Fox.
Jetsons, The, 1990 D: Joseph Barbera and William Hanna, Hanna Barbera.
Lost in Space, 1998 D: Stephen Hopkins, New Line Cinema.
Nixon, 1995 D: Oliver Stone, Buena Vista Pictures.
Peacemaker, The, 1997 D: Mimi Leder, DreamWorks SKG.
Platoon, 1986 D: Oliver Stone, Hemdale Film Corporation.

Children: A Higher Standard

Friends, 1994–present. Bright/Kauffman/Crane Prods. and Warner Bros. TV.
South Park, 1997–present. Comedy Partners and Comedy Central.

The Virulence of Violence

Cops, 1989–Present, 20th Century Fox TV.
Hard Copy, 1989–1999, Syndicated.
NYPD Blue, 1993–present, ABC TV.

Index

Name and topic index. Film titles are listed by chapter in the Filmography.